SPEECH
AND CORTICAL
FUNCTIONING

ACADEMIC PRESS RAPID MANUSCRIPT REPRODUCTION

Proceedings of a Symposium
Held at the University of British Columbia
April 1972

SPEECH AND CORTICAL FUNCTIONING

Edited by

JOHN H. GILBERT

Division of Audiology and Speech Sciences
Faculty of Medicine
University of British Columbia
Vancouver, Canada

Academic Press New York and London 1972

ACADEMIC PRESS, INC.
111 Fifth Avenue, New York, New York 10003

United Kingdom Edition published by
ACADEMIC PRESS, INC. (LONDON) LTD.
24/28 Oval Road, London NW1

LIBRARY OF CONGRESS CATALOG CARD NUMBER: 72-88342

PRINTED IN THE UNITED STATES OF AMERICA

CONTENTS

CONTENTS

PARTICIPANTS

A. Cohen, Faculty of Arts (English Department), Rijksuniversiteit te Utrecht, Kromme Nieuwe Gracht 29, Utrecht, The Netherlands

Eli Fischer-Jørgensen, The Institute of Phonetics, Faculty of Philosophy, Københavns Universitet, Frue Plads, Copenhagen K, Denmark

Victoria A. Fromkin, Department of Linguistics, University of California, Los Angeles, California 90024

Osamu Fujimura, Research Institute of Logopedics and Phoniatrics, Faculty of Medicine, University of Tokyo, Hongo, Tokyo, Japan

Harold Goodglass, Department of Psychology, Veterans Administration Hospital, Boston, Massachusetts 02130

Arthur S. House, Institute for Defence Analysis, Von Neuman Hall, Princeton, New Jersey 08440

Doreen Kimura, Department of Psychology, University of Western Ontario, London, Ontario, Canada

Peter Ladefoged, Linguistics Department, University of California, Los Angeles, California 90024

Ilse Lehiste, Department of Linguistics, Dieter Cunz Hall of Languages, Ohio State University, Columbus, Ohio 43210

A. M. Liberman, Department of Psychology, University of Connecticut, Storrs, Connecticut 56268

Peter F. MacNeilage, Department of Linguistics, The University of Texas, Austin, Texas 78712

Brenda Milner, Department of Neurology and Neurosurgery, McGill University, Montreal, Quebec, Canada

Sven Ohman, Faculty of Arts, Universitet l Uppsala 75, 751 05 Uppsala, Sweden

Wayne A. Wickelgren, Department of Psychology, University of Oregon, Eugene, Oregon 97403

OBSERVERS

A-P. Benguerel	University of British Columbia
J. B. Delack	University of British Columbia
J. D. Edwards	University of British Columbia
R. P. Gannon	University of British Columbia
John H. Gilbert	University of British Columbia
D. D. Greenwood	University of British Columbia
A. G. Hannam	University of British Columbia
André Roch Lecours	University of Montreal
Otfried Spreen	University of Victoria
J. A. Wada	University of British Columbia

PREFACE

Since *Sound Pattern of English* appeared in 1968, its underlying phonetic theory has been subjected to the scrutiny of phoneticians well versed in speech acoustics, physiology, perception, and neurology. This scrutiny has been both extensive and intensive, supporting Benjamin Lee Whorf's contention that "speech is the best show man puts on." In 1970 it appeared that a review of the show would be appropriate; and ultimately the symposium "Speech Production, Speech Perception: Their Relationship to Cortical Functioning" took place at the University of British Columbia in April 1972, under the auspices of the Medical Research Council of Canada.

The title of the symposium was not chosen without trepidation, for, like the physicist who indicated in an introductory lecture that he would talk on "the universe, and other things," speech and cortical functioning is a vast topic. The examination of speech processes appears, at the present time, to be delineable into four major areas: speech physiology, speech acoustics, speech perception, and cortical functioning. These were the basic units for the $2\frac{1}{2}$-day symposium.

Each principal speaker was assigned a discussant; the format of this volume follows the symposium schedule. Apart from minor editing, each chapter stands much as it was presented, in an attempt to retain the informality of the meeting.

No symposium is successful without the full support of its participants; my thanks are due to all who came and made the $2\frac{1}{2}$ days a fruitful exchange of information. Unfortunately, Professor Brenda Milner's paper was not available for publication in these proceedings. For the financial support of the Medical Research Council of Canada and the Dean of Medicine's Fund, we are extremely grateful. I should also like to acknowledge the helpful comments and suggestions of Arthur House, Vicki Fromkin and Ilse Lehiste, in the early planning of the symposium, and I am extremely grateful to my associate André-Pierre Benguerel for his support and encouragement.

SPEECH
AND CORTICAL
FUNCTIONING

Chapter I

SPEECH PHYSIOLOGY

Peter F. MacNeilage

Departments of Linguistics and Psychology
University of Texas at Austin

INTRODUCTION

The area of speech physiology is a diverse one.
We do not appear to be in a position to formulate a
general theory of the physiological control of speech
production. In fact, although we have seen some
theoretical models of aspects of the control of speech
production which have had physiological implication,
none has succeeded in engaging the support or perhaps
even the interest of the majority of people working
in this field. We are still primarily at a data-
gathering stage, or at most at the stage of formulating microtheories the authors of which would be well
advised not to take their work too seriously. This
review of the present status of speech physiology is
designed to reflect the state of affairs I have just
described. It is an attempt to summarize the well-
established facts in this area, especially those
established recently, and consider the main points of
view with respect to these facts, without attempting
to force unwarranted advocacy of any particular view,
and without neglecting significant unanswered questions.

Readers of this review may also wish to avail
themselves of some other review articles with related
themes which have been published recently. Four of
these appear in Volume 12 of the series Current
Trends in Linguistics, edited by T.A. Sebeok and pub-

lished by Mouton and Co. (1972). They are: Physiological Aspects of Articulatory Behavior, By K.S.
Harris; Laryngeal Research in Experimental Phonetics,
by M. Sawashima; On Time and Timing in Speech, by L.
Lisker; and a Study of Prosodic Features, by P.
Lieberman. In addition, note the chapter on Experimental Phonetics by C.W. Kim in the book, A Survey
of Linguistic Science, edited by Dingwall and published by the University of Maryland Press. Mono-
graphs by Ohala (1970) and Lehiste (1971) also deal
extensively with issues discussed here. Some chapters
in the forthcoming book, Normal Speech, Hearing and
Language, edited by F.D. Minifie, T.J. Hixon, and F.
Williams, and published by Prentice-Hall, Inc., will
also deal with related themes. The papers by Daniloff, Hixon, and Netsell should be of particular interest.

Respiratory Mechanisms

Although we have learned a great deal about respiratory function in speech during the past few years
(Hixon, 1972), there has not been a great advance in
understanding of specifically linguistic aspects of
respiratory function since the pioneering work of
Draper, Ladefoged and Whitteridge in the late fifties.
(Draper, Ladefoged and Whitteridge; 1957, 1958, 1960;
Ladefoged, 1960, 1962, 1963, 1967, 1968; Ladefoged,
Draper and Whitteridge, 1958; Ladefoged and McKinney,
1963). Ladefoged (1968) presents the following summary of the general course of respiratory events associated with an utterance:

> ...In general, we found that during the
> first part of an utterance beginning after
> a deep inspiration, the external intercos-
> tals remain in action, regulating the pres-
> sure of the air below the vocal cords by
> checking the descent of the rib cage, thus
> counteracting the relaxation pressure. As
> the lung volume decreases, the action of
> the external intercostals diminishes and
> eventually ceases altogether when the lung

2

volume is slightly less than the volume
after a normal inspiration, at which moment the relaxation pressure is sufficient
to provide the power required for a normal
conversational utterance. From then on,
expiratory activity is needed to maintain
the pressure below the vocal cords, and
accordingly the internal intercostals come
into action with gradually increasing intensity. When the lung volume is a little
below that at the end of a normal expiration, the action of the internal intercostals is supplemented by various other
muscles, such as the external obliques,
rectus abdominis, and latissimus dorsi.
Ladefoged also noted that most speech is not preceded
by deep inspiration or prolonged as long as in the
example he describes above. Under these conditions
no action of the external intercostals or of muscles
other than the internal intercostals was usually observed.

The actions described here are necessary to pre-
serve a relatively constant level of subglottal pressure during most of an utterance. However, typically
superimposed on this average level of subglottal pressure were found transient increases in pressure
which were correlated with transient reductions of
electromyographic activity of the external intercostals if they were active during the period, and increases in activity of the internal intercostal muscles if they were concurrently active. The circumstances governing these occurrences are of particular
interest. Perhaps the most well-known hypothesis
related to this phenomenon is that of Stetson (1951)
who believed that each syllable was accompanied by a
"chest pulse," a belief that is still occasionally
stated as fact in introductory textbooks (e.g. Gleason, 1967; Abercrombie, 1967). Ladefoged and his
associates (Ladefoged, Draper and Whitteridge, 1958)
have shown quite conclusively that neither a burst of
internal intercostal muscle action nor a transient

increase in subglottal pressure is an invariant ac-
companiment of the syllable. Ladefoged, et al. did
find that a burst of intercostal muscle activity preceded each syllable during repetition of a single
stressed syllable. However, during connected speech
the bursts do not accompany every syllable, but occur
mainly preceding the principal stresses of the utterance, with some variation correlated with degrees of
stress. Some other findings also deserve attention.
Occasionally a single increase in muscle activity
spanned a group of articulations including two vowels
separated by a consonant closure (e.g. in "pity" or
"around"). Sometimes two bursts of activity were observed in a single syllable, e.g. in "sport" and
"stay" and other words beginning with a fricative-
plosive sequence. Bursts of activity usually preceded [h] and long vowels. In other words, some aspects
of intercostal activity appeared to be related to the
pattern of individual articulatory segments as well
as to stress. These latter findings contradict the
usual conclusion that the subglottal mechanism is too
sluggish to produce changes associated with individual segments.

A theory of stress which could account for this
particular pattern of results is not known to us. In
fact there is a good deal of difference of opinion
about how to define stress, which is beyond the scope
of this paper but adversely affects any consideration
of stress from the point of view of speech physiology.
(Problems of stress are discussed from various points
of view by Bolinger, 1958; Lieberman, 1967, 1971:
Chomsky and Halle, 1968; Fry, 1970, Ohala, 1970; Kent
and Netsell, 1971; Lehiste, 1971; and Vanderslice,
1968). There is some agreement that in clear cases
of stress four physical correlates are typically involved in English; fundamental frequency, intensity,
segment duration, and vowel quality, with fundamental
frequency being the most effective perceptual cue
(Fry, 1970). What we require is a set of rules determining when stress if applied, how many different degrees of stress must be postulated, and what is the

relative role of respiratory, laryngeal and articulatory mechanisms in generating the above physical correlates. One of the main problems in analysis of respiratory contributions to stress is that these contributions must be made in the context of entire utterances whose length and overall intonation contour also involve adjustments in the respiratory mechanism in order to maintain the required control of lung volume and subglottal pressure. We are at present a very long way from formulating these rules.

The role of physiological mechanisms in speech is to produce acoustic signals which have communicative significance. It is therefore of interest, in this context, to ask what are the acoustical effects of particular manouvers of the respiratory system. It is well accepted that subglottal pressure (ps), or more accurately, amount of pressure drop across the glottis, (transglottal pressure drop (P_T) is positively related to both intensity and fundamental frequency (Fo) of the speech signal. Hixon and his associates have recently done some elegant parametric work on the effect of changes in transglottal pressure drop (typically produced in natural speech by differences in subglottal pressure, at least during vocalic segments) on Fo and intensity of the speech wave. (Hixon, Mead and Klatt, 1970; Hixon, 1971) By applying the output of a low frequency loudspeaker either to the external entrance to the airway (the mouth) or to the body wall of the respiratory apparatus (enclosed in a body plethysmograph), they were able to effect sinusoidal variations in transglottal pressure drop in 10 subjects.* The latter technique is a more sophisticated form of the old technique of unexpectedly punching a phonating subject in the chest. It allows greater experimental control of the timing and amplitude of the intervention than the old method, although perhaps having less human interest value as

---

*Use of such a 'large' number of subects is as meritorious as it is rare in speech physiology research.

a technique. Use of this technique has made it possible to resolve the question of whether relationships between subglottal pressure change and Fo
change obtained during steady phonation are a good
estimate of the relationships which hold during
speech, as it can be used under both conditions. It
also has an advantage over the technique of inferr-
ing the contribution of subglottal pressure to Fo by
simply observing the relation between the two variables in running speech (Lieberman, 1967). The latter technique has two difficulties: the difficulty of
disambiguating the relative influence of Ps and vocal cord tension changes on Fo, and the difficulty
of assessing the indirect contribution of glottal
adjustments to subglottal pressure (Ohala, 1970) (increases in glottal impedance produce increases in
subglottal pressure).

Hixon et al's results concerning the relation
between changes in transglottal pressure drop (P_T)
and changes in Fo ($\Delta Fo/ \Delta P_T$) add to a consensus
arising from the work of several investigators (Isshiki, 1959; Ladefoged, 1963; Ohman and Lindqvist, 1966
Fromkin and Ohala, 1968; Ohala, 1970). They found
that "...($\Delta Fo/ \Delta P_T$) values exceeded 5 Hz/cm of H_2O
in only one subject and in the speech range of Fo
they were typically 2-4 Hz/cm H_2O." Their findings
were similar whether the changes in P_T were induced
via the body wall or the airway, and similar whether
the subject was engaged in steady phonation or production of monosyllables. It is of special interest,
in view of Lieberman's contention (1967, 1971) that
effects of transglottal pressure drop quite often
exceeded 5 Hz by considerable amounts, that Hixon et
al. failed to replicate the range of 3-18 Hz/cm H_2O
found by Lieberman, Knudson and Mead (1969) even in
the particular experimental subject used by Lieberman
et al. Given a dynamic range of Fo during speech of
about one octave and a modal value of approximately
120 Hz in men, and given that the range of subglottal
pressures observed during speech is approximately 8
cm of water, then a good deal of observed variance in

6

Fo cannot be accounted for in terms of respiratory influences on subglottal pressure.

Hixon (1971) has also found that intensity levels are relatively more responsive to changes in P_T than fundamental frequency, but unlike Fo, the amount of change was proportional to the prestimulus intensity level. At the 10% point in subjects' intensity range, a 1 cm change in P_T resulted in approximately a 3 dB change in sound pressure level, whereas at the 90% level, a 1/2 dB change was more characteristic. Prestimulus Fo level was found to have very little influence on intensity change.

Complementary to these results are some interesting unpublished observations of Shipp. Using inspection of meter readings of his own output as a means of control, he attempted, while holding subglottal pressure level constant, to vary one of the two parameters, Fo or intensity, while also holding the other constant. He found that while he was able to effect easily observable changes in Fo with Ps and intensity constant,* he was unable to produce any consistent intensity change with Ps and Fo held constant. These results support the implication of Hixon's work that whereas intensity variations in speech are very largely of subglottal origin, there is quite an appreciable capacity to vary Fo with maneuvers at the glottal level. The results are also consistent with the observation that patients with paralysis of the respiratory musculature find it difficult to speak loudly (Peterson, 1956, cited by Lehiste, 1971; Draper, Ladefoged and Whitteridge, 1960) but were reported in one case (Peterson) to produce stress patterns which sounded normal to the listener. This was presumably achieved almost entirely by control of the other 3 acoustic correlates of stress in English-laryngeal control of Fo, and upper articulatory control of segment duration and vowel quality.

The results described here have at least one

---

* A range of up to 1 1/2 octaves was possible.

major linguistic implication. There are many languages in which fundamental frequency is systematically manipulated as an independent variable (Lehiste,
1971 pp. 83-105). The large number of tone languages
constitute one example, and other languages with what
have been called "accent" systems constitute another.
To my knowledge, in these languages the correlation
of intensity changes with Fo changes is at most low
and typically inconsistent. This is not surprising
in the light of our considerable ability to affect
Fo changes, without amplitude changes, by laryngeal
maneuvers. On the other hand, I know of no language
in which intensity is used systematically as an independent variable. Where intensity does appear to
have a linguistic function, as for example for stress
in English, it is probably at least moderately correlated in most cases with Fo. These considerations
suggest that the speech mechanism is not capable of
continuously varying the amount of decoupling of larynx from lungs necessary to have intensity changes
play a major role independent of concurrent Fo
changes which Ps changes tend to produce. I will
further consider this question of the interaction between respiratory and laryngeal components of the
speech mechanism in the next section.

Laryngeal Mechanisms

Lieberman's Hypotheses

The most far-reaching claims about the relative
role of the respiratory and laryngeal components in
the control of prosodic aspects of speech to be made
recently have been made by Lieberman (1967). He
postulated the existence of an "archetypal unmarked
breath group", which was supposedly an innate and universal maneuver of the respiratory apparatus, and
was reflected in the infant's cry. In adult speakers
it was manifest in simple declarative sentences. "Joe
ate his soup: was the main example used by Lieberman.
It was Lieberman's contention that the characteristic
changes in Fo produced in sentences of this type were

8

a result of subglottal pressure changes with laryngeal maneuvers playing, by implication, a minor role. First of all, Lieberman pointed out that the subglottal pressure curve tends to match the Fo curve in declarative sentences, remaining fairly constant through most of the sentence but falling considerably at the termination. Lieberman contended further that the phenomenon of prominence, or major sentence stress (which, for example, in "Joe ate his soup", would be placed on "soup"), was also a result of changes in subglottal pressure. Finally, Lieberman postulated the "marked" breath group, which occurred in yes-no questions and took the form of a laryngeal maneuver to increase vocal cord tension and therefore Fo in the terminal part of the sentence. His evidence for this contention was his observation that on these occasions, Fo increased while Ps was decreasing, which, incidentally, provides further documentation of the possibility of the independence of laryngeal Fo control from the respiratory component during speech.

One value of Lieberman's hypotheses is that at least some of them are sufficiently specific to enable specific tests. Ohala (1970) has provided confirmatory evidence that Fo increases in the terminal phases of yes-no question forms, are produced by laryngeal maneuvers. Using electromyography, he found increases in activity in thyroarytenoid, cricothyroid and lateral cricoarytenoid muscles paralleling Fo increase and Ps decrease, which suggested that increases in vocal cord tension were occurring.

Other aspects of Lieberman's hypotheses have been called into question, particularly by Ohala (1970). From a reanalysis of the data Lieberman studied on infant cry, Ohala finds insufficient grounds for Lieberman's claim that this data provides evidence of an unmarked breath group. Ohala's dissatisfaction arose both from the small sample of data considered, and from the heterogeneity of that data with respect to the hypothesis. He also raised the question of whether infant cry was an appropriate

9

homologue of adult speech.

In addition to confirming Lieberman's evidence
that there are subglottal pressure increases accompanying sentence prominence as Ladefoged's work had
also shown, Ohala and his associates (particularly
Hirano) have found electromyographic evidence for
concurrent Fo-raising laryngeal maneuvers. The electromyographic findings were analagous in pattern to
those accompanying terminal Fo raising, namely concurrent activity of the cricothyroid, vocalis and lateral cricoarytenoid muscles. These findings along
with those of Hixon, et al., on the limitations of
changes in P_T in changing Fo, lead to the conclusion
that there is a considerable amount of laryngeal contribution to the implementation of sentence prominence.*

It does not provide a great advance in our knowledge to note that laryngeal maneuvers are more important in sentence prominence than Lieberman had
supposed, for, as Ohala (1970) has pointed out, this
view had a good deal of acceptance before Lieberman
formulated his alternative view. What we require at
this stage is research showing in more detail what
the relative contribution of larynx and lungs to Fo
actually is, under a variety of conditions. A step
in this direction has recently been made by Lieberman
Sawashima, Harris and Gay (1970). They were able to
confirm the finding of laryngeal involvement in sentence prominence in simple declarative sentences by
means of recording of cricothyroid muscle activity in
one subject. But they did not observe cricothyroid
activity accompanying sentence prominence in questions
which involved terminal Fo raising. (It may also be

---

*Incidentally, the greatest reported contribution of
laryngeal maneuvers to Fo change under any speech
condition to my knowledge can be seen in Fig. 34 b of
Ohala's monograph, where an Fo increase of 50 Hz over
a 200 ms period is preceded by a Ps increase of no
more than I cm of water.

that little Fo change accompanied prominence.) An additional requirement at present is for studies of a number of subjects. The fact that it is possible to vary Fo by more than one means, tends to make one suspect generalizations about the relative role of lungs and larynx which are based only on one or a few subjects but intended to apply to the whole population.

With respect to the terminal fall in Fo in declarative sentences, Ohala has observed increases in activity of the sternohyoid muscle, again suggesting laryngeal involvement, this time of the extrinsic musculature in Fo control. Two recent reviewers (Harris, 1971; and Sawashima, 1971) have noted other studies which have not been successful in finding a relation between sternohyoid activity and Fo lowering. Harris considers that the laryngeal contribution to Fo lowering may be a passive one, consisting of cessation of activity in muscles mediating Fo raising. In this regard Ohman (1967) has noted abrupt decreases in cricothyroid activity preceding Swedish word accents which require Fo lowering.

In summary, Lieberman appears to have been correct about the role of the larynx in terminal Fo raising, wrong about the degree of laryngeal involvement in sentence prominence, and his hypothesis about terminal Fo lowering is still being evaluated. However, no convincing evidence is available to support his notion of an innate universal archetypal breath group, partly because the notion is not formulated in a manner allowing its test (Ohala, 1970, p.80).

Other Studies of Laryngeal Function

A good deal of progress has been made in the past few years in the understanding of the relation between the anatomy of the larynx and its function, though much remains to be learned. Most information has come from 3 sources; anatomical studies, direct and indirect observation of laryngeal movements, and electromyographic studies. These studies and their methodology have been reviewed by Sawashima (1971) and their implications for laryngeal function will be

11

briefly summarized below.

It is relatively well established that the main laryngeal maneuvers used to change fundamental frequency are changes in the length, thickness, and longitudinal tension of the vocal folds. Within the modal or chest register which includes the range of fundamental frequencies ovserved in normal speech, it is generally agreed that most of the increase in vocal fold length is achieved by a maneuver known as "closing the cricothyroid visor".

This movement is achieved by a rotation of the cricoid cartilage about a horizontal transverse axis of rotation at the cricothyroid joint (Sonesson, 1970). This results in the anterior part of the cricoid being raised towards the anterior part of the thyroid cartilage (thus closing the visor). The posterior part of the cricoid is tilted backwards. As the vocal folds run between the anterior part of the thyroid cartilage and the arytenoid cartilages which are mounted on the posterior of the cricoid cartilage, the result of this rotation will be lengthening of the vocal folds and an increase in their tension.

It appears that a further tension increase is produced by contraction of the muscles within the vocal folds themselves. In a particularly comprehensive recent study of steady phonation within the chest register conducted on 16 subjects, Shipp, McGlone and Morrisey (1971) have shown a positive relation between increase in fundamental frequency and increase in contraction of the cricothyroid and thyroarytenoid muscles, as judged from electromyograms. The cricothyroid muscle is likely to be the one most involved in the visor-closing action and the thyro-arytenoid muscle is situated within the vocal folds.*

As Sawashima (1971) points out, a number of earlier investigators have come to similar conclusions.

*Some electromyographers such as Shipp prefer to indicate that they are recording from the thyroarytenoid muscle which is a term for the entire body (cont'd)

Shipp did not find any systematic increases in activity of the interarytneoid muscle or the posterior cricoarytenoid muscle with increase in Fo. (Note that the interarytenoid muscle has been considered to be a vocal cord adductor and the posterior cricoarytenoid an abductor). Other investigators have found some changes in interarytenoid and posterior cricoarytenoid activity during phonation in the chest register, and some action of the lateral cricoarytenoid (another supposed vocal cord adductor) has also been noted. But these changes are typically smaller than changes noted in the cricothyroid muscle and in musculature within the vocal folds. They also seem to be less consistent across subjects and often confined to the higher reaches of the frequency range. The role of the extrinsic laryngeal muscles--what Sonninen (1968) has called the external frame function--in producing Fo changes in either direction is not at present clear (Harris, 1971; Sawashima, 1971). It appears that a unique solution to the problem of how the extrinsic laryngeal muscles operate is not available from mechanical inferences alone and the necessary combined study of laryngeal movements and extrinsic muscle activity has not been done.

As was pointed out earlier, it has been shown by Ohala and his associates that increases in activity of the vocalis, cricothyroid and lateral cricoarytenoid accompany increases in Fo associated with prominence and yes-no question intonation in running speech. However little systematic work on electromyographic correlates of Fo in running speech has yet been done which would enable us to evaluate the relative role of each laryngeal muscle in the various

---

(cont'd) of muscles within the vocal folds. Others such as Hirose (1971) indicate that they are recording from the vocalis muscle which is a small medially placed subdivision of the thyroarytenoid. To my knowledge nobody has yet shown a functional difference between the vocalis and the remainder of the thyroarytenoid muscle.

situations in which Fo change is produced.

There is very little agreement about the exact nature of the role of the larynx in control of vocal intensity either in steady phonation or in running speech. Experiments typically reveal rather small changes in action of laryngeal muscles with intensity changes. This is consistent with our earlier conclusion that respiratory factors play the dominant role in intensity control.

Consider now the operation of abduction and adduction of the vocal cords, and more specifically the movement of the arytenoid cartilages which bring about these adjustments. It now seems clear from the morphology of the cricoarytenoid joint that the degree of posterior separation of the vocal cords is not controlled by the rotation of the arytenoid cartilages about a vertical axis as some earlier descriptions had suggested. As Sawashima (1971) puts it,

> "The structure of the cricoarytenoid joint permits the arytenoid cartilages two principal types of motion. One of them, the main type, is a rotating motion around the longitudinal axis of the joint; the other is a longitudinal sliding motion parallel to the axis."

The cricoid facet of the cricoarytenoid joint is a convex surface the axis of which runs in a ventrolaterocaudal to dorsomediocranial direction. The arytenoid facet is a reciprocally concave surface. Sonesson (cited by Sawashima) considers the movements of the arytenoid cartilages to be controlled by the individual laryngeal muscles in the following manner:

> "(1) the thyroarytenoid and the lateral cricoarytenoid muscles contribute to the adduction of the arytenoid cartilages and their linear sliding in the ventrolaterocaudal direction (for what he considers to be a maximum of 2 millimeters); "(2) the arytenoid muscle causes the adduction of the arytenoid cartilages and their linear sliding in the dor-

14

somediocranial direction; (3) the posterior
cricoarytenoid muscle contributes to the abduction of the arytenoid cartileges with
little effect on their linear sliding motion."

Electromyographic studies of segmental articulation have added to the broad outline of functions
attributed to the intrinsic laryngeal muscles by Sonesson, although in this area there is still relatively little data available, and evidence of small differences between muscles should probably await replication.

A recent study of 2 subjects by Hirose (1971)
has shown quite clearly that the posterior cricoarytenoid muscle is active in the abduction of the vocal
cords for voiceless stop consonants and fricatives in
intervocalic position and for the voiceless stop [p]
in final position. In addition I have found in an
unpublished study of data from Shipp's laboratory
that there was always posterior cricoarytenoid activity for intervocalic voiceless stops and fricatives
in the records of a number of subjects producing dis-
yllables in citation form. The abduction of the vocal cords for voiceless stop consonants and fricatives and their behavior for voiced obstruents has
been observed in transillumination studies and direct photography, and the results of these studies
have been summarized by Sawashima (1971).

Hirose (1971) has observed EMG activity of the
vocalis, interarytenoid and lateral cricoarytenoid
muscles preceding the initiation of voicing in dis-
yllables beginning with a vowel. These effects are
visible in the results shown by Ohala (1970) in
utterances beginning with [b], and have also been
reported by Hiroto, Hirano, Toyozumi and Shin, (1967)
and observed by me (in the thyroarytenoid and interarytenoid) in Shipp's data. Hirose has also found
that the interarytenoid appears to be more directly
opposite in function to the posterior cricoarytenoid
than the vocalis or the lateral cricoarytenoid. It
shows much more reduction of activity preceding
voiceless stops than preceding voiced stops, when the

15

reduction is only slight. On the other hand, the vocalis and the lateral cricoarytenoid show only slight but equal reductions preceding both voiced and voiceless stop consonants. The interarytenoid also mirrors the posterior cricoarytenoid more than the other two muscles in showing more increase in activity (as PCA activity reduces) after voiceless stops than after voiced stops. These data, though requiring confirmation, suggest to Hirose that there may be a functional differentiation between these three muscles. Whereas the interarytenoid is more strictly an adductory muscle, the remaining two muscles maybe also concerned with other adjustments. Elsewhere Hirose and his colleagues have also suggested there may be a functional differentiation between the lateral cricoarytenoid and the vocalis (Hirose, Simada and Fujimura, 1970). They found in one subject that "...the vocalis is particularly active in voicing and has the characteristic of contracting and relaxing in a relatively fast manner, while the lateralis shows relatively continuous activity during the entire period of the utterance." It is of interest that the reduction in activity of all these muscles preceding voiced stop consonants is consistent with the hypothesis of Halle and Stevens, (1967) that there may be a different mode of voicing during voicedstop consonants than during vowels. On the other hand the lack of difference in vocalis and lateral cricoarytenoid activity for voiced and voiceless stops (together with the fact that the cricothyroid muscle is minimally involved in segmental gestures (Hirose, 1971))is contrary to the claim of Halle and Stevens, (1971) that voiced and voiceless stops differ in vocal cord stiffness.

Articulatory Mechanisms

During the past few years, there has been a raped increase in the number of studies of articulatory dynamics (Laver, 1970), and the development of a number of new techniques for their measurement. Accompanying this work, there has been an increase in the

16

realization, which began with the earlier acoustic phonetic studies, that there is enormous variability in articulatory gestures as a function of their phonetic and linguistic context. This has led in turn to an increasing realization of the inappropriateness of conceptualizing the dynamic processes of articulation itself in terms of discrete, static, context-free linguistic categories, such as "phoneme" and "distinctive feature".* This development does not mean that these linguistic categories should be abandoned -as there is considerable evidence for their behavioral reality (Fromkin, 1971). Instead, it seems to require that they be recognized, even more than before, as too abstract to characterize the actual behavior of articulators themselves. They are therefore at present better confined to primarily characterizing earlier pre-motor stages of the production process, as revealed by speech errors, and to reflecting regularities at the message level (Fant, 1962) of the structure of language, such as those noted by phonologists. Parallel to this decrease in relevance of the units of linguistic theory to the dynamics of articulation, there has arisen a need for new concepts to characterize articulatory function, concepts more appropriate to the description of movement processes than stationary states. It seems desirable that in the future, these concepts be integrated with or made compatible with traditional linguistic-unit concepts. But this should not be a one-way street. If a goal of linguistic theory is to characterize what speakers do, then the concepts of that theory must be compatible with the facts of speech production. I will discuss this point in more detail later in the paper.

In the nineteen fifties, perhaps the major impetus to studies of articulatory dynamics came from the pioneering work of Haskins Laboratories' re-

---

*Lisker (1971) has a particularly good exposition of this point.

searchers, in which they established the importance
of formant transitions arising from articulatory dynamics and delicate timing cues arising from dynamic
interaction of laryngeal and articulatory structures
(Liberman, 1957), as cues to speech perception. These
discoveries led to increasing interest in the articulatory processes underlying the cues. Concern with
articulatory processes was given further impetus by
the motor theory of speech perception (Liberman,
Cooper, Harris, MacNeilage and Studdert-Kennedy, 1967)
which claimed that perception of some linguistic categories resulted from the listener making reference
to a particular kind of motor information underlying
his own articulation. In other words, the perceptual
theory was accompanied by an assertion about the commands underlying speech production, which naturally
invited tests. This in turn led to the initiation,
at Haskins Laboratories, of electromyographic studies
of articulation (Cooper, Liberman, Harris and Grubb,
1958; Lysaught, Rosov, and Harris, 1961).

In the nineteen sixties, perhaps the most important event was the publication of a monograph by a
number of Russian authors (Chistovich, Kozhevnikov,
Alyakrinskiy, Bondarko, Goluzina, Klass, Kuz'min,
Lisenko, Lyublinskaya, Fedorova, Shuplyakov, and
Shuplyakova) entitled: "Speech: Articulation and
Perception", which was translated (badly) by the U.S.
Department of Commerce in 1965. In my opinion, this
monograph came to grips, for the first time, with the
general problem of articulatory dynamics, in the context of the production of entire utterances, and presented a number of very ingenious hypotheses and experimental approaches bearing on this problem. It perhaps demonstrated for the first time that conceptual
tools appropriate to the study of articulatory dynamics could be formulated free from the inherent constraints imposed by static linguistic-unit concepts
that were themselves formulated primarily for reasons
other than explanation of articulatory processes.

These developments, along with a number of others
have given rise to the increasing interest in details

of the articulatory process in the past few years.In
the following paragraphs, I will attempt to summarize
the present state of knowledge in this area and to
evaluate the explanatory concepts which have arisen.
Before beginning, I should emphasize again that we
are still primarily at a fact-gathering stage in this
area. Consequently, there are many facts available
which appear to have no principled basis at present.
Nevertheless, I will present many of these facts as
there is no satisfactory means of unfavorably pre-
judging their ultimate significance as an excuse for
ignoring them. I will begin by reviewing some recent findings on the function of the soft palate.
The Soft Palate or Velum

In most languages the soft palate has only one
linguistically distinctive function, namely to distinguish between nasal and non-nasal segments. However, a closer look at the soft palate has revealed
a number of further aspects of its function which
bear on the general question of articulatory dynamics.
Also because of its inaccessibility and its rather
complex morphology and for clinical reasons, much
effort has been expended in attempting simply to find
out how the palate actually moves, and how this movement is controlled by contraction of the palatal musculature.

There is a good deal of agreement that the rad-
ial movement of the velum in a posterior-superior direction which results in a closure of the velopharyngeal port for non-nasal segments is achieved primarily by contraction of the levator palatini muscle.
Combined cinefluorographic and electromyographic studies (Lubker, 1968; Fritzell, 1969) have shown correlation coefficients of approximately 0.8 between
amount of velar elevation and amplitude of EMG activity in the levator palatini muscle. Velar elevation and levator EMG amplitude have also been regularly shown to be directly proportional to vowel
height, although not so regularly related to the
front-back dimension of vowels (Berti, 1971).
Lubker (1968) is probably right in postulating that

19

the higher EMG levels for high vowels reflect a maneuver compensating for their greater susceptibility
to nasalization. Palatal elevation and levator EMG
activity have been found to be greater for obstruents
than for vowels. But within the class of obstruents,
no differences have been consistently observed. For
example, Berti (1971) found higher EMG amplitudes for
voiced stops than for voiceless stops in one of her
two subjects, but no difference in the other. On the
other hand, Lubker, Fritzell and Lindqvist (1971)
found higher EMG amplitudes during voiceless stops
in the one subject they investigated intensively.

A number of coarticulation effects, of both
left-to-right and right-to-left variety have been observed in cinefluorographic studies of palatal movement and electromyographic studies of the levator
palatini. Coarticulation effects stretching across
more than one segment will be discussed later. The
most systematic study of coarticulation effects on
adjacent segments is a study of left-to-right effects
in EMG activity of their one subject by Lubker, et al.
(1971). It is extremely provocative that most of the
numerical data they present on non-nasal segments
following other segments (see Fig. IIA-4) is consistent with one generalization; the average amount of
EMG activity for the second of two segments is proportional to the ratio between the average amount of
peak activity observed during speech in general for
segment two and segment one. For example, most activity is observed for voiceless stop consonants following nasals, as voiceless stops showed the most
activity in general and nasals the least. Conversely,
the non-nasal segments showing least activity in general were open vowels, and they showed their least
activity when they followed voiceless stop consonants.
These results, although based on only one subject,
suggest two generalizations about left-to-right coarticulation over adjacent segments in the levator palatini muscle which are probably applicable to other
articulatory systems as well: (1) the production
system is constrained to approximate a particular

articulatory configuration for each member of a given segment class, whenever it occurs, at least in careful speech.; (2) the amount of EMG activity associated with a segment on any given occasion is proportional to the mechanical work required to approximate the required articulatory configuration. This second generalization is perhaps stating the obvious. But what is of interest in the particular case is that the levator, unlike most other articulatory muscles, is only involved in one task during speech so that its degree of contraction can be related in a straight forward manner to the accomplishment of that task.

When considering other muscles of the palatopharyngeal complex, we find that the present picture is not nearly as straightforward as it is with the levator palatini.

There is disagreement in the literature as to whether the tensor palatini is operative during speech, and among those who think it is, there is disagreement as to its role (see Fritzell, 1969, for a review of this literature). However, in a recent comprehensive electromyographic study of twelve subjects, Fritzell has found that:

"The activity of the tensor during connected speech varied considerably (Figs. 13 and 14). In 7 out of the 12 recordings from this muscle there was very little activity or none at all. In those instances where a fair degree of activity was recorded, there was little agreement between subjects. Apart from the onset of activity before the onset of sound and a peak of activity in the beginning of the sentences, no consistent mode of 'behavior' was found."

The two most recent studies of the palatopharyngeus and the superior pharyngeal constrictor (Fritzell 1969; and Berti, 1971) appear to be in agreement with the earlier finding of Harris, et al. (1962) that these muscles like the levator are active for oral gestures and relatively inactive for nasal gestures. In addition, Berti has observed in the data of some-

21

times one, sometimes two subjects, that EMG activity
is inversely correlated with highness and backness
of vowels and is higher for voiceless than voiced
consonants.

Fritzell (1969) and Lubker, et al. (1971) are
agreed that palatoglossus activity can be observed
to accompany nasalization suggesting that it acts
antagonistically to the levator, in lowering the
soft palate. Berti did not observe this activity in
either of two subjects. Fritzell (1969) and Berti
(1971) agree on the presence of EMG activity in the
palatoglossus muscle during segments involving high
back tongue positions, namely [n], [g], [k], [u].

The differences of opinion as to the role of
these muscles could be due to two main sources: a.
problems of gaining a satisfactory recording from a
muscle; and b. individual differences between subjects in their pattern of use of muscles. It is
highly likely, given the techniques of localization
of muscle recording used in these studies and the
morphology of these muscles, that when workers claim
to have observed a pattern of activity from a given
muscle, they are usually correct; i.e. there is probably a minimum number of false positives reported in
the literature. The main problem therefore lies in
accounting for the negative findings. In muscles
that are very small, such as the palatoglossus, or
very inaccessible, such as the tensor, it is possible
that electrodes may sometimes be suboptimally placed
with respect to the muscle fibers of interest. This
problem could perhaps sometimes be diagnosed by increasing the receptive field of the electrode by
changing from bipolar to monopolar recording. On
the other hand, it is entirely conceivable that there
are individual differences in use of different speech
muscles. They may arise for example, from individual
differences in overall morphology of the speech apparatus which result in differences in the functional
demand placed on different subcomponents of the
speech apparatus. A major challenge that is emerg-
ing for researchers in speech physiology, when they

22

use several subjects in their experiments, is to develop speech production theories which take these individual differences into account rather than ignoring them.

Segment Durations and Articulatory Dynamics

Segment durations provide useful information about dynamics in that they provide clues as to the temporal organization or serial ordering of speech production. In the past few years, this information, usually derived from acoustic measurements, has been supplemented by more direct information about articulator movements expressed in terms of displacement, velocity and acceleration. In the following paragraphs, I will review some of this information and consider its significance.

Segments can be conceived of as possessing intrinsic durations that relate to the means of their own articulation (Lehiste, 1971, p. 18). Within the class of vowels, some of the variance in duration of different vowels in comparable contexts is accounted for by amount of jaw opening, more open vowels having longer durations (House, 1961). The articulatory process thus appears to be subject to the mechanical constraints inherent in moving this large articulator increasing distances, as most consonants require relatively closed jaw positions. But it is of interest that partially successful efforts appear to be made to overcome this constraint. It has been shown that maximum velocity of jaw opeing and closing movements required for the vowel in the set [i], [ε], [æ] (Sussman and Smith, 1971). Furthermore, Lindblom has shown compensatory vowel-shortening movements of the lower lip when open vowels are followed by bilabial stop consonants (Lindblowm, 1967). It is as if the central mechanism strives for equality of segment duration but with either an inability to achieve it, or a lack of necessity for completely achieving it, which Lindblom has suggested may be based on perceptual tolerances (Lindblom, 1967).

When different phonetic contexts are considered, most of the variance in vowel duration is related to the identity of the following consonant, with voiced consonants preceded by longer vowels than voiceless, and fricatives by longer vowels than stop consonants. An important clue to the reason for these differences, at least in stop consonants, was provided by Chistovich et al. (1965). They found that average velocity of the lip closing movement was faster for voiceless bilabial stops than for voiced (140-vs- 125 mm per second). On the basis of some measurements of this effect in English, Chen (1970) has concluded that the greater rate of lower lip movement in voiceless bilabial stops could make a difference of 27 ms. in vowel duration. Chen found that this value was similar to the differences in vowel duration preceding voiced and voiceless stops in a number of languages. These differences in closure movements for bilabial stop consonants probably result from the fact that a more forceful articulator movement is required in the voiceless stop to counteract the greater aerodynamic forces about to be imposed on the upper articulators by air flow in the open glottal condition necessary for voicelessness.

However, rates of lip movement would not be expected to be relevant to differences in voicing of alveolar and velar stops as they do not actively involve the lips. In this connection, it must be borne in mind that rate of lower lip movement is a combined result of actual lower lip movement with respect to the lower jaw and lower jaw movement itself. Ohala, Hiki, Hubler and Harshman (1968) have concluded that rates of lower jaw closing movements are greater for voiceless stop consonants in general than for voiced, though they only presented a single illustration of each type stop. We have recently gathered information on this question in three subjects (Kim and MacNeilage, 1972) and found that although actual lower lip movement rates were not greater for bilabial voiceless stops, lower jaw movement rates for all three voiceless stops significantly exceeded those of their voiced counterparts when they followed the open vowel [a]. In the case of [k] and [g], other structures also appear to bear some of the differential dynamic burden. Minifie (personal communication) has observed more EMG activity in muscles running from the hyoid bone to the styloid process during [k] than during [g]. I have also observed this in an unpublished study of one subject, but did not observe such an effect in [t,d] or [p,b].) It appears then that velocity differences in jaw movement are related to the need to counteract aerodynamic forces. It therefore seems that mechanical constraints are responsible for differences in vowel duration due to following stop-consonatal context just as they are responsible for durational effects of vowel openess.*

This explanation appears to cover the facts of vowel duration effects of following stop consonants in many languages, but not all. It is well known that differences in vowel duration preceding voiced and voiceless stop consonants in English and French can considerably exceed 27 ms. (House, (1961), for example, finds a mean value of approximately 130 ms). In fact, it has been shown by Denes (1955) in an experiment using synthetic speech, that English-speaking listeners used the differences in vowel length as a perceptual cue to the voicing of the following consonant. Furthermore, it has been shown by Chen that in English utterances involving the sequence vowel-sonorant ([m,r,l[), -stop, vowels as well as sonorants are shorter in duration before voiceless stops. This change in the vowel obviously cannot be due to any physiological effect of the terminal stop consonant. Findings of this kind make it necessary to postulate

---

*The interesting theoretical question thus becomes; why does the means of coping with the aerodynamic contingencies result in a shortening of vowel segment duration in the voiceless case? It is not the only possible means.

that an inherent mechanical constraint on speech production has in some sense 'triggered' differences in
vowel duration in some languages which exceed the
immediate effect of the constraint itself, and can
in some cases, achieve perceptual significance.*

This explanation unfortunately does not appear
to account for the differences in vowel duration preceding voiced and voiceless fricatives even though
voicing differences in fricatives are associated with
similar aerodynamic contingencies to voicing differences in stops (Malecot, 1970). Kim and I (1972)
found no systematic differences in our three subjects
between velocities of jaw closing for voiced and
voiceless fricatives. The argument that compensation
for aerodynamic force differences is exerted primarily at the point of constriction does not seem prom-
ising either. All three of our subjects showed
greater net lip closing velocities for [v] than for
[f]. Differences in vowel duration due to voicing
of following fricatives thus remains unexplained,
unless one appeals to a totally ad hoc 'output regularity' constraint that makes vowels behave in the
same way with respect to the voicing distinction in
all obstruents.

So far, we have observed the effects of two
different types of mechanical constraint on articulatory dynamics. In the case of intrinsic differences
in vowel duration, there appears to be a simple constraint of articulatory mass, directly proportional
to displacement and partially compensated for by
velocity of movement. In the case of vowel duration
differences conditioned by voicing of following stop
consonants, we have observed an interaction between
phonatory and articulatory mechancial contingencies.

---

* A similar case of differences in Fo associated with
voiced voiceless stops 'triggering' the development
of differences in word tone even though the earlier
consonant distinction has disappeared, has been described by Mohr (1970).

26

The greater vowel durations preceding fricatives than preceding stops appear to be associated with a third distinct type of mechanical effect--the effect of required precision of movement on rate of movement. Stevens and House (1963) have postulated, on the basis of spectrographic evidence that articulator movements are slower during transitions from vowels into fricatives than in transitions from vowels into stops. They speculated that the slower movements for fricatives might result from the fact that a greater precision of articulator placement is required for fricatives--namely an optimally narrow constriction-- than for stops where "overshoot" of an articulator following occlusion will have a negligible effect on the acoustic signal. Kim and I have shown that al- though the lower jaw does not appear to move more slowly for fricatives than stops, the only articulat- or we measured which directly participated in con- striction (namely the lower lip) did move more slow- ly for labiodental fricatives than bilabial stops in all three subjects. Thus, longer durations of vowels before fricatives might be at least partly due to longer durations of movements of the articulators directly involved in the fricative constriction, rel- ated to the precision required for fricative produc- tion. This would not be surprising in the light of Fitts' (1954) finding that in simple skilled movements there are trading relations between the three vari- ables: 1. speed of movement; 2. precision of the termination of the movement; and 3. amount of dis- placement required. It appears that in this case, some speed may have been traded for precision.

Vowel durations are also affected by the place of articulation of the following consonant. Both Fischer Jørgensen (1964) and Peterson and Lehiste (1960) have shown that vowels are shorter preceding bilabial stop consonants than before velar or alveo- lar stops. Peterson and Lehiste also found this effect of place of articulation for durations of both long and short vowels before fricatives, and for long vowels before nasals, i.e. the labiodental fricatives

27

[f] and [v] and the bilabial nasal [m] were preceded
by shorter vowels than other segments of comparable
manner and voicing. There is also in this literature
some tendency for vowels to be shorter before palatal
and velar consonants than before alveolar consonants
though there are some exceptions to this trend.

These findings can be most profitably considered along with the durations of the consonants themselves, i.e. the time period of occlusion of the
vocal tract for stops and nasals and the period of
optimal vocal tract constriction for fricatives.
There is a very good consensus that the period of
occlusion is longer in all phonetic contexts for bilabial stops than for alveolar or velar stops (see
summary in Lehiste, 1971, pp. 27-30). The fact that
this effect is context-free suggests that it is an
intrinsic property of bilabial stops. Still another
mechanical contingency appears to be involved here.
As the lips and jaw are to some extent mechanically
independent of the tongue, which is the major articulator for vowels and most consonants, they are
apparently under less time constraint than the tongue
which is typically involved in segments adjacent 'on
both sides' to a given one. The lips and jaw are
therefore free to produce longer occlusions than lips
and jaw are therefore free to produce longer occlusions than the tongue. The fact that vowel duration
is less before bilabials than before other stops, and
the fact that vowels are shortened more by following
stops than by preceding stops suggests that the mechanical freedom of the lip and jaw system is manifest
more in anticipation of its target position for bilabial stops than in perseveration in that position.
Of course, the fact that an articulator is free to
produce a longer occlusion is not an explanation of
the fact that it produces a longer occlusion.

Although the literature is less clear on this
point than on the characteristics of bilabial stops,
there is some consensus that vowels are shorter before
velar stop consonants than before alveolars. And as
in the case of bilabials, there is some evidence that

28

the consonants which shorten the vowel more, namely
velars, are themselves longer in duration than alveolars with comparable voicing. Lehiste has suggested
a mechanical explanation for these findings, namely
that the tongue tip, being the more mobile articulat-
or, can move faster, thus producing shorter closure
durations. Whether this explanation is correct would
seem to depend on the overall timing demands imposed
on an utterance, which are not at present clear, but
will be discussed more in later paragraphs. In the
absence of that knowledge, one could equally well argue that being a faster articulator, the tongue tip
could carry out closing and opening gestures more
quickly, thus leaving more time for occlusion than is
available for velars.

I would like to continue by reviewing data on
the influence of place of articulation on fricative
durations but I don't know of enough data on this topic to make any general statement possible.

It is well known that manner of articulation
has some consequences for duration. Lehiste (1971)
has reviewed data on flaps, taps, and trills--point-
ing out that some aspects of their duration, which
are always relatively short, are understandable in
terms of the way in which they are produced. Fricative and stop durations do not show any clear general
differences.

The presence of voicing affects segment durations of obstruents. Voiced stops and fricatives are
typically shorter in duration than their voiceless
equivalents. I do not know of any satisfactory explanation for this.

Suprasegmental Influences on Segment Duration

So far, this has been a review of two types of
variables affecting segment duration: Intrinsic variables in the case of vowels and consonants, and effects of immediate segmental context in the case of
vowels. Information is obviously incomplete on even
these limited topics. Some of our areas of ignorance
have been already pointed out in the course of this
review. We are apparently far from the point where

29

we can say whether segment durations are in general more influenced by preceding than following phonetic contexts, or even whether there can be a sensible answer to this question. The question may be too general to permit a single enlightening answer.

Even within the class of monosyllables, vowels presumably differ in duration, depending on whether or not they are bounded by consonants, though to my knowledge, this question has not been systematically investigated, probably largely because of the difficulty of deciding on where unbounded vowels actually begin and end. Durational influences of adjacent consonants on each other have received little attention. In this regard, a recent study of Haggard (1971) deserves some attention. He points out that it is well known that consonants in clusters 'reduce' in duration to a point somewhere between the sum of their values when produced singly, and the mean of those values. The only attempts at formulating rules for these reductions have been made in connection with the synthesis of speech (e.g. Mattingly, 1968), but these rules are rather ad hoc and not based on a careful study of durational variation of individual consonants when in clusters. Haggard has made such a study of 8 subjects producing a set of six English cluster types in monosyllables. Even though this is a limited sample of English consonant cluster types, a number of his findings and conclusions are of interest. His data show first, that consonants do not invariably reduce their duration in clusters. Second, there are a number of positional effects within the monosyllables which influence consonant durations. Postvocalic, absolute final consonants appear to have longest durations and are reduced by approximately 20% when in final consonant clusters, even though they still retain their absolute final position. There appears to be a much smaller difference between absolute initial consonants when pre-vocalic and when cluster-initial, i.e. less shortening in cluster-initial position. Consonants internal in clusters also appear to reduce very slightly in duration whether in initial or final position. Haggard also documented a number of specific effects of place and manner of adjacent consonants on the duration of given consonants, but these probably deserve replication and extension before being made to carry a heavy theoretical burden.

So far, we have considered durational variations which are observable in monosyllabic words. But there remains an enormous class of durational effects associated with higher-order aspects of the production of utterances, and indicating the existence of an elegant heirarchy of speech timing mechanisms. I will now outline some of these durational variations. They have recently been reviewed in more detail by Lehiste (1971). She also reviews contrastive uses of duration in languages other than English, which will not be considered here.

There is a tendency in many languages for the duration of syllabic nuclei to vary inversely with the number of syllables in a word. This tendency is quite marked, for example in Hungarian (Tarnoczy, 1965, cited by Lehiste, 1971, p.40) and also occurs in English (Lehiste, 1971). I do not know how frequently this effect has been observed in other languages.

The lengthening* of final syllables is another well known suprasegmental effect, and has recently been systematically explored by Oller (1971). He has confirmed the popular impression that final syllable lengthening is greater when a word occurs in the final position of an utterance. He also finds a slight (20 ms) lengthening even when the word is produced in a non-final position in a phrase. In English, lengthening of the syllable appears to take place predominantly within the vowel. However, in a study of one dialect of Finnish, Oller found very little final vowel lengthening but relatively more final consonant lengthening. It appears then, that final syllable

---

* This term is arbitrary. One could as well talk about shortening of non-final syllables.

lengthening is not uniform in pattern in different languages, and this makes the phenomenon difficult to ascribe, in any striaghtforward way, to an inherent production constraint. It is also difficult to explain it as the provision of a perceptual cue (Oller, 1971).

In English, though not in a number of other languages, stress appears to be typically accompanied by lengthening of syllable nuclei (Fry, 1955), and probably by systematic, though small, changes in surrounding consonants. It is rather well known that in English and some other languages the longer duration of more heavily stressed syllables is accompanied by more movement of articulators toward target positions (Lindblom, 1963). Studies of articulatory dynamics have suggested that these articulator movements also tend to be of higher velocity for stressed syllables (MacNeilage, 1970; Kent and Netsell, 1971). Electromyographic studies have shown that stressed syllables are accompanied by higher levels of muscle activity in some articulators than unstressed syllables (Harris, Gay, Sholes and Lieberman, 1968; Harris, 1971; Slis, 1972). Kent and Netsell's study suggests that these differences are not accompanied by differences in the amount of coarticulation of the affected gestures with adjacent gestures.

Segment duration also seems to vary inversely with utterance length, at least in English. Gaitenby (1965) has shown that increasing the total utterance in which a given phrase is embedded reduces the duration of the phrase.

A final determinant of segment duration is speaking rate. Increases in speaking rate are accompanied by decreases in segment duration, with the decrease in the vowel being proportionately greater (Chistovich, et al., 1965; MacNeilage and DeClerk, 1968). These decreases are achieved not by an increase of rate of articulator movement--rates either remain constant (Lindblom, 1964; MacNeilage and DeClerk, 1968) or decrease (Chistovich, et al. 1965)--but by a reduction in the amount of articulator displacement

32

towards target. The consequences of speaking rate increase thus may be analagous to those of stress decrease.

It is of interest to note two variables that might have been imagined to have durational consequences, but apparently do not. Lehiste (1971, (b)) has concluded that morpheme boundaries and syntactic boundaries did not have any systematic effects on segment durations separable from effects that could be ascribed to the syllabic structure of the utterances.

Chistovich et al's View of Articulatory Dynamics

We do not yet have available satisfactory theoretical formulations about any of the main individual aspects of articulatory timing that have been summarized here. In fact, general interest in articulatory timing within the field of speech physiology has only developed within the past few years, largely as a result of contributions by Lashley (1951) (whose general view of the problem of output timing has, in my opinion, yet to be improved upon (MacNeilage and MacNeilage, 1971), Chistovich et al. (1965), Lenneberg (1967), Allen, (1968), and Lehiste, (1971). Chistovich and her colleagues have made the most specific and influential attempts to develop a model of articulatory timing. A convenient and appropriate way to evaluate the present state of theorizing in this area is to summarize the views of the Russian group and then consider how subsequent studies, stimulated largely by the Russian work, bear on these views.

Chistovich et al. postulate that the largest unit of speech timing is the syntagma. This is defined as "a sentence or part of a sentence distinguished by meaning". It is produced as a single output bounded by pauses, and has an average length in free speech of 7 syllables.

Within the syntagma, Chistovich, et al., postulated that the basic articulatory unit was the articulatory syllable which differed considerably from traditional linguistic conceptions of the syllable. The articulatory syllable consisted of a vowel and however

33

many consecutive consonants preceded it. This claim
was based largely on the finding that the lip rounding gesture for the vowel /u/ began "simultaneously"
with first consonant when either one or two consonants preceded the vowel. This same result was still
found, even when a conventional syllable or word
boundary fell between the two consonants. The coin-
cidence between lip-rounding onset and the first consonant led Chistovich et al. to consider lip rounding
onset as an objective sign of the beginning of the
syllable. Further hypotheses governed the interrel-
ations between gestures within the syllable. The
most basic assumption was that all movements required
for the syllable are 'assigned' at the beginning of
the syllable. Movements which are not antagonistic
to other movements, such as lip-rounding during consonants, are accomplished simultaneously (with a minor 'triggering' rule to account for appropriate se-
quencing of consonant clusters). Where antagonism
exists, movements required for the vowel are delayed.
A cinefluorographic study by Daniloff and Moll (1968)
confirmed the findings of Chistovich for one and two
consonants preceding rounded vowels, and also found
that the vowel-rounding gesture extended back to the
beginning of three and four consonant sequences as
well (e.g. in the four consonant sequence in "con-
strue").

More recently, Moll and Daniloff (1971) have
discovered some rather damaging counterexamples to
the Russian concept of the articulatory syllable.
They found that "in sequences in which a nasal consonant is preceded by one or two vowel sounds, the
velar opening gesture for the nasal is initiated near
the beginning of primary articulatory movement toward
the first vowel in the sequence." In addition, Dixit
and MacNeilage (1972) have found that in Hindi, nasal
vowels and nasal consonants exhibit similar right-to-
left coarticulatory effects which extend over at least
three segments--consonants or vowels--if none of these
preceding segments are obstruents. These results suggest that the temporal scope of right-to-left coartic-

ulation effects is not consistently related to any
postulated 'left-hand' boundary of a syllable, if
this boundary is defined in terms of consonant-vowel
relations. Results such as this also call into question the generality of the hypothesis of MacNeilage
and DeClerk (1969), based on analysis of a small set
of CVC monosyllables, that the CV unit is more "cohe-
sive" than the VC unit because there is more right-to-
left coarticulation of V on preceding C_1 than of C_2
on preceding V.

It appears, therefore, that although there is no
reason to abandon the view of Chistovich, et al.,
that the syllable is in some sense a basic articulatory unit, the position of the left-hand boundary of
the syllable cannot be established by examination of
right-to-left coarticulation effects alone. The question now arises as to what overall pattern the right-
to-left effects exhibit. The principle suggested by
Chistovich, et al., that movements not contradictory
to other movements can be coarticulated with these
movements has some appeal from the intuitive point of
view. For example, right-to-left nasality effects
presumably do not extend into obstruents because the
resultant nasal leak would prevent the formation of
the aerodynamic prerequisites for some acoustic cues
for obstruents, e.g. friction in fricatives, bursts
in stops. But it is difficult to give a formal definition to the notion "contradictory." In addition,
we have observed one instance in which anticipatory
movements are contradictory to preceding gestures.
(Sussman, MacNeilage and Hanson, 1972). We have observed that the amount of closing of the jaw for an
intervocalic bilabial stop consonant decreases as the
amount of opening required for the following vowel increases. This decrease in jaw closing is contradictory to the demand for lip closure for the bilabial
stop because of the dependance of lower lip position
on jaw position. The fact that it is contradictory
is illustrated by the activity pattern of the mentalis
muscle which is associated with lip elevation for the
bilabial stop. This muscle shows an increase in act-

35

ivity for the bilabial stop, as the amount of opening required for the following vowel increases. It thus appears to be compensating for the reduction of the jaw closing movements.

Another question of considerable interest is why do articulatory effects extend so far to the left. It is obviously not due to mechanical demand in any simple sense of the term, because the 'same' gestures which spread over four segments on some occasions are produced in little more than half a segment on others. Moll and Daniloff have suggested that right-to-left coarticulation may have perceptual benefits in that it may provide useful anticipatory cues to the identity of later segments. This possibility is consistent with the fact that left-to-right effects appear to be typically a good deal more restricted in their temporal scope than right-to-left effects (MacNeilage, 1972). There may be two perceptually-based reasons for this finding. First, left-to-right effects are restricted because there is little perceptual advantage in continuing to provide cues for segments whose main acoustic effects have already been transmitted. Second, the provision of such cues may, because of the potentially confusing effects of their co-occurrence with anticipatory cues for later segments, reduce the usefulness of the anticipatory cues.

This explanation should not be accepted uncritically. It has troubling teleological connotation. In addition, Dixit and MacNeilage (1972) have found that left-to-right effects of nasality in Hindi have a temporal scope at least equal to that of right-to-left effects, which is a counterexample to the general finding that R-L effects have greater temporal scope than L-R effects. Nevertheless, it still appears that the overall pattern of both R-L and L-R effects is better explained in terms of its perceptual consequences than in terms of any simple view of articulatory necessity. Furthermore, the apparent counterexample of Hindi may simply reflect the fact that the general principles governing the temporal scope of both types of coarticulation in a given language are a result of the total

36

inventory of perceptual cues to segmental forms and
their phonotactic distribution in that language.
However, it should be noted that perceptually based
solutions are not without theoretical inconvenience.
The more comprehensive, and language-specific, perceptually motivated articulatory events are, the more
they are likely to mask inherent articulatory constraints on the production process.

Correlational Studies

Chistovich, et al., distinguished between two
types of models or principles which could govern the
temporal organization of speech output.* In the
first type of model, commands are issued from a central location at regular intervals, This has been
called a comb model. In the second type, the timing
of peripheral events subsequent to the first one is
determined by some signal arising from the immediately preceding event (the so-called chain model). Note
that there is an important difference in control principles between these two models. The first can be
regarded as open-loop in that the commands and their
timing are autonomously controlled from higher centers. On the other hand, the second is a closed-loop
model in that the timing (although not the form) of
output gestures is determined by feedback from previous events. Chistovich et al. attempted to make an
empirical choice between these two models on the basis of the durations exhibited by speech segments in
repeated productions of the same utterance. They
reasoned that speech segment durations would be affected in two ways depending on which type of model
was controlling production. First, if the chain model was correct, there would be no reason to expect
any correlation between the duration of a given segment and the duration of the immediately following
one. On the other hand, the constant timing of higher

---

*The general form of these two types of models has
often been postulated. See Ohala (1970, p 118) for
a review.

order outputs in the comb model was taken to mean
that if the actual duration of a given peripheral
gesture was shorter than its average, the manifesta-
of the next gesture would be correspondingly longer
as required for it to terminate as 'planned' by the
higher-order timing scheme. Second, the resultant
negative correlation between adjacent durations in
the comb case should result in the sum of the vari-
ances of individual segments in an utterance being
larger than the variance of the total utterance. Both
these predictions from the comb model were upheld in
Chistovich's analysis. Sums of variance for syllables, and for individual segments, were greater than
the variance of the entire utterance in the case of
the phrase, "Tonya topila banyu" repeated 100 times
by two subjects. Negative correlations were found
between segments in the same syllable, for segments
straddling 'their' syllable boundary (V-C) and for
adjacent syllables. The highest average negative
correlation was between vowel and following consonant
and although this was across the postulated syllable
boundary, Chistovich, et al., made no comment on it.
More recently, Lehiste (1971, (c)) has also found
generally higher and more consistent negative correlations between vowel and following consonant in English monosyllables (which, interestingly, reduced in
magnitude if the 'same' syllable was not the final
syllable, e.g. "steady" instead of "stead").

Perhaps these results mean that there is indeed
a syllable boundary between vowel and subsequent consonant as Chistovich, et al., propose, despite the
fact that coarticulation is not 'controlled' by the
V-C boundary, as we have seen. It may be that the
lower negative correlations between segments within
the syllable indicates a lesser temporal cohesiveness
of intrasyllabic organization, which would naturally
result in considerable temporal mismatching of the
syllable boundary (hence the high negative correlations) if that boundary is controlled by central timing which is comparatively regular and can not 'toler-
ate' peripheral delay. However, I do not feel that

38

such speculation is justified at present because so
little data is available and there are a number of
reasons for interpreting it with caution. First,
there is reason to question whether there is a simple
one-to-one relation between particular patterns of
variance in unit durations, and correlation between
units, on the one hand, and either of the two models
on the other. Ohala (1970) has reviewed some of
these questions. Secondly, Haggard has pointed out
that the type of correlation to be expected depends
partly on whether the two adjacent segments are hom-
organic, partly on whether the articulatory demands
of the two gestures are compatible and partly on whether the vocal tract is changing to a more closed or
to a more open position between segments. For example
he argues quite convincingly that in a sequence such
as [p ə], even if the events governing [p] closure,
[p] closure termination, and [ə] termination in a
series of repetitions are all random, there will still
be a negative correlation between [p] and [ə] durations because the 'earlier' the release of the [p]
occurs, the longer the vowel will be, other things
being equal. Haggard's attempt to predict the form
of correlations from articulatory dynamics (and his
claims to have confirmed some of these predictions)
deserve study because they address themselves to a
very important question in speech physiology, although one that has often been ignored, because
bothering with these extremely small variations in
segment duration appears to some as mere bristle-
counting. The question can be formulated in the following manner; the mechanism responsible for sequen-
cing of speech sounds must program articulatory gestures that satisfactorily interface pairs of adjacent
segments. Segment durations and details of articulatory dynamics give clues as to how this interfacing
takes place. It seems quite clear at present that
the means by which this interfacing is achieved is
extremely complex and dependent on the type of segments being interfaced and their position in words.
However it also seems clear that simple attempting an

either-or choice between comb and chain models of
articulatory dynamics is far too superficial a way to
approach the problem of speech organization. It is
discouraging to some of us but stimulating to others
to realize that we will have to undertake the task of
resolving these 'molecular' puzzles of segment dynamics in order to obtain a satisfactory theory of
temporal organization of speech. It is my conviction
that the climate of opinion that has led to the emphasis on invariance and the neglect of contextual
variability in speech physiology, has led us away
from the most important single clue to the nature of
the speech production mechanism.

The Control of Gestures Within a Syllable

A good deal of work has been done on the general
question of the control principles underlying segmental articulatory gestures themselves. I have reviewed this work in detail elsewhere (MacNeilage, 1970;
MacNeilage and MacNeilage, 1971) and will merely summarize these reviews here.

In the early sixties a number of authors independently formulated models of speech production in
which the phoneme (segment) was the basic unit. Segment production was conceived as either the issuing
of a single invariant motor command (or one of a small
subset of allophonic variants) per phoneme (Liberman,
Cooper, Harris, MacNeilage and Studdert-Kennedy, 1967;
Halle and Stevens, 1964; Ohman, 1966; Moll and Shriner, 1967) or as the result of central specification
of targets or vocal tract configurations (Lindblom,
1963; Ladefoged, 1967 b; Stevens and House, 1963).
These models were unanimous in attributing the well
known lack of phonemic invariance in the acoustic signal to mechanical and neurosmuscular limitations of
the production apparatus and temporal overlap in commands. In the few years since the formulation of
these models it has become quite clear, largely from
electromyographic studies of articulator movement
(e.g. Fromkin, 1966; Ohman, 1967; MacNeilage and
DeClerk, 1969) that the notion of invariant motor commands is untenable at the neuromuscular level and un-

40

testable (at present) at higher levels of the nervous
system. The finding of a lack of invariance at the
peripheral level is quite consistent with the review
of data presented earlier on segmental influences on
articulatory dynamics which shows the interfacing of
segments to be such a complex and context dependant
process. In addition, this review suggests that rather than being a passive victim of its neural and
mechanical limitations the articulatory mechanism has
a host of elegant strategies which help it achieve
its aim under different circumstances.

In 1969, Wicklegren put forward a different type
of "motor command" hypothesis, namely that there are
as many commands ("context sensitive allophones") as
there are interfaces between segments. This hypothesis has drawn criticism like a magnet on a number of
grounds, mostly valid to varying degrees in my opinion. (Halwes and Jenkins, 1971; Lenneberg, 1971;
MacKay, 1970; MacNeilage, 1970; MacNeilage and Mac-
Nailage, 1971; Whitaker, 1970) The most important of
these criticisms are: I. the hypothesis is little
more than a restatement of the facts and is virtually
untestable, 2. It contains no principle for distinguishing between different allophones and hence does
not recognize important phonetic generalizations that
emerge from the facts, (to take a single example, the
allophones of [/p/, /t/, and /k/] following open vowels have in common a faster rate of jaw movement than
their voiced cognates because they share aerodynamic
contingencies related to voicelessness): 3. It dis-
allows the potential for creativity in the production
mechanism which allows it to 'spontaneously' reorgan-
ize its articulatory movements in order to remain in-
telligible in situations such as talking with the
teeth clenched, or with food in the mouth. Incidentally this same criticism can be levelled at the other
"motor command' theories also.

The alternative hypothesis that there are targets
governing segmental articulation remains tenable in
my opinion. There is a large body of evidence which
I have reviewed in the earlier papers that we have

"space coordinate systems" (Lashley's (1951) term) in the brain which we use to conceptualize three dimensional space, and guide movements in three dimensional space. One of the most important pieces of evidence for the existence of targets comes from our ability to speak intelligibly with the teeth clenched which, I have argued (1970) can be done without changes of targets of moving articulators but would require on-the-spot generation of whole sets of new motor commands. I have suggested the possibility (1970), as had others before me, that relatively invariant articulator positions might be achieved by operation of the so-called gamma loop (Matthews,(1964) which could allow a muscle to assume a single length for a given segment regardless of its segmental context. More recent work has suggested that the target mechanism must be a good deal more complex than I had proposed. Nooteboom (1970) and Lindblom and Sundberg (1971) have pointed out that in teeth-clenched speech the fact that the jaw is fixed means that many muscles need to assume different lengths than usual in order to shape the vocal tract in a similar way for a given vowel (for example, muscles lowering the tongue for a low vowel which involves considerable jaw opening (e.g. [a]) must shorten more when the jaw, to which the tongue is attached, does not lower. The gamma loop mechanism of equalizing muscle length is therefore inadequate to the task of obtaining an analagous vowel target position with the jaw fixed in position. Furthermore Nooteboom has argued that we are able to produce quite different configurations of the resonant cavities of the vocal tract in order to produce a vowel with similar acoustic properties. This suggests to Nooteboom that there is an auditory perceptual component to the target assignment mechanism because the match being produced under restriction is more an acoustic match than an articulatory match.
Closed-Loop Control of Articulation
        The role of closed-loop, or feedback, control in articulation has been a recurrent theme in this paper and in the area of speech physiology in general. It

42

should be said at the outset that despite a considerable amount of research and speculation on this subject, there is at present no simple yes-or-no answer to the question of whether closed-loop control operates during speech. If one considers the results of a large number of neurophysiological studies of sensorimotor function, the overwhelming impression is that closed loop control is a universal property of behavior. But most neurophysiological studies are of limited direct relevance to speech in that they have been done on other species than man and under highly artificial conditions, typically including physical restraint. Furthermore, the activity being studied is initiated by the experimenter--often with electrical stimulation--rather than in a natural manner by the animal itself.

Neurophysiologists themselves have only recently begun to turn their attention to the implications of their findings of these types of experiments for the understanding of normal voluntary motor function in intact animals and are concluding that at present they know very little about it. (Brooks, Jasper, Patton, Purpura and Brookhart, 1970). The main function which closed-loop control most probably serves if it serves any in ongoing speech is an extremely delicate one of correcting aspects of ongoing articulator movements, some of which are completed in considerably less than 100 milliseconds. Considering the delicacy of this possible function, the types of investigation of closed loop-control that have been made on speech have been extremely gross. They have consisted mostly of either observation of the effects of accidental (pathological) impairment of sensory pathways, or experimental intervention in the operation of these pathways. These investigations and others have given rise to at least a certain amount of information about the role of feedback control of speech which I will now summarize.

It seems unlikely that moment to moment auditory feedback plays an important role in control of running speech, largely because speech movements for the

43

most part precede their main acoustic effects in time
and the firing of the motoneurons controlling the
muscles largely precedes the movement. Unfortunately
it is not possible to simply eliminate auditory feedback in an experiment. More complex interventions
consist of masking the self-generated acoustic signal
with a high intensity noise (McCroskey, 1958) or al-
tering its usual time of arrival either by acceleration (Peters, 1954) or delay (Lee, 1950). Effects on
speech have been measured up until very recently in
terms of rather gross criteria such as distortions,
omissions and additions, overall speech rate and intensity.

Effects of masking noise and acceleration have
been found to be rather minor. Effects of delayed
auditory feedback have been quite considerable, even
to the point of reducing some subjects to complete
incoherence. However in all these cases the interven-
consists of <u>changing</u> the arrival time of most auditory input and not eliminating it, and the effects observed may be due to the nature of the changes rather
than to the fact that normal feedback is necessary.
This interpretation is suggested by the fact that
there is an optimal delay interval of 0.2 seconds
which produces the maximum disturbance in delayed auditory feedback situations. Such a time-locked effect
would not be predicted simply from the notion that
normal feedback is essential to normal production.
Thus it suggests that factors other than mere loss of
sensory information are involved. In fact the delay
producing most disturbance does not even seem to be
related to the structure of the speech material, as
supposed by those who noted that 0.2 seconds is similar to the duration of the syllable. Huggins (1968)
has shown that the interval producing maximum disturbance does not change when the utterances spoken have
particularly long or particularly short syllables.

With respect to <u>somatic sensory</u> control, it seems
to me that closed loop control is essential to the initiation of speech. The command necessary for an articulator to reach a fixed speech-initial position

44

must be conditional upon the pre-speech position of that articulator which no doubt varies from occasion to occasion. We have shown that this is true for the jaw in one subject (MacNeilage, Krones and Hanson, 1969).

The sensory intervention studies have a number of methodological problems. Borden (1971) has recently provided evidence that the nerve block procedure used by Ringel and Steer (1963) and by Scott and Ringel (1971) to produce a characteristic spectrum of speech deficits short of unintelligibility may also paralyse certain muscles. However, it is at present difficult to reconcile the spectrum of deficits with the malfunction of the particular muscles that may be impaired. Selective block of gamma efferent fibers has been shown to affect the parameters of displacement, velocity and acceleration of movements (Smith, 1969; Abbs, and Netsell, 1970) though apparently not affecting speech intelligibility (Abbs, Personal Communication). There are two unanswered questions about these experiments. One is about the extent to which the changes in movement pattern are specific to the gamma block condition. The second is whether the pattern of effects could have been predicted from the hypothesized operational characteristics of the gamma loop. With respect to the first question, Sussman has also found changes in velocity and displacement of jaw movements in subjects speaking under delayed feedback (Sussman and Smith, 1971) and following topical anesthetic of the lips (unpublished study) and some of these changes have been analagous to those found by Abbs and Netsell. Would white noise also produce such changes? In addition it is necessary to ask whether Abbs and Netsell would have found similar changes in simple repetitive jaw movements (diadachokinesis) not involving speech control mechanisms?

Smith and Lee (1971) have recently produced evidence unfavorable to a gamma loop control hypothesis for speech. They showed that an artificially introduced increase in resistance to lip closure during the production of bilabial stop consonants is not

45

followed in a few milliseconds by an increase in muscle contraction, as would be predicted from the load compensating property of the gamma loop. On the contrary, they observed EMG inhibition in many cases.

There are some experiments which suggest that the gamma loop does operate during respiration both in cats (Euler, 1966) and in humans. Nathan and Sears (1960) reached the latter conclusion after observing a reduction of intercostal muscle activity on the affected side as compared to the intact side in a patient after unilateral deafferentation, which would, of course, block the operation of the gamma loop. In addition, Sears and Newsom Davis (1968) have shown that from 30 to 80 milliseconds after introducing an unexpected resistance to air flow during phonation in humans, there is an increase in muscle contraction in the internal intercostal muscles. This suggests to them that the gamma loop could operate in normal speech to compensate for changes in respiratory load resulting from changes in impedence at laryngeal and upper articulatory sites. However, similar changes have not yet, to my knowledge actually been observed in speech (see for example McGlone and Shipp, 1972) and there is some question (Martensson, 1968) whether the latencies reported are short enough to be the result of gamma loop action.

Perhaps the clearest indication that the gamma loop can operate in human voluntary behavior comes from an experiment by Dewhurst (1967). He showed that when an unpredictable increase is made in a load supported by the human biceps muscle, compensatory muscle contraction begins about 20-30 ms. after the load increase--about the time necessary for transmission around the gamma loop. Although this result is suggestive, it was obtained in circumstances dissimilar to speech in that they involved isometric and not isotonic contraction. Moreover, it is not clear from Dewhurst's description whether subjects evolved this response during the experiment or exhibited it from the beginning.

It is clear from this review that we do not at

46

present have a satisfactory answer to the question of
whether closed loop control operates during on-going
speech, although the review can easily give rise to
some suggestions for further research. Unfortunately
one problem that plagues this type of research as
well as any other that attempts to infer normal nervous system function from the results of intervention
(Brooks, et al., 1970) is that of redundancy in central nervous system control mechanisms. As Brookhart
(1970) has put it:

> If one inactivates a spark plug in an automo-
> bile engine, it may be observed that the en-
> gine makes unusual noises, vibrates excess-
> ively and loses power. The inference that
> the function of the spark plug was to inhi-
> bit noise generation, vibration and power
> loss would be much more difficult to reach
> if an auxilliary spark plug existed and be-
> came functional when the primary failed.
> This kind of functional redundancy in the
> motor control pathways almost certainly
> makes more difficult the understanding of
> normal functional modes through the obser-
> vation of abnormally functioning systems.

Speech researchers must determine whether there is an
auxilliary spark plug in sensory intervention experiments. If there is one it may take the form of either increased reliance on other available sensory return or increased precision in open loop control functions, and possibly both. The results of the experiments on speech with fixed jaw position certainly suggest that we have a versatile control mechanism.

Speech Physiology and Cortical Function

In considering the neurophysiology of speech in
general, we again encounter the fact that up until
very recently most neurophysiological work on the motor system had limited relevance to normal voluntary
behavior. Perhaps the most encouraging recent development in neurophysiology from the point of view of

the speech physiologist has been the advent of studies involving simultaneous recording of single CNS
neurons and electromyograms during the voluntary performance by animals of relatively skilled motor tasks
which can be considered similar to speech in some respects. The most well known work of this kind has
been done by Evarts (Evarts, 1967) and his colleagues
who have recorded from precentral motor cortex and
points in cortico-cerebello-cortical pathways while
monkeys made regular goal directed flexion and extension movements of the wrist under various loads. The
most typical motor cortex neuron from which they recorded exhibited firing patterns related to the force
developed by the muscle, although a number of other
less interpretable firing patterns were also observed.
Another example of this approach is the work of Humphrey and his associates (Humphrey, Schmidt and Thompson, 1970). They have succeeded in recording from up
to 5 motor cortex neurons simultaneously and, using
multiple regression procedures, have been able to predict the form of the corresponding peripheral movement from cortical neuronal firing patterns with a
high degree of accuracy. Despite the recent tendency
to de-emphasize the relative importance of the precentral motor cortex in voluntary movement as opposed to
the importance of other motor centers and pathways
(Rosner, 1970), these results demonstrate again that
the motor cortex plays an important role in normal
voluntary movement. Furthermore when it is considered
that there are extensive monosynaptic links between
the larger motor cortex neurons and cranial motoneurons (Kuypers, 1964) and that there is a l:l relation
between an action potential in a cranial motoneuron
and the muscle action potential in the muscle fibers
which it innervates, the possibility emerges that electromyographic studies of speech production may provide an important indirect index of cortical motor
function--in fact the least indirect neurophysiological link available in normal users of speech. A number
of my colleagues and I have begun to explore this possibility by making electromyographic recordings of

single motor units in the speech musculature. Our
initial intention is to attempt to 'calibrate' single
motor units in various muscles by observing their
waveforms, and their firing frequencies under isometric (motor unit training)* and isotonic (speech gesture) conditions with special reference to the possibility of functional differentiation of motor units
into tonic and phasic types (Granit, 1970). A central aim is to determine the overall composition of a
burst of firing accompanying a speech gesture and
note the relative role of the 2 variables known to be
involved--the time pattern of recruitment of motor
units, and their firing frequencies. The methodology
and preliminary results of these studies have been
described elsewhere (Hanson, 1971; Sussman, Hanson
and MacNeilage, 1971; MacNeilage, Sussman and Hanson,
1972; MacNeilage and Szabo, 1972). However, an example of one of our preliminary findings may be of
some interest. In muscles running to the tongue and
the hyoid bone from the anterior mandible, a rather
wide range of modal firing frequencies (from 13 to
36 per second) has been observed for single motor units in motor unit training studies. However some of
these same units have been observed to fire at up to
6 times their modal isometric firing frequencies when
involved in a speech movement, and there is scarcely
any overlap between their isometric and isotonic firing frequencies. These latter firing rates, approach-
ing 200 per second, are higher than any reported in
the literature to our knowledge, with the exception
of reports of firing frequencies of up to 350 per second from the extrinsic eye muscles (Marg, Tamler and
Jampolsky, 1962).

The division of firing into two frequency ranges
is strongly reminiscent of the "primary" and "secondary" ranges of firing shown by Kernell (1965) with a
more direct method of 'calibration' of cat motoneur-

* The paradigm for motor unit training studies has
been described by Basmajian (1963).

ons, namely by intracellular stimulation. This finding raises a number of interesting questions about
possible differences in the means of motor control in
the two cases. One possibility which is relevant to
issues already discussed in this paper is that these
two firing conditions make different use of closed
loop control from somatic sensory receptors. Mac-
Neilage (1971), Tokizane and Shimazu (1964) have suggested that slower, more regular rates of firing in a
given muscle are relatively more under spinal (closed
loop) control whereas faster firing rates are more
under cortical (open loop) control. They have partially documented their claim by showing that blockage
of the gamma loop by procaine considerably impairs
the regularity of motor units firing at low rates.
An obvious implication of these findings and hypotheses for the question of closed loop control of speech
is that experiments should be done in which the effect of sensory block on single motor unit firing
frequencies is observed in both isometric and isotonic conditions.

There is one further recent experimental development which I wish to cite because it appears to per-
tain to the issue of the cortical component of speech
physiology. Sussman (1971) has shown that if subjects
are required to track a slowly varying control tone
presented to one ear with a second tone, generated in-
directly by their own lateral tongue movements, and
presented to the other ear, they do significantly better if the tone they generate themselves is presented
to their right ear which projects 'more strongly' to
the left hemisphere. Furthermore a control condition
where the right hand generates one signal shows no
such ear preference. It is tempting and plausible to
interpret this finding, with Sussman, as indicating
the presence, in the left hemisphere, of a specialized
speech related mechanism for the integration of auditory and somatic sensorimotor information, thus providing a sensorimotor addition to the more well known
specialized auditory mechanism (Studdert-Kennedy and
Shankweiler, 1970).

Postscript: Speech Physiology and Linguistic Theory

A satisfactory theory of the physiology of speech production obviously must be compatible with the main phenomena of language function. One might imagine that the converse would also be self-evident, namely that a satisfactory linguistic theory must be compatible with the main phenomena of speech physiology. However speech physiology, and for that matter phonetics in general, has occupied and still does occupy a rather marginal position within linguistic science. For example, from the standpoint of generative phonology, which is what has come to be known as the "standard" view of phonological aspects of linguistic theory, it has been made clear by Chomsky and Halle (1968) that many aspects of the speech signal are of little theoretical interest (coarticulation phenomena are specifically singled out for mention in this regard). They consider the linguistically significant aspects of speech to be embodied in a "phonetic transcription" (p. 295) according to the perception of the language user. Lisker (1971) has pointed out that this view involves an interest in speech which is confined to linguistically distinctive properties of parts of the speech signal, and that this in turn involves the characterization of the speech signal in terms of discrete static entities, a characterization which I hope this review has indicated to be unrealistic at the phonetic level in many ways. One consequence of the view, which was pointed out by Lisker (and Laver, 1970) is a lack of interest in the dynamics of speech production and of the important variable of timing in speech. As Lisker has put it in discussion of the generative phonologists' "phonetic transcription":

> "Underlying the linguist's graphical representation of a sentence is a model of the speech piece as a temporal sequence of articulatory states, their acoustic resultants or their neural-command antecedents, which are themselves largely "timeless" (Abercrombie,

51

1967: 42, 80-81), in that a particular segment is no more to be characterized by the
time interval over which its defining physical properties are maintained than its graph-
ical representative is by the space it may
occupy on the line of print."

(Lisker, 1971, p. 152)

The generative phonologists lack of concern with
many aspects of the speech signal is one way in which
they indicate their opinion that speech physiology
has limited relevance to linguistic theory. The fact
that aspects which are of interest are perceptual
ones further reduces the relevance of speech physiology. This is especially so in the case of stress
in which it is implied that under certain conditions
stress distinctions made on perceptual grounds might
not have any basis in the speech signal:

"A person will normally not be aware of
many properties manifest in the signal,
and, at the same time, his interpretation may involve elements which have no
direct physical correlates."

(Chomsky and Halle, 1968, p.294)

It would perhaps be possible to defend such a-
priori restriction of the scope of linguistic theory
if the resultant formulation did not seriously suffer
from the restriction. A defense might be made on the
tactical grounds that it is difficult at this early
stage in the development of linguistic science to
formulate a complete theory covering all linguistic
phenomena. But in the present case the restriction
of scope results in some serious limitations. One
limitation is that a specification of the phonological component on perceptual grounds is not verifiable
in that it does not suggest means for objective test.
Furthermore, Chomsky and Halle, in fact attempt to
specify the phonological component almost entirely in
articulatory terms, not in perceptual terms, which
reflects rather unfavorably on their arguments for
the primacy of the perceptual approach to their theoretical framework. This inconsistency results from

ignoring the needs expressed by a number of writers (e.g. Lieberman, 1970; Ladefoged, 1971) to explicitly separate perceptual and articulatory explanations in phonological theory and to recognize that each has considerable explanatory power but for different sets of data.

It is unfortunate that where Chomsky and Halle provide articulatory underpinnings to their phonological view the resultant formulations are in many cases not only uninformed with respect to current phonetic knowledge, but lacking in obvious phonetic implications. For example they state:

"The feature 'tenseness' specifies the manner in which the entire articulatory gesture of a given sound is executed by the supraglottal musculature. Tense sounds are produced with a deliberate, accurate, maximally distinct gesture that involves considerable muscular effort; nontense sounds are produced rapidly and somewhat indistinctly."

(p. 324)

Although the terms "deliberate", "accurate", "maximally distinct", "rapidly", and "somewhat indistinctly" have a number of vague mentalistic, physical and auditory-perceptual connotations, they are undefined in phonetics. In the case where an articulatory meaning can be most safely inferred, namely that tense sounds are produced with slower rates of articulator movement than lax sounds, the data which were available (Chistovich et al., 1965) were contrary to the hypothesis (rates of movement are greater in closure for [p] than [b]).

In addition, Lisker and Abramson (1971) have argued that the difficulty of including speech timing considerations in linguistic models has adversely affected Chomsky and Halle's attempt to specify the phonological component in phonetic terms. According to Lisker and Abramson, this is evidenced by Chomsky and Halle's use of combinations of 4 simultaneous articulatory features (often with questionable phonetic justification) to attempt to account for a number of aspects of stop consonant production that Lisker and Abramson account for quite well in terms of the <u>time relations</u> between release of occlusion and onset of voicing.

The work of Lisker and Abramson and a number of others (e.g. Ohman, 1967; Stevens, 1969; Lindblom, 1971; McAllister, 1971; Ohala, 1971) suggests that many aspects of the sound pattern of languages can be best understood in terms of facts of speech production dynamics. The fact that it has proven difficult to give a definition of phonological concepts like "least effort" and "naturalness" in terms of phonetic facts, does not necessarily mean that phonetics is irrelevant to phonological concerns. It may just mean that these concepts have been formulated in a manner that does not allow phonetic evaluation, thus limiting their usefulness in phonology as well as phonetics.

It seems likely that the integration of speech physiology with linguistic theory would be well served by following Ladefoged's (1971) suggestion that "the proper goal of phonology is to attempt to describe the sound patterns that occur in a language." The adoption of this goal would place more value on verification of phonological hypotheses by reference to phonetic data. It would also de-emphasize the distinction between competence and performance (Chomsky and Halle, 1968, p.3) which has too often in the past been used as an excuse to ignore directly observable aspects of language function (as performance variables) which are inconvenient to a theoretical view. The value of acknowledging the importance of performance variables in the formulation of linguistic theory has been made especially evident by recent studies of speech errors. (e.g. Boomer and Laver, 1968; MacKay, 1969; Fromkin, 1970). These studies provide important clues to the organizing principles that underlie the production of language and by doing so, provide guidelines (well-stated in the above papers) for the construction of explanatory models in both speech physiology and linguistic theory, thus giving an import-

ant impetus towards a much needed unification of the
two disciplines.

ACKNOWLEDGEMENTS

    Preparation of this paper was supported in part
by Grant GU-1598 and Grant GS-3218 from the National
Science Foundation. I would like to thank Prakash
Dixit and Harvey Susman who read the manuscript and
made helpful comments. I would also like to thank
Hajime Hirose for his comments on the section on respiratory and laryngeal mechanisms. Finally I would
like to thank Dr. Thomas Hixon for discussing his
work with me at length, and to thank Dr. Thomas Shipp
for permission to examine the data from his laryngeal
experiments."

REFERENCES

Abbs, J.H. and Netsell, R. The inferential role of
the gamma role of the gamma loop in speech
production: a new application of an old technique. Paper presented at the Annual Convention
of the American Speech and Hearing Association,
New York City, Nov. 21, 1970.

Abercrombie, D. Elements of General Phonetics.
Chicago: Aldine Publishing Co., 1967.

Allen, G.D. The place of rhythm in a theory of
language. U.C.L.A. Working Papers in Phonetics,
1968, 10, 60-84.

Basmajian, J.V. Control and training of individual
motor units. Science, 1963, 141, 440-441.

Berti, F.B. The velopharyngeal mechanism: an electromyographic study - a preliminary report.
Status Report on Speech Research (Haskins Laboratories), SR-25/26, 1971, 117-129.

Bolinger, D.S. A theory of pitch accent in English.
Word, 1958, 14, 109-149.

Boomer, D.S. and Laver, J.D.M. Slips of the tongue.
British Journal of Disorders of Communication,
1968, 3, 1-12.

Borden, G.J. Some effects of oral anesthesia on
speech: a perceptual and electromyographic analysis. Paper presented at the Annual Convention of the American Speech and Hearing Association, Chicago, Nov. 17-20, 1971.

56

Brookhart, J.M. In Brooks, V.B., et al., 1970, op cit.

Brooks, V.B., Jasper, H.H., Patton, H.D., Purpura, D.P. and Brookhart, J.M. Symposium on cerebral and cerebellar motor control. Brain Research, 1970, 17, 539-552.

Chen, M. Vowel length variation as a function of the voicing of the consonant environment. Phonetica, 1970, 22, 129-159.

Chistovich, L.A., Koxhevnikov, V.A., Alyakrinskey, V.A., Bondarko, L.V., Goluzina, A.G., Klass, Yu. A., Kuz'min, Yu. I., Lisenko, D.M., Lyub- linskaya, V.V., Dedorova, N.A., Shuplyakov, V.S. and Shuplyakova, R.M. 1965. Rech': Artik- ulyatsiya i vospriyatiye, ed. by Kozhevnikov, V.A. and Chistovich, L.A., Moscow and Leningrad: Nauka. Trans. as Speech: Articulation and Perception. Washington. Clearinghouse for Federal Scientific and Technical Information. JPRS. 30, 543.

Chomsky, N. and Halle, M. The Sound Pattern of Eng- lish. New York: Harper & Row, 1968.

Cooper, F.S., Liberman, A.M., Harris, K.S., and Grubb, P.M. Some input-output relations ob- served in experiments on the perception of speech. Proceedings of the Second International Congress of Cybernetics, Namur, Belgium. 1958.

Daniloff, R. and Moll, K. Coarticulation of lip rounding. J. Speech and Hearing Res., 1968, 11, 707-721.

Denes, P. Effect of duration on the perception of voicing. J. Acoust. Soc. Amer., 1955, 27, 761-764.

Dewhurst, D.J. Neuromuscular control system. IEEE Transactions on Biomedical Engineering, 1967, 14, 167-171.

Dixit, R.P. and MacNeilage, P.F. Coarticulation of nasality: evidence from Hindi. Oral paper presented at the 83rd Meeting of the Acoustical Society of America, April 18-21, 1972.

Draper, M.H., Ladefoged, P., and Whitteridge, D. Expiratory muscles involved in speech. J. Physiol., 1957, 138, 17P-18P.

Draper, M.H., Ladefoged, P., and Whitteridge, D. Respiratory muscles in speech. J. Speech and Hearing Res., 1958, 2, 16-27.

Draper, M.H., Ladefoged, P., and Whitteridge, D. Expiratory muscles and airflow during speech. Brit. Med. Journal, June 18, 1960, 1837-43.

Euler, C.V. Proprioceptive control in respiration. In R. Granit (Ed.), Muscular Afferents and Motor Control. New York: John Wiley, 1966.

Evarts, E.V. Representation of movements and muscles by pyramidal tract neurons of the precentral motor cortex. In Yahr and Purpura (Eds.) Neurophysiological Basis of Normal and Abnormal Motor Activities. New York: Raven Press, 1967.

Fant, C.G.M. Descriptive analysis of the acoustic aspects of speech. LOGOS, 1962, 5, 3-17.

Fischer-Jørgensen, E. Acoustic analysis of stop consonants. Miscellanea Phonetica, 1954, 2, 42-59.

Fitts, P.M. The information capacity of the human motor system in controlling the amplitude of movement. Journal of Experimental Psychology,

1954, _47_, 381-391.

Fritzell, B. The velopharyngeal muscles in speech:
an electromyographic and cinefluorographic
study. Acta Oto-laryngologica, Supplement 250,
1969.

Fromkin, V.A. Neuromuscular specification of linguistic units. Language and Speech, 1966, _9_,
170-199.

Fromkin, V.A. The non-anomalous nature of anomal-
ous utterances. Language, 1970, _47_, 27-52.

Fromkin, V.A. and Ohala, J. Laryngeal control and
a model of speech production. Reprints of
the Speech Symposium, Kyoto, 1968.

Fry, D.B. Duration and intensity as physical correlates of linguistic stress. J. Acoust. Soc.
Amer., 1955, _27_, 765-768.

Fry, D.B. Prosodic phenomena. In B. Malmberg (Ed.)
Manual of Phonetics, Chapter 12. Amsterdam:
North-Holland Publishing Co., 1970.

Gaitenby, J.H. The elastic word. In Status Report
on Speech Research (Haskins Laboratories),
SR-2 (1965).

Gleason, H.A. An Introduction to Descriptive Linguistics. New York: Holt, Rinehart and Win-
ston, 1967.

Granit, R. The Basis of Motor Control. New York:
Academic Press, 1970.

Haggard, M.P. Speech synthesis and perception.
Progress Report No. 5, 1971, Psychological Laboratory, Cambridge.

Halle, M. and Stevens, K.N. Speech recognition: a model and a program for research. In J.A. Fodor and J.J. Katz (Eds.), The Structure of Language, Englewood Cliffs, N.J.: Prentice-Hall, 1964.

Halle, M. and Stevens, K.N. On the mechanism of glottal vibration for vowels and consonants. Quarterly Progress Report, Research Laboratory of Electronics, M.I.T., 1967, 85, 267-271.

Halle, M. and Stevens, K.N. A note on laryngeal features. Quarterly Progress Report, Research Laboratory of Electronics, M.I.T., 1971, 101, 198-213.

Halwes, T. and Jenkins, J.J. Problem of serial order in behavior is not resolved by context-sensitive associative memory models. Psych. Rev., 1971, 78, 122-129.

Hanson, R.J. Computer aided analysis of single motor unit muscle action potentials. Proceedings of the DECUS Fall Symposium, San Fransisco, Nov., 1971, 45-48.

Harris, K.S. Physiological aspects of articulatio behavior. In T.A. Sebeok (Ed.), Current Trends in Linguistics (Vol. 12). The Hague: Mouton and Co., 1972.

Harris, K.S., Gay, T., Sholes, G.N. and Lieberman, P. Some stress effects on llectromyographic measures of consonant articulation. In Status Report on Speech Research (Haskins Laboratories), SR 13/14, 137-152. (Also presented at the Kyoto Speech Symposium of the Sixth International Congress on Acoustics, August 29, 1968).

Harris, K.S., Schvey, M.M. and Lysaught, G.F. Component gestures in the production of oral

and nasal labial stops. J. Acoust. Soc. Amer.,
1962, 34, 743. (Abstract)

Hirose, H. An electromyographic study of laryn-
    geal adjustments during speech articulation:
    a preliminary report. In Status Report on
    Speech Research (Haskins Laboratories), SR-25/26,
    1971.

Hirose, H., Simada, Z. and Fujimura, O. An electro-
    myographic study of the activity of the laryn-
    geal muscles during speech utterances. Research
    Institute of Logopedics and Phoniatrics Annual
    Bulletin, 1970, 4, 9-26.

Hiroto, I., Hirano, M., Toyozumi, Y. and Shin, T.
    Electromyographic investigation of the intrin-
    sic laryngeal muscles related to speech sounds.
    Annals of Otology, Rhinology and Laryngology,
    October, 1967, 76, 861-872.

Hixon, T.J. Respiratory function in speech. In F.
    Minifie, T.J. Hixon and F. Williams (Eds.),
    Normal Speech, Hearing, and Language. Engle-
    wood Cliffs, N.J.: Prentice-Hall, Inc., 1972
    (In Press).

Hixon, T.J. Oral paper presented in the session on
    "Mechanical Aspects of Speech Production",
    Annual Conventionoof the American Speech and
    Hearing Association, Chicago, Nov. 17-20, 1971.

Hixon, T.J., Mead, J. and Klatt, D.H. Influence of
    forced transglottal pressure changes on vocal
    funcamental frequency. Paper presented at the
    80th meeting of the Acoustical Society of Amer-
    ica. Houston, Nov. 3-6, 1970.

House, A.S. On vowel duration in English. J. Acoust.
    Soc. Amer., 1961, 33, 1174-1178.

Huggins, A.W.F. Delayed auditory feedback and the temporal properties of the speech material. Zeitschrift fur Phonetick, Band 21, Heft 1/2, 1968.

Humphrey, D.R., Schmidt, E.M. and Thompson, W.D. Predicting measures of motor performance from multiple cortical spike trains. Science, 1970, 170, 758-761.

Isshiki, N. Regulatory mechanism of the pitch and volume of voice. Oto-Rhino-Laryngology Clinic. (Kyoto), 1959, 52, 1065-1094.

Kent, R.D. and Netsell, R. Effects of stress contrasts on certain articulatory parameters. Phonetica, 1971, 24, 23-44.

Kernell, D. Synaptic influence on the repetitive activity elicited in cat lumbosacral motoneurons by long-lasting injected currents. Acta Physiol. Scand., 1965, 63, 409-410.

Kim, J. and MacNeilage, P.F. (Unpublished observations), 1972.

Kuypers, H.G.J.M. The descending pathways to the spinal cord, their anatomy and functions. In J.C. Eccles and J.P. Schade (Eds.), Organization of the Spinal Cord. Amsterdam: Elsevier, 1964, 178-202.

Ladefoged, P. The regulation of subglottal pressure. Folia Phoniatrica, 1960, 12, 169-175.

Ladefoged, P. Sub-glottal activity during speech. In A. Sovijarvi and P. Aalto (Eds.), Proceedings of the IVth International Congress of Phonetic Sciences. The Hague: Mouton and Co., 1962, 73-91.

Ladefoged, P. Three Areas of Experimental Phonetics.
    New York: Oxford University Press, Inc., 1967.

Ladefoged, P. Some physiological parameters in
    speech. Language and Speech, 1963, 6, 109-119.

Ladefoged, P. Linguistic phonetics, In U.C.L.A.
    Working Papers in Phonetics, 1967, 6.

Ladefoged, P. Linguistic aspects of respiratory
    phenomena. In Annals of the New York Academy
    of Sciences, 1968, 155, 141-151.

Ladefoged, P. Phonological features and their phonet-
    ic correlates. In U.C.L.A. Working Papers in
    Phonetics, 1971, 21.

Ladefoged, P., Draper, M.H. and Whitteridge, D.
    Syllables and stress. Miscellanea Phonetica,
    1958, 3, 1-14.

Ladefoged, P. and McKinney, N. Loudness, sound
    pressure and subglottal pressure in speech. J.
    Acoust. Soc. Amer., 1963, 35, 454-60.

Lashley, K.S. The problem of serial order in behav-
    ior. In L.A. Jeffress (Ed.), Cerebral mechan-
    isms in behavior (the Hixon symposium). New
    York: Wiley, 1951.

Laver, J. The production of speech. In J. Lyons
    (Ed.), New Horizons in Linguistics. Baltimore:
    Penguin Books Inc., 1970, Chapter 3.

Lee, B.S. Effects of delayed speech feedback. J.
    Acoust. Soc. Amer., 1950, 22, 824-826.

Lehiste, I. Suprasegmentals. Cambridge: The M.I.T.
    Press, 1970.

Lehiste, I. The temporal realization of morphological and syntactic boundaries. Paper presented at the 81st Meeting of the Acoustical Society of America, Washington, D.C., April 20-23, 1971.

Lehiste, I. Temporal organization of spoken language. Form and Substance: Phonetic and Linguistic Papers presented to Eli Fischer-Jørgensen. Akademisk Forlag, Copenhagen, 1971.

Lenneberg, E.H. Biological Foundations of Language. New York: John Wiley & Sons, Inc., 1967.

Lenneberg, E.H. The importance of temporal factors in behavior. In Horton, D.L. and Jenkins, J.J. (Eds.), The Perception of Language. Columbus, Ohio: Charles E. Merrill Publishing Co., 1971, 174-184.

Liberman, A.M. Some results of research on speech perception. J. Acoust. Soc. Amer., 1957, 29, 117-123.

Liberman, A.M., Cooper, F.S., Harris, K.S., MacNeilage, P.F., and Studdert-Kennedy, M.G. Some observation on a model for speech perception. In W. Wathen-Dunn (Ed.), Models for the perception of speech and visual form. Cambridge, Mass.: M.I.T. Press, 1967.

Lieberman, P. Intonation, Perception, and Language. Cambridge: The M.I.T. Press, Research Monograph No. 38, 1967.

Lieberman, P. Towards a unified phonetic theory. Linguistic Inquiry, 1970, 307-322.

Lieberman, P. A study of prosodic features. In T.A. Sebeok (Ed.), Current Trends in Linguistics, 12. The Hague: Mouton and Co., 1972.

Lieberman, P., Knudson, R. and Mead, J. Determin-
    ation of the rate of change of fundamental fre-
    quency with respect to sub-glottal air pressure
    during sustained phonation. J. Acoust. Soc.
    Amer., 1969, 45, 1537-1543.

Lieberman, P., Sawashima, M., Harris, K.S. and Gay,
    T. The articulatory implementation of the
    breath-group and prominence: crico-thyroid mus-
    cular activity in intonation. Language, 1970,
    46, 312-327.

Lindblom, B.E.F. Spectrographic study of vowel re-
    duction. J. Acoust. Soc. Amer. 1963, 35,
    1773-1781.

Lindblom, B.E.F. Articulatory activity in vowels.
    STL-QPSR 2/1964. Royal Institute of Technol-
    ogy Stockholm, Sweden, 1-5.

Lindblom, B.E.F. Vowel duration and a model of lip
    mandible coordination. STL-QPSR, 4/1968.
    The Royal Institute of Technology, Stockholm,
    Sweden, 1-29.

Lindblom, B.E.F. Numerical models in the study of
    speech production and speech perception: some
    phonological implication. Paper presented at
    the VIIth International Congress of Phonetic
    Sciences, Montreal, August 22-28, 1971.

Lindblom, B.E.F. and Sundberg, J. Neurophysiological
    representation of speech sounds. Paper present-
    ed at the XVth World Congress of Logopedics and
    Phoniatrics, Buenos Aires, Argentina, August,
    1971.

Lisker, L. On time and timing in speech. In T.A.
    Sebeok (Ed.), Current Trends in Linguistics,
    (Vol. 12). The Hague: Mouton and Co., 1972.

Lisker, L. and Abramson, A.S. Distinctive features and laryngeal control. Language, 1971, 47, 767-785.

Lubker, J.F. An electromyographic-cinefluorographic investigation of velar function during normal speech production. The Cleft Palate Journal, 1968, 5, 1-18.

Lubker, J.F., Fritxell, B. and Lindqvist, J. Velopharyngeal function: an electromyographic study. In Abstracts of the VII International Congress of Phonetic Sciences, Montreal, August 22-28, 1971.

Lysaught, G., Rosov, R.J. and Harris, K.S. Electromyography as a speech research technique with an application to labial stops. J. Acoust. Soc. Amer., 1961, 33, 842 (Abstract).

MacAllister, R. The nuclear stress rule and the description of English stress. Paper presented at the VIIth International Congress of Phonetic Sciences, Montreal, August 22-28, 1971.

MacKay, D.G. Spoonerisms: the structure of erro s in the serial ordering of speech. Neuropsychologia, 1970, 8, 323-350.

MacNeilage, P.F. Motor control of serial ordering of speech. Psych. Rev., 1970, 77, 182-196.

MacNeilage, P.F. Indirect inferences about somatic afferent control mechanisms from neuroanatomy and neurophysiology: the possibility of sensory influences on single motor unit firing patterns. Paper presented at the Annual Convention of the American Speech and Hearing Association, Nov. 18, 1971, Chicago.

MacNeilage, P.F. Coarticulation: its theoretical and practical implications. Invited paper in preparation for publication in the Journal of Speech and Hearing Disorders (1972).

MacNeilage, P.F. and DeClerk, J.L. Cienflourographic study of speaking rate. Paper presented at the 76th meeting of the Acoustical Society of America, Cleveland, Ohio, Nov. 19-22, 1968.

MacNeilage, P.F. and DeClerk, J.L. On the motor control of coarticulation in CVC monosyllables. J. Acoust. Soc. Amer., 1969, 45, 1217-1233.

MacNeilage, P.F., Krones, R. and Hanson, R. Closed-loop control of the initiation of jaw movement for speech. Paper presented at the 78th meeting of the Acoustical Society of America. San Deigo, Nov. 4-7, 1969.

MacNeilage, P.F. and MacNeilage, L.A. Central processes controlling speech production during sleep and waking. Paper presented at the Conference on the Psychophysiology of Thinking, Hollins College, Virginia, Oct. 18-21, 1971.

MacNeilage, P.F., Sussman, H.M. and Hanson, R.J. Parametric study of single motor unit waveforms in upper articulatory musculature. Paper presented at the 83rd meeting of the Acoustical Society of America, April, 1972.

MacNeilage, P.F. and Szabo, R.K. Frequency control of single motor units in upper articulatory musculature. Paper presented at the 83rd meeting of the Acoustical Society of America, April, 1972.

Malecot, A. The lenis-fortes opposition: its physiological parameters. J. Acoust. Soc. Amer.,

1970, 47, 1588-1592.

Marg, E., Tamler, E. and Jampolsky, A.   Activity of
    a human oculaorotary muscle unit.   Electroen-
    cephalography and Clinical Neurophysiology,
    1962, 14, 754-757.

Martensson, A.   In discussion of Sears, T.A. and
    Davis, J.N.   Annals of the New York Academy of
    Sciences, 1968, 155, 202.

Matthews, P.B.C.   Muscle spindles and their motor
    control.   Physiol. Rev., 1964, 44, 219-288.

Mattingly, I.G.   Synthesis by rule of general Amer-
    ican English.   Unpublished doctoral disser-
    tation, Yale University, 1968.

McCroskey, R.L.   The effect of specified levels of
    white noise upon flicker fusion frequency.
    U.S.N. Sch. Aviat. Med. Res. Rep., 1958, Proj.
    No. NM 18 02 99, Sub. I, No. 80. ii, p. 10.

McGlone, R.E. and Shipp, T.   Comparison of sub-
    glottal air pressures associated with /p/ and
    /b/.   J. Acoust. Soc. Amer., 1972, 51, 664-665.

Mohr, B.   Intrinsic variations of acoustic para-
    meters of speech sounds.   Project on Linguistic
    Analysis (Berkeley: University of California),
    1969, 2.9, M 1-44.

Moll, K.L. and Daniloff, R.G.   Investigation of the
    timing of velar movements during speech.   J.
    Acoust. Soc. Amer., 1971, 50, 678-684.

Moll, K.L. and Shriner, T.H.   Preliminary investig-
    ation of a new concept of velar activity dur-
    ing speech.   The Cleft Palate Journal, 1967,
    4, 58-69.

Nathan, P.W. and Sears, T.A. Effects of posterior
    root section on the activity of some muscles
    in man. J. Neurol. Psychiat., 1960, 23, 10-22.

Nooteboom, S.G. The target theory of speech pro-
    duction. IPO Annual Progress Report, 1970,
    5, 51-55.

Ohala, J.J. Aspects of the control and production
    of speech. U.C.L.A. Working Papers in Phon-
    etics, 1970, 15.

Ohala, J.J. The role of physiological and acoustic
    models in explaining the direction of sound
    change. Project on Linguistic Analysis (Berkel-
    ey: University of California), 1971, 2.15, 25-
    40.

Ohala, J.J., Hiki, S., Hubler, S. and Harshman, R.
    Transducing jaw and lip movements in speech.
    Paper presented at the 76th meeting of the Ac-
    oustical Society of America, Cleveland, Ohio,
    Nov. 19-22, 1968.

Öhman, S.E.G. Coarticulation in VCV utterances:
    spectrographic measurements. J. Acoust. Soc.
    Amer., 1966, 39, 151-168.

Öhman, S.E.G. Word and sentence intonation: a
    quantitative model. STL-QPSR 2-3/1967, Royal
    Institute of Technology, Stockholm, Sweden,
    20-48.

Öhman, S.E.G. Peripheral motor commands in labial
    articulation. STL-QPSR 4/1967. Royal Instit-
    ute of Technology, Stockholm, Sweden, 30-63.

Öhman, S.E.G. and Lindqvist, J. Analysis-by-synth-
    esis of prosodic pitch contours. STL-QPSR
    1/1966, Royal Institute of Technology, Stock-
    holm, Sweden, 1-6.

Oller, D.K. The duration of speech segments: the effect of position in utterance and word length. Unpublished doctoral disseration, The University of Texas at Austin, 1971.

Peters, R.W. The effect of changes in side-tone delay and level upon rate of oral reading of normal speakers. J. Speech and Hearing Dis., 1954, 19, 483-490.

Peterson, G.E. Some curiosities of speech. Paper presented at the University of Michigan Summer Speech Conference, Ann Arbor, Michigan, 1956.

Peterson, G.E. and Lehiste, I. Duration of syllable nuclei in English. J. Acoust. Soc. Amer., 1960, 32, 693-703.

Ringel, R.L. and Steer, M.D. Some effects of tactile and auditory alterations of speech output. J. Speech and Hearing Res., 1963, 6, 369-378.

Rosner, B.S. Brain functions. In P.H. Mussen and M.R. Rosenweig, Annual Review of Psychology, 1970, 21, 555-594.

Sawashima, M. Laryngeal research in experimental phonetics. In T.A. Sebeok (Ed.), Current Trends in Linguistics (Vol. 12). The Hague: Mouton and Co., 1972.

Scott, C.M. and Ringel, R.L. Articulation without oral sensory control. J. Speech and Hearing Res., 1971, 14, 804-818.

Sears, T.A. and Davis, J.N. The control of respiratory muscles during voluntary breathing. Annals of the New York Academy of Sciences, 1968, 155, 183-190.

Shipp, T., McGlone, R.E. and Morrissey, P. Some

physiological correlates of voice frequency and intensity change. In Abstracts of the VIIth International Congress of Phonetic Sciences, Montreal, August 22-28, 1971.

Slis, I.H. Articulatory effort and its durational and electromyographic correlates. Manuskript No. 194/2, Institute for Perception Research, The Netherlands, 1971.

Smith, J.L. Fusimotor neuron block and voluntary arm movement in man. Unpublished doctoral dissertation, University of Wisconsin, 1969.

Smith, T.S. and Lee, C.Y. Peripheral feedback mechanisms in speech production models? Paper presented at the VIIth International Congress of Phonetic Sciences, Montreal, August 22-28, 1971.

Sonesson, B. The functional anatomy of the speech organs. In B. Malmberg (Ed.), Manual of Phonetics. Amsterdam: North-Holland Publishing Co., 1970, 45-75.

Sonninen, A. The external frame function in the control of pitch in the human voice. Annals of the New York Academy of Sciences, 1968, 155, 69-90.

Stetson, R.H. Motor Phonetics. Amsterdam: North-Holland Publishing Co., 1951.

Stevens, K.N. The quantal nature of speech: evidence from articulatory-acoustic data. In E.E. David and P.B. Denes (Eds.), Human Communication: A Unified View, 1969 (In Press).

Stevens, K.N. and House, A.S. Perturbation of vowel articulation by consonantal context: an acoustical study. J. Speech and Hearing Res., 1963,

6, 111-128.

Studdert-Kennedy, M. and Shankweler, D. Hemispheric specialization for speech perception. J. Acoust. Soc. Amer., 1970, 48, 579-594.

Sussman, H.M. The laterality effect in lingual-auditory tracking. J. Acoust. Soc. Amer., 1971, 49, 1874-1880.

Sussman, H.M., Hanson, R.J. and MacNeilage, P.F. Studies of single motor units in the speech musculature: methodology and preliminary findings. J. Acoust. Soc. Amer., 1972 (In press).

Sussman, H.M., MacNeilage, P.F. and Hanson, R.J. Labial and mandibular dynamics during the production of bilabial stop consonants. 1972 (In preparation).

Sussman, H.M. and Smith, K.U. Jaw movements under delayed auditory feedback. J. Acoust. Soc. Amer., 1971, 50, 685-691.

Tokizane, T. and Shimazu H. Functional Differentiation of Human Skeletal Muscle. Springfield: Charles C. Thomas, 1964.

Vanderslice, R. The prosodic component: lacuna in transformational theory. Paper presented at the RAND Corporation, Seminar in Computational Linguistics, sponsored by the National Science Foundation, June, 1968.

Whitaker, H.A. Some constraints on speech pro tion models. Paper presented at the First Essex Symposium on Models of Speech Production, Sept. 24-25, 1970.

Wicklegren, W.A. Context-sensitive coding, associative memory, and serial order in (speech) behavior. Psych. Rev., 1969, 76, 1-15.

Chapter 2

Discussion Paper on Speech Physiology

Victoria A. Fromkin

Department of Linguistics
University of California at Los Angeles

INTRODUCTION

Peter MacNeilage has presented an extensive and detailed state of the art paper on Speech Physiology. I would like to comment on this important paper from the point of view of a linguist, interested in the nature of language and language use or behavior. In other words, I would like to address myself to the question - how can a study of physiological processes illuminate the probjems of linguistic performance and the underlying structure of language?

In attempting an answer, it should be noted that the reverse of this question is also of interest. Lashley, one of America's leading physiological psychologists before his death in 1957, had planned to undertake an extensive study of linguistics. We hoped that this would help him find answers to the problem of brain function which was, of course, his main concern. MacNeilage's paper deals primarily (but not exclusively) with questions of the peripheral physiology of speech. Yet, an understanding of peripheral motor behavior is enhanced by an understanding of higher order brain functions. Linguistics may direct us to some answers.

Looking at the problem from another side, Edward Sapir clearly pointed out that

"There are, properly speaking, no organs of speech: there are only organs that are inci-

73

dentally useful in the production of speech
sounds. The lungs, the larynx, the palate,
the nose, the tongue, the teeth, and the
lips, are all so utilized, but they are no
more to be thought of as primary organs of
speech than are the fingers to be considered as essentially organs of piano playing
or the knees as organs of prayer. Speech is
... an extremely complex and ever-shifting
network of adjustments -- in the brain, in
the nervous system, and in the articulating
and auditory organs. Physiologically, speech
is an overlaid function, or, to be more precise, a group of overlaid function." (Sapir,
E. 1921, 1949)

This being the case, in order to understand the
speech production process a knowledge of the basic
physiology of these organs 'utilized' by the speech
producing mechanism is necessary but not sufficient.

I say 'not sufficient' because it is also well
known that a distinction must be made between the lower motor mechanism necessary for the occurrence of
speech and the higher nervous activity essential for
the control of these lower mechanisms. This was
clearly pointed out in 1826 by Bouillaud in his discussions on aphasia:

"Since certain movements of the tongue, such
as those of prehension, mastication, degluti-
tion, et cetera, persist, although those necessary for the articulation of sounds are ab-
olished by lesion of the anterior lobes of the
brain, it follows that the tongue has in the
nerve-centre several sources of distinct action." (Bouillaud, J. 1926)

This point is underscored by MacNeilage when he
points out that where the levator palatini muscle is
actively involved in movements of the soft palate,
the tensor palatine is either inactive or randomly active during speech. One might then conclude that similar muscular movements are activated differently for
speech and non speech. MacNeilage has carefully dif-

ferentiated these gestures.

One is again reminded of the insights of Sapir when he stated:

"In view of the utterly distinct psychological backgrounds of the two classes of sound production (speech and non speech) it may even be seriously doubted whether the innervation of speech-sound articulation is ever actually the same type of physiological fact as the innervation of "identical" articulations that have no linguistic context". (Sapir, E. 1925)

It will be in light of these possible differences that I would like to single out certain of the questions discussed by MacNeilage in an attempt to answer the questions raised earlier.

RESPIRATORY MECHANISMS AND LARYNGEAL FUNCTIONS

The fact that speech is an overlaid function is clearly shown by reference to respiratory mechanisms. The main function of the intercostal muscles is to cause an increase or decrease in the volume of the chest by moving the ribs and the diaphragm muscles which push down on the viscera during inspiration. The non-speech motivation (if I may use this teleogical term) of the respiratory control centers in the brain is to regulate the level of blood oxygen and carbon dioxide which is achieved by changing the ventilation rate of the lungs by varying the rate and/or depth of respiration. In normal breathing only the muscles of inspiration are used, and expiration occurs passively due to elastic recoil once the action of the inspiration muscles has ceased (Moore, 1966). The maintenance of the blood-gas level must also of course be controlled during speech. But there is an additional motivation behind respiratory control during speech -- namely the maintenance of the necessary sub- and supra-glottal pressure difference to permit vocal cord vibration.

To ensure adequate ventilation in spite of chan-

ges in muscle power, airway resistance or driving
pressures requires a complex system involving gamma
and alpha cells. This, of course, is outside the
scope of the present discussion. But, it is clear
that because of the different 'functions' of the respiratory muscles for speech and non speech, different
controls are involved, or at least, the speech mechanism involves additional controls. That is, air
flow and pressure requirements for speech production
implies that the feedback mechanism responsible for
the necessary blood-gas levels is supplemented by
other speech dependent processes. It is equally
clear that the bursts of muscular activity 'which immediately precede each (stressed) syllable' (Ladefoged, 1967) must be pre-programmed in order to produce
increases in intensity levels which Hixon (1971)
showed to be 'responsive to changes in P_T (and) proportional to the prestimulus intensity level.'

The relationship between the respiratory and
laryngeal components which MacNeilage discusses has
great importance for linguists concerned with an adequate set of distinctive features for describing linguistic sounds and phonological rules.

Ladefoged (1963) has clearly shown how the two
mechanisms are both related and independent:

"The pitch (or, to be more precise, the rate
of vibration of the vocal cords) during a
syllable largely depends on two factors: the
tension of the vocal cords, and the rate of
flow of air through the glottis. During a
voiced stop or fricative the rate of flow
decreases; consequently the pitch goes down,
unless the speaker makes the delicate adjustment in the tension of the vocal cords which
would compensate for the decrease in flow.
Conversely, during the first part of a vowel
after the release of a voiceless stop or
fricative there is a high rate of flow,
which results in an increase in pitch as long
as there is no counter-acting adjustment in
the tension of the vocal cords."

76

This relationship between pitch phenomena (particularly in tone languages) and segmental features of
speech sounds, has recently given rise to a new set
of distinctive features within the framework of generative phonology. (Halle and Stevens, 1971; Halle,
1971)

Unlike Ladefoged, Halle and Stevens attribute the
increased rate of vibration accompanying a raise in
pitch solely to the stiffness of the vocal cords. In
addition, because of the noted relationship between
pitch phenomena and glottal stricture features of
segments, i.e. the cases where a vowel occurs with a
high tone after voiceless stops but with a low tone
after voiced stops, they suggest that such segments
fall into a single natural class by virtue of the suggested feature 'stiff vocal cords'. That is, high
tone vowels and voiceless stops are specified as
[+stiff vocal cords] and mid or low tone vowels and
voiced (or lax) obstruents are specified with the
feature value [-stiff vocal cords]. In addition, low
tone vowels and regularly voiced and 'breathy voiced'
obstruents (the latter are called aspirated by Halle
and Stevens) are distinguished from the other segments by being specified with the feature value [+
slack vocal cords]. The use of these features can
create many difficulties in writing the phonological
rules of languages, (see Fromkin, 1972). The reasons
for such difficulties may well be that the physiological explanation provided is not in keeping with the
physiological facts. As Ladefoged (1972) has pointed
out:

"Halle and Stevens do not produce any evidence
for their claim that the pitch tends to rise
after voiceless consonants because voiceless
consonants have stiff vocal cords...There are
two other reasons why there may be increase in
pitch after voiceless consonants. Firstly:
voiceless consonants may have a higher larynx
position than the corresponding voiced consonant. ...This may result in a stretching of
the vocal cords; but it seems curious to call

this stretching a stiffening of the vocal
cords. Secondly, the increase in pitch
may be due to the increase in the flow
rate which is associated with voiceless
sounds." (Ladefoged, 1972)

He adds: "... a correct feature system must
make it possible to separate out differences in phonation type, which are due to
differences in glottal stricture, from
differences in pitch which depend on another mechanism."

He suggests that "marking conventions" (Chomsky
and Halle, 1968) he used to reveal the connection in
some languages between glottal stricture features and
pitch features, synchronically as well as historical-
ly.

It is of interest to contrast the use of these
alternative feature sets in phonological description.
Ngizim, a Chadic language, has tone rules which relate both to voicing and tone of segments, (Schuh,1972)
One rule raises a low tone on a vowel when the vowel
follows a high tone if and only if the segment preceding the low tone is not a voiced nonglottalized
obstruent; this rule is illustrated under (1) and (2).

(1) a. geji k sekwai   [geji-k sekwai]
        'sickle handle'

    b. dlugun kaawa   [dlugun kaawa] 'name of a
        game'

    c. na danke-wu   [na danku] 'I sewed'
(2) a. kuter gaskam   [kuter gaskam] 'tail of the
        rooster'

    b. na zaage-wu   [na zaagu] 'I waited'

(= high tone, = low tone, and = drop tone or 'lowered high', and no tone marking = mid tone)

In (1a.) the /e/ of the last word is raised because it is preceded by voiceless obstruents. In
(1b.) the low tone on /a/ is raised because it too is
preceded by a voiceless obstruent which is preceded by
a sonorant /n/. In (1c.) the /d/ an implosive or lar-
yngalized obstruent does not block the tone raising.
In (2) however the raising does not occur because of

78

the presence of the /g/ and /z/ in (a.) and (b.) respectively.

The Halle/Stevens features specify the relevant
segments as in (3):

(3) obstruents b_1 b   p p^h b   ?b
     glides   w,y
     vowels   V   V   V

	b_1 / w,y / V	b / V	p / V	p^h	b	?b
spread glottis	-	-	-	+	-	-
constricted glottis	-	-	-	-	+	+
stiff vocal cords	-	-	+	+	-	-
slack vocal cords	-	+	-	-	-	+

I do not know whether the voiced stops in Ngizim
are of the lax [(b_1)] variety or the regularly voiced
[(b)]; nor does Schuh's description indicate whether
the 'glottalized' b (or d, in the example given)are
implosive sounds or laryngealized sounds. In this
case and in others it is not decisive phonologically,
since as Ladefoged points out no language contrasts
these two classes of sounds.

The tone raising rule would be given informally
as in (4).

(4) V   V   /V p_h
                     p
                     b_1
                     b
                     ?b

In other words the tone is raised if it occurs
after all segments except /b/, (bilabials are used il-
lustratively), I include the Halle/Stevens segment b_1
as permitting tone raising because the raising does
occur after sonorants, and glides have the same specification in (3) as the obstruent b_1.

Using the features as given in (3) this rule
would be written as (5)

79

(5)   +syl   +syl   +syl
        −stiff   +stiff   +stiff   −syl
        +slack   −slack   −slack   −constricted
                                      −stiff
                                      −slack

$\overline{(b_I, w, y)}$

−constricted
+stiff
−slack

(p, p^h)

+constricted
−stiff
+slack

$\overline{(\ b,\ ?b)}$

We can ignore the feature value for Spread Glottis, since it seems to be redundant for this rule.

If the underlying glottalized segment is /ʔb/ (i.e. [−Constricted, −stiff, +slack] then the rule can be written as (5)

(6) V   [+stiff, −slack / +stiff $\overset{V}{\text{constricted}}$
                                 −slack   slack

In other words this rule would state that a tone is raised if it occurs after a segment which is either [−constricted, −slack] or [+constricted, +slack], but not after a segment which is [−constricted, +slack]. If, however, the 'restricting' or 'blocking' consonant is /b/, i.e. [+constricted, −slack], then the alpha variable notation cannot be used in this way but rather as (6')

(6') V   +stiff $\overset{V}{+\text{stiff}}$ −constricted
         −slack   −slack   −slack

                                    [+constricted]

Neither of the rules reveal the assimilatory nature of the process which the suggested new features are supposed to capture.

Using Ladefoged's feature Glottal Stricture the

segments would be specified as in (7):

(7) /p/ or /p^h/   [0 Glottal Stricture] (voiceless)
   /b/   [1 Glottal Stricture] (voiced)
   /b/ or /b/ [2 Glottal Stricture] (creak)*

In addition there would be tone features assigned to the vowels (in this case [+ High Tone] and
the /b/ could, if desired be specified as an implosive). The rule could be stated as in (8).

(8) V   V / V [I Glottal Stricture]

where [I Glottal Stricture] represents the compli-
ment of [I Glottal Stricture] i.e., either [0 Glottal
Stricture] or [2 Glottal Stricture].

It is true that the statement of the rule using
the Ladefoged features does not reveal why the voiced
obstruant should block the pitch raising. But the
reasons are not revealed using the Halle/Stevens features either. And neither sets of features 'explain'
why the laryngealized obstruent or implosive should
permit the rise. However, Ladefoged's features have
the virtue of not providing wrong physiological explanations. The relationship between the voiced and
voiceless obstruents and the tone change can be revealed by a universal marking convention as in (9):

(9)
             +High   Voiced C
  u Tone
             -High   Voiceless C

The reasons why such a rule exists is explained
in the Ladefoged quote given above.

Of course using such a Marking Convention also
implies that the marked situation will occur in some

---

* The values assigned are based on the fact that
there are just three contrasting glottal strictures
in the language. Phonetic rules would specify the
particular kind of glottal stricture related to these
values, (See Ladefoged, 1971). It is possible however to use the same values in all descriptions. Then
we would substitute '4' for '1' and '6' for '2'.

languages. And, in fact, in Kanakura (Newman, 1972) there seems to be a restriction on the tones of verbs such that those with initial voiced obstruents always have high tone on the first vowel while those with initial voiceless or glottalized obstruents always have low tone on the first vowel. Tones of verbs with initial sonorants are not predictable. Examples are given under (10), (11) and (12).

(10)	dape	'to collect'		
	gemi	'to fill'		
	boi	'to shoot'		
(11)	tupe	'to send'		
	seni	'to remember'		
	demi	'to be able'		
(12)	ade	'to eat (meat)	ate	'to dip out'
	lukure	'to disperse'	lapere	'to hold down'
	maane	'to return'	muule	'to smooth'

It is obvious that much more research is necessary to discover all the complexities involved in the inter-dependence of respiratory features and glottal strictures. We can see the importance of physiological research in the explanation of synchronic and diachronic linguistic rules.

The results of the investigations of EMG activity of the laryngeal muscles conducted by Hirose (1971) are also of interest in relation to the proposed Halle/Stevens features. In this experiment the stimulus words all consisted of two syllables with the first syllable stressed in some, and the second syllable in others. VCVC and CVCV utterances were used. The unstressed vowel was [ə] and the stressed [ʌ]. As MacNeilage pointed out, stress in English is realized both by increased intensity and by increases in Fo. Hirosi found that the posterior cricoarytenois (PCA) was active only in the articulation of the voiceless consonants; its role 'as an abductor in speech articulation' was demonstrated. The Interarytenoid (INT) on the other hand is activated for voiced segments, although more so for vowels than for voiced obstruents. The Thyroarytenoid (VOC) and Lateral Cri-

coarytenoid (LCA) activity decreased for consonant
segments (both voiced and voiceless) and 'increased
for vowel segments particularly ...for stressed vowels.' (p. 113) Finally, the Cricothyroid (CT) 'shows
a temporary increase in EMG activity for the stressed
vowel. I reprint Hirosǰ's table which sums up their
findings:

(13)

	Abductor	Adductor	
			VOC
	PCA	INT	LCA
Vowel	-	++	+/ ++*
Voiced C	-	+	-
Voiceless C	+	-	-

(*The ++ represents in this case greater activity for
stressed vowels).
This table is interesting in that the action of
these muscles can be correlated with features required
for the natural classes used in phonological descriptions. (This is of course an oversimplification.)
Vowels and voiced consonants are in the same 'class'
by virtue of the activity of the INT, and the lack of
activity of the PCA. The reciprocal of these 'features' distinguish the voiceless consonants. And the
class of consonants can be distinguished from that of
vowels by the activity of the VOC and LCA in the case
of the vowels, not found during the articulation of
the consonants. Interestingly enough, none of these
laryngeal muscles seem to class the voiceless consonants with the high pitched or in this case, stressed
vowels, i.e. the cricothyroid muscle activity which
is closely related to rising Fo was absent during the
articulation of voiceless consonants.
It is interesting to note that in the earlier set
of features proposed by Chomsky and Halle (1968) it
was suggested, as MacNeilage points out, that "there
may be a different mode of voicing during voiced stop
consonants and during vowels." This may be supported
(as further suggested by MacNeilage) by the fact that
a number of muscles particularly active in voicing of
vowels show a 'reduction in activity...preceding voiced stop consonants.' In the new proposed set of fea-

tures no mention is made of the feature Spontaneous
Voicing and, as is shown by(13) above, no feature or
combination of features distinguishes voiced obstruents as a class from vowels as a class. In addition,
as MacNeilage goes on to say, 'the lack of difference in vocalis and lateral cricoarytenoid activity
for voiced and voiceless stops...is contrary to the
claim of Halle and Stevens (1971) that voiced and
voiceless stops differ in vocal cord stiffness.'

Slis and Damste (1967) also showed through transillumination data that whereas the glottis was open
for voiceless consonants, the glottal stricture was
the same for the voiced plosives, fricatives and the
adjoining vowels.

An EMG study of VCV Japanese syllables (Hiroto
et al. 1967) shows an increase in the activity of the
abductor muscle and a decrease in adductor muscles
for voiceless consonants and no change in the cricoarytenoid m. No differences in the EMG patterns were
observed between Voiced C's and Vowel (p. 109).

Ladefoged's explanation for the effect of voiced
and voiceless obstruents on tones seems therefore to
be more adequate than the 'explanation' provided by
the Halle/Stevens features.

There is another phenomenon called 'downdrift'
associated with tone languages which requires a physiological explanation. It has been found that there
are many tone languages which display an overall tone
lowering, i.e. subsequent high tones are lower in
pitch than preceding ones when a low tone intervenes,
and the low tones also decrease in pitch. This is
exemplified by the examples under (14) and (15).

(14) Hausa: Sànnú dà áikì 'Greetings at your
                 3 1 4 2 5   work'

1	nu	
2		ai
3	San	
4	da	
5		kì

(15) Twi: kòfí Hwèhwέ Kwàbènà 'Kofi looks for
            4 1   5 2   6 6 3   Kwabena'

1	fi
2	hwε
3	na
4	ko
5	Hwe
6	Kwabe

This 'downdrift' phenomenon is related to Mac-Neilage's discussion on the mechanisms involved in the raising and lowering of Fo. He points out that the evidence is quite clear that prominence (in both the unmarked and marked breath group) is accompanied by laryngeal activity. But the data regarding Fo lowering is ambiguous. It is possible that different mechanisms are responsible for Fo lowering depending upon whether the lowered pitch has contrastive function in the language. MacNeilage points to "The fact that it is possible to vary Fo by more than one means (which) tends to make one suspect generalizations about the relative role of lungs and larynx which are based only on one or a few subjects..." Since Fo can be varied by different means, it is possible that laryngeal activity is responsible for lowering Fo for a contrastive low 'tone' in languages such as exemplified above, but that the 'downdrift' lowering is due to the 'cessation of activity in muscles mediating Fo raising' as suggested by Harris, (1971). Examples (14) and (15) above show that the successive lowering of high tones and low tones have no communicative significance or contrastive function. In fact, as can be seen, it is often the case that the high tone occuring late in the utterance has a pitch equal to an earlier low tone. The contrast is maintained because of the relative pitch differences between sequential high and low tones.

My own view is that in languages with contrasting tone, high tones and low tones must be under both

85

open and closed loop controls -- in that the pitch of
the syllable must depend on the pitch of the previous
contrasting tone. I would also hypothesize that laryngeal activity maybe responsible for the lowering of
Fo for low tones. On the other hand, the continually
decreasing Fo -- the downdrift phenomenon -- may be
the manifestation of Lieberman's 'unmarked' breath
group in tone languages.

Again, physiological evidence is of key importance. We need subglottal pressure data, EMG data,
and air flow data obtained from speakers of such tone
languages as described here, before an answer is ar-
rived at.

ARTICULATORY MECHANISMS

The discussion on the Velum, again shows how
phonological processes (i.e. the structure of grammars and linguistic change) are influenced and constrained by physiological processes.

MacNeilage correctly states: 'In most languages
the soft palate has only one linguistically distinctive function, namely to distinguish between nasal and
non-nasal segments.' What is of interest is the fact
that in many languages where the nasality of certain
segments is 'distinctive' nasality of others is non-
contrastive. I cannot think, for example, of a single
language which contrasts oral and nasal vowels before
nasal consonants. This is as true of languages in
which there are oral-nasal vowel contrasts as those
where vowel nasality is always 'allophonic'. The explanation for this linguistic 'universal' has been
discussed by Ohala, (1971). Using a nasograph* he
showed that vowels adjacent to nasal consonants are

---

* "The instrument consists of a light and light sensor encased in a transparent tube...inserted into the
subject's nose and pharynx such that the light is in
the pharynx and the light sensor in the nasal cavity.
Greater or lesser velar elevation allows less or more
light to impinge on the light sensor and thus develop
relatively a greater or lesser voltage which can be
recorded..." (p.32)

nasalized, i.e. the velum is lowered either in anticipation of the following nasal consonant or remains
lowered after the release of the nasal consonant. He
suggests that this is because the velum moves slower
than do other articulators. In addition he refers to
the study of House and Stevens (1956) which reveals
that 'although opening the velopharyngeal port obviously does distort the spectrum of a vowel it does
not seem to distort it so much that it loses its dis-
tinctiveness'. Ohala concludes: 'If this is true it
suggests that the early lowering of the velum is al-
lowed because it does not destroy the acoustic identity of the vowel' (p. 32).

Thus a physiological/acoustic explanation is
provided for linguistic facts. Given that vowels are
redundantly nasalized before nasal consonants, this
redundant feature on vowels may be interpreted by later generations as the distinctive feature, with the
subsequent dropping of the nasal consonants, and a
phonemic contrast between nasal and oral vowels resulting. The 'sluggishness' of certain of the articulators has in this case linguistic significance dic-
tating as it were what is to be found in languages of
the world.

In discussing the velopharyngeal muscle complex
MacNeilage points out the variability of various muscle activity. He states: "it is entirely conceivable
that there are individual differences in use of different speech muscles" and believes (correctly, I
think) that "speech production theories..(must) take
these individual differences into account rather than
ignoring them."

THE REPRESENTATION OF SOUNDS

In his discussion of Articulatory Mechanisms,
MacNeilage, pointing to the "enormous variability in
articulatory gestures as a function of their phonetic
and linguistic context" notes the "inappropriateness
of conceptualizing the dynamic processes of articulation...in terms of discrete, static, context-free
linguistic categories, such as "phoneme" and "dis-

tinctive feature". He adds, however, that such 'linguistic categories should (not) be abandoned--as
there is considerable evidence for their behavioral
reality...Instead, ...they are...at present better
confined to primarily characterizing earlier pre-motor stages of the production process...'

While I have no disagreement with MacNeilage's
conclusions it is clear that at some point the units
at these 'earlier pre-motor stages' must be understood and furthermore that their relation to the units necessary to explain the dynamics of articulation
require edification.

The various models of speech production and perception discussed by MacNeilage all assume that at
some stage in the speech production or perception
process an utterance is composed of discrete units.
The representation of the units differentiates the
Haskins "motor command" hypothesis from the "target
hypothesis". Wickelgren's model in which he posits
context sensitive allophonic type units does not specifically deal with whether these are represented in
terms of motor commands or targets.

The debate concerning the representation of
speech sounds in the brain is not a new one.

Pribram (1971) reviews the controversy saying
that there are those who:

"...maintain that anatomically a point-point-
representation of muscles and even slips of
muscles exists in the motor region, that the
motor cortex is a keyboard upon which all
other activity -- and indeed all willed action
-- plays. By contrast..others have pointed
out that the receptive fields of neighboring
cortical units cover a wide sample of muscles...and that electrical excitations of the
motor cortex produce movements, integrated
sequences of muscle contractions, and that
the movement produced by a particular excitation depends in part on the state of the
brain and the position of the limbs...The
interpretation made of these neurophysiolog-

ical data has always been that movements,
not muscles, were represented in the motor
areas."(p. 238-240)

The difficulties inherent in the 'motor command'
position were also discussed by Hughling Jackson and
by Walshe (1943). Walshe was particularly interested
in Jackson's hypothesis concerning the representation
of movements rather than muscles in the motor cortex.

"That muscles are not therein represented in
the cortex is illustrated daily by every case
of residual meiparesis, where we may see the
extensors of the wrist paralyzed as prime
movers in an attempted voluntary extension
of the wrist but powerfully active as syner-
gists in every forceful grasping movement of
the fist. Were a direct representation of
muscles in question, this familiar clinical
phenomenon could not occur."

MacNeilage argues for the target hypothesis in
which specifications are, in accordance with Lashley,
"not specific movements but directions of movement in
relation to goals or targets specified within space
co-ordinate systems."

One can accept the 'target hypothesis' and at
the same time view the 'targets' in a different light.

Pribram, for example, concludes on the basis of
various experiments and observations that:

"...the motor regions of the cortex were
critically involved in the control of
neither individual muscles nor specific
movements. Rather, the motor cortex seemed
to play some higher order role in directing
action -- action defined not in terms of
muscles, but of the achievement of an external representation of a psychological set
of Plan." (p.241)

These observations are very much in keeping with
Ladefoged's (1972) proposal, namely, that for the
production of some speech sounds the achievement of
the Plan is in terms of the auditory or acoustic representation.

89

As is well known, there is no simple correlation between articulatory gesture and acoustic or auditory output, i.e. different articulations may produce the same output. In a recent study by Ladefoged et al. (1972) it was clearly shown that not only may different muscles be utilized to produce the same articulatory gesture or "target", as is put forth by MacNeilage, but different articulatory gestures may be used to produce the same auditory "target". Cinefluograms of six subjects pruducing ten sentences of the form "Say h_d again" with all the English vowels used in the frame were analyzed. Measurements were taken of (1) tongue height, (2) mandible height, (3) tongue root advancement (4) hyoid height and (5) tongue lift. "A considerable degree of variation in the articulatory gestures used by the different subjects" was found (p. 64). The details of the results are all given in this paper. To summarize, it was found that Lindblom and Sundberg's (1971) proposal "that the primary difference among the front vowels is simply one of relative jaw opening" is untenable. Only two subjects behaved as predicted by Lindblom and Sundberg. The other subjects did not use "the degree of jaw opening as the main method of distinguishing between front lax vowels." (p. 70).

Furthermore, the suggestion of Perkell (1971) that the "distinctive feature" correlated with "tenseness" of vowels is "advanced tongue root" was also not supported. While tongue root advancement is one way of "bunching up the tongue" it is not the only one.

Finally, in a study of vowel differences (Lindau et al. 1972), in which radiographic data from two West African languages (Twi and Igbo), two East African languages (Dho-Luo and Ateso) and two Germanic languages (English and German) it was found that tongue height in different languages may result from three different mechanisms: lifting, jaw opening and advanced tongue root.

These studies vividly support the notion that 'target representations' may also be acoustic or auditory spacial configurations. As Ladefoged states:

90

'We...feel...that acoustic properties and their
sensory counterparts (or more likely the corresponding neurological processes) become part
of the producing process, mediating between the
possible articulatory gestures and their ultimate production. Articulatory gestures are organized within the sensory-motor cortex. The
information available at this level includes not
only sensory feedback information revealing dynamic and static information about the state of
the muscles, but also neural projections from
the auditory cortex. A speaker may be able to
use an auditory image at a suitable tongue
position without reference to any stored pattern
of articulatory gestures.' (p. 73)

It is interesting to note that similar conclusions were reached by Nooteboom as pointed out by Mac-
Neilage.

This position is in agreement with one accepted
in the neuro-physiological literature.

'In humans the nature of the cortex is revealed
in terms of its ability to generate symbolic
patterns, i.e. those associated with speech production. This can be considered a special case
of neuromuscular tracking of an internally generated 'auditory' signal...the number of basic
motor pattern elements available for this task
is not clear, but apparently it is finite and a
function of the particular language." (McRuer et
al. 1968)

The research of Ladefoged et al. provide some
evidence for the "number of basic motor pattern elements available for this task" and also support the
notion that "it is finite and a function of the particular language".

Ladefoged does not suggest in his "auditory theory of speech production" that the only representation of "phonemes" is in auditory terms. Rather he
shows that some "sound patterns...are more easily explicable by reference to acoustic rather than to articulatory data." and that this seems particularly

relevant to the linguistic description of vowels.
He concludes:

> "Considerations of this kind lead us to sug-
> gest that it is inappropriate to speak of a
> dichotomy between auditory and articulatory
> theories. At the sensory-motor level of
> the cortex, which is where phonetic units
> are encoded for the production of speech,
> both articulatory and auditory images are
> available:..."

I cannot see how the physiological data can be
explained in any other terms. This being the case,
it seems clear that a universal phonetic feature system needed by linguists to account for the sound
patterns of languages should not be restricted to articulatory based features. When the original Jakobson
Fant and Halle feature system was proposed, these
features were acoustically based. In an attempt to
overcome the inadequacies of this set, a new feature
set was proposed in which all the features were defined in articulatory or physiological (or pseudophys-
iological) terms (Chomsky and Halle, 1968). While
linguists do not have a monopoly on pendulum swinging
they are very adept at the process. What we need is
an adequate set of features and more and more evidence
such as the physiological evidence discussed above
and phonological evidence points to the need for both
articulatory and acoustic or auditory representation
of features.

As to phonological evidence, Hyman (forthcoming)
presents a strong case for resurrecting the feature
Grave. He shows that in Feʔ Feʔ reduplication, a
back vowel ([+grave]) is the reduplicated vowel when
the morpheme initial consonant is either a velar or
a labial ([+grave]).

Again we see how physiological and linguistic
research combine to advance our understanding of language and linguistic behavior.

How these features and segments are realized in
actual dynamic speech production is discussed at
length by MacNeilage. We of course know very little

about the transformations which must occur between the higher more abstract representations and the articulatory movement toward the targets aimed at. But I think we are beginning to get a better idea of the kind and size of abstract units which must be posited if we are to account for linguistic behavior.

MacNeilage does not address himself directly to the nature of the more abstract units. He was particularly concerned with whether the representation of any such units was in terms of "motor commands" or "targets" concluding that the evidence supports the "target" hypothesis. It is in this light that he levels his criticisms against Wickelgren's model. I think however that the 'motor command' aspect of this model is not the crucial question. Wickelgren's 'unordered context sensitive allophones' could be represented by 'targets' rather than 'commands'. The question is whether the speech sounds by which meaningful utterances are realized are at any level represented by such units. I think there are data which can not be accounted for by positing such units.

For example, in the paper contributed to this volume, Wickelgren suggests that 'the units of representation in the lexicon...are concepts, not words or morphemes' and that 'a plural concept such as "birds" is represented by the conjunction of two concept representatives, "bird" and "plural".' Furthermore he assumes 'that a concept (word) is represented by a set of structural (articulatory and auditory) units at some lower phonetic level(s) of the nervous system.' These structural units are his 'unordered set of context-sensitive allophones ... such that each allophone...(is) an ordered triple of immediately adjacent phonemes.' He does not tell us how the concept 'plural' is to be represented in this way. Presumably 'birds' will be represented as $_\#b_\wedge$, $_b\wedge_r$, $_\wedge r_d$, $_r d_z$, $_d z_\#$. I do not know how the plural 'morpheme' can be represented in any other way, in order for the [z] (which is unordered) to be 'primed' by the articulation of the <u>d</u>. But evidence from

93

speech errors reveals a number of problems which are exemplified under (16).

(16) a. She has one uncle and two aunts
              [ʌŋkəl]   [ænts]
          She has one aunt and two uncles
              [ænt]   [ʌŋkəlz]
      b. Can you pick up the things [θiŋz] →
          Can you thing up the picks [piŋs]
      c. Wage hikes [weyĭ hayks]
          Wake higes [weyk hayjez]

These examples show that there are many errors in which words (or morphemes) are transposed without their plural endings. And furthermore that the plural ending is realized by its correct morphophonemic phonetic form after the word switch occurs. I cannot see how Wickelgren can account for the 'switch' from the intended plural $+^s_\#$ in aunts (16a.) to the $_1{}^z_\#$ which no longer occurs in the utterance produced. Perhaps he would suggest that the 'concept' aunt and the 'concept' uncle gets switched prior to their being 'translate(d)...into a sequence of articulatory gestures'. But even if one had any idea how this 'translation process' worked, some ordering must be assumed in order that the 'plural concept' is realized at the end rather than at the beginning of the word.

We can look at the particular example Wickelgren presents to illustrate his model and again see a number of difficulties. He suggests (Wickelgren 1969 a, b, and this volume) that 'the spelling of the immediate constituents of the word "struck" would be $\#^s{}_\pm, {}_s{}^t{}_r, {}_+{}^r{}_\Lambda, {}_r{}^\Lambda{}_k, {}_\Lambda{}^k{}_\#$. The spelling of the phrase deep structure would then presumably be as in (17)

(17) $\#^d{}_i, {}_d{}^i{}_p, {}_i{}^p{}_s, {}_s{}^t{}_r, {}_+{}^r \, , {}_r{}^ \, {}_k, {}^k{}_{\check{c}} \, , {}_k{}^{\check{c}}{}_\partial,$
$_{\check{c}}{}^\partial{}_r, {}_\partial{}^r{}_\#$

Instead of uttering the above, however, the

94

speaker produced steep dructure which would be represented in Wickelgren's schema as (18)

(18) $\#^s+$, $_s{}^t{}_i$, $_+{}^i{}_p$, $_i{}^p{}_d$, $_p{}^d{}_r$, $_d{}^r{}_\wedge$, $_r{}^\wedge k$, $_\wedge{}^k\check{x}$, $_k{}^{\check{c}}\partial$,
$_{\check{c}}{}^{\partial}r$, $_\partial{}^r\#$.

Notice that none of the underlined 'context-sensitive allophones' (CSA) in (17) occur in the actual
utterance (18) and the underlined CSA's in (18) are
'unrepresented' in the intended utterance. Given
such units it is very difficult, if not impossible,
to explain such speech errors. However, if one posits
that words, morphemes etc. are represented at some
level by phonemic type segments (or traditional phonetic allophones) the error is shown to be one of dis-
ordering of units as in (19).

(19) /d i p s t r ʌ k č ə r / →/s t i p d r ʌ k č

ə r /

Furthermore the suggestion that the units are 'unordered' fails to reveal why effected segments in
speech errors are constrained in that, for the most
part, syllable place is maintained (Fromkin, 1971).

I am not suggesting that phonemic type segments
are the only units which underlie the dynamics of production. I think it is necessary to posit a hierarchy
of units including syntactic phrases, words, morphemes, syllables, phonemes, allophones, and distinctive features (Cf. Fromkin, 1971). What I am suggesting is that the particular kind of allophones posited
by Wickelgren are not among the units needed.

Finally, I think it is important to note that despite the 'abstractness' of linguistic units, and despite the fact that a representation in terms of a
linear string of such units may be inappropriate to
characterize the dynamic processes of articulation,
they can not be dismissed as figments of the linguists
imagination and must be included in an overall explanatory model of speech production.

VICTORIA A. FROMKIN

TEMPORAL FACTORS IN SPEECH PRODUCTION

MacNeilage has summarized the important contributions of many researchers concerning segment durations
and articulatory dynamics. Again, I would like to
select out of this excellent discussion a few questions as they relate to linguistic grammars, i.e.
phonemic contrasts and phonological rules.

In discussing the lengthening of vowels before
voiced as opposed to voiceless segments, he notes the
finding of Chen (1970) and others that in some languages the increased duration exceeds what can be explained by physiological causes. Here again we find
some support for the 'auditory theory of speech production'. If, as has been shown, 'English speaking
listeners (use) the differences in vowel length as a
perceptual cue to the voicing of the following consonant' then, despite the fact that vowel duration is a
'redundant' feature in English, one must posit that
such length contrasts are 'preprogrammed'. In other
words, at 'the sensory-motor level of the cortex,
which is where phonetic units are encoded for the production of speech' duration must be in some way specified. It would not be surprising if in the process
of language change such languages would begin to use
vowel length duration 'phonemically' with a neutrali-
zation of the voiced/voiceless contrast of obstruents
in final position arising. In English this may already be happening, with the devoicing or partial devoicing of final voiced stops and the contrast maintained in the vowel. We would expect to find this
rarer in languages where the duration difference does
not exceed the 27 ms reflecting the greater rate of
lower lip movement in voiceless stops, where such a
difference does not provide enough of a perceptual
contrast.

In noting that net lip closing velocities for [v]
was greater than for [f] MacNeilage states: "Differences in vowel duration due to voicing of following
fricatives thus remains unexplained, unless one appeals
to an ad hoc "output regularity" constraint that

96

makes vowels behave the same with respect to the voicing distinction in all obstruents." I see no reason why this is an 'ad-hoc' explanation, given that the language imposes constraints on the speech-production mechanism just as the physiology imposes constraints. In fact, it would be odd if such a constraint did not occur, given that the actual durations of vowels in English exceed the predicted physiological differences. To suggest that there is a duration rule excluding the labio-dental fricatives would not make sense. In our concern for physiological explanations of linguistic phenomena we should not ignore the linguistic explanations for physiological phenomena.

The data concerning variability of segment durations also relates to other questions of synchronic and diachronic phonology. The 'trade-off' between number of consonants and vowel length has been discussed by many investigators. In addition the relation between the syllable durations and number of syllables in an utterance have also been discussed.

We find such phenomena reflected in historical sound change and in synchronic phonology.

The Vowel Shortening rules in Early Middle English and in Modern English reflect these processes, as illustrated below:

(20) Early Middle English

$$V \rightarrow [-long] \; / — CC \begin{cases} C \\ ..V..V \end{cases}$$

gōdspell → godspell   ō/

brǣmblas → bræmblas

blēdsian → bledsian

(21) Modern English

$$V \rightarrow [-long] \; / — C \begin{cases} C \\ ..V..V \end{cases}$$

keep → kept

vain → vanity

severe → severity

(See Kiparsky, 1968)

Linguists can describe the vowel shortening before two or three consonants and in tri-syllabic words but explanations are provided by reference to physiological data.

The reverse situation, as noted above, is also true. MacNeilage refers to a study of one dialect of Finnish where "Oller found very little final vowel lengthening but relatively more final consonant lengthening. Therefore....final syllable lengthening does not appear to be uniform in pattern in different languages, and this makes (the)...phenomena difficult to ascribe, in any straight-forward way, to an inherent production constraint." I agree with this statement and again believe that the linguistic system may provide explanations where the physiological system cannot. The situation in Finland may be due to the fact that consonant length is contrastive, although further investigation is required before this can be offered as the explanation for the data.

CONCLUSION

I would like to conclude with a brief discussion of the overall production mechanism. It is clear that the muscular movements, articulatory shapes which they give rise to, and the acoustic output are very late stages in a complex set of psychological and neuro-physiological events in speech production. Since this conference is concerned with the relationship of speech production and perception to cortical functioning, the representation of language in the brain is also of interest, since to understand the overall process one must have some understanding of the many transformations which occur between the act of ideation and the final acoustic output. A study of the neurophysiology of the cortex will not in itself answer our questions. It will not reveal the 'reality' of linguistic units and rules, i.e. of the internalized grammars which speakers use. On the other hand we are interested in a model of reality in the Galileo sense rather than a model which posits that 'There is no need for these hypotheses to be true, or even to be at all like the truth...one thing

is sufficient for them - that they should yield calculations which agree with the observations.' (Osiander, as quoted by Popper, 1965)

Obviously we want our hypotheses to be true,
whether they refer to higher-order units and processes or peripheral mechanisms.

I have attempted to show, in my comments, the relationship between linguistic theory and speech physiology. Physiological data can explain many facts and
help to constrain linguistic models. But linguistic
models are also relevant and necessary in our search
for physiological models.

MacNeilage states; "we are still primarily at a
data gathering stage, or at most at the stage of formulating microtheories." It is obvious, however, that
our data-gathering must be directed and it is here
where linguistic theory can help. Perhaps we are not
so 'data-rich and so theory poor' as Rosenblith (1967)
suggests. But it would be well to keep in mind his
statement that:

'The kinds of things that the rational man can
say about language - the kinds of deep structures, the abstract operations he can concaten-
ate...are still untestable. They are untestable
precisely because we do not have as yet a technology of what I might call his cognitive measurement...I am struck with the fact of the gap
that exists at the present time between the
highly developed quantifigable kind of technol-
ogies of measurements, and the basic facts of
language. My feeling is that...one cannot talk
any more about the human brain without really
trying to understand what linguists mean when
they talk about language behavior.' (p. 96)

This is of course very much the position taken
by Lashley, and I think it is the correct position up
to a point. The point of course being that one cannot explain certain linguistic facts without the kind
of information reported on so ably by MacNeilage.

While we strive to provide the data and informa-

tion which I believe are necessary in the development
of linguistic (particularly, phonological) theory,
and while I believe free and sharp criticism is a
necessary ingredient of any science, I think we ex-
perimentalists must recognize the enormous insights
provided by linguistic theory. The new goals set by
Chomsky in 1957 have provided a framework for much
of our work. The attempts in the recent years to
develop a theory of 'markedness', one which will reveal and account for notions of 'naturalness', have
stimulated much phonetic research. The attempt to
find evidence to support or disprove 'psychological
reality' of abstract units and rules posited by linguists can only have positive effects in our work.

   Those of us who are concerned with linguistic
performance and in testing linguistic hypotheses have
perhaps more of a burden than the linguists whose
"freedom and the lack of constraints on making of
theories and making of models are restricted only by
their own intelligence." (Rosenblith, 1967, p. 97).
I have often envied the syntactician who looks for
sentences to prove or disprove some hypothesis such
as the A over A constraint on transformations. I
think all of us will say 'Amen' to Rosenblith's "hope
that they (the linguists) won't exploit their position by turning away from the laboratories instead
of turning towards them."

   We are turned towards the laboratories and we
are finding some answers. If we keep in mind the
importance of relating linguistic constructs and empirical verifications, more answers may be forthcoming.

ACKNOWLEDGEMENTS

   Preparation of this paper was supported in part
by USPHS Grant NS 09780, ONR Contract NR 049-226,
NSF Grant GS 2859, UCLA intramural research funds and
a Grant from the UCLA African Studies Center.

REFERENCES

Bouillaud, J. cited by H. Head in Aphasia and Kindred Disorders of Speech, Vol. I, Cambridge: Cambridge Univ. Press., 1926, 16.

Chen, M. Vowel length variation as a function of the voicing of the consonant environment: Phonetica, 1970, 22, 129-159.

Chomsky, N. and Halle, M. The Sound Pattern of English, New York: Harper & Row; 1968.

Fromkin, V.A. Tone features and tone rules. Studies in African Linguistics, U.C.L.A., 1972, March.

Haggard, M.P. The use of voicing informati n. Progress Report No. 2, 1970, Psychological Laboratories, Cambridge.

Halle, M. Theoretical issues in phonology in the 1970's. Paper presented at the VIIth Intern. Cong. of Phonetic Sciences, August, 1971.

Halle, M. and Stevens, K. A note on laryngeal features. Quarterly Progress Report, Research Laboratory of Electronics, M.I.T., 1971, 101, 198-213.

Head, H. Aphasia and Kindred Disorders of Speech, Vol. I, Cambridge: Cambridge Univ. Press, 1926.

Hirose, H. An electromyographic study of laryngeal adjustments during speech articulation: a preliminary report, 1971, SR-25/26, 107-116.

Hiroto, I., Hirano, M., Yoyozumi, Y. and Shin, T.
Electromyographic investigation of the intrin-
sic laryngeal muscles related to speech sounds.
Ann. Otol. Thinol. Laryng. 76, pp. 861-872, 1967.

House, A. and Stevens, K.N. Analog Studies of the
Nasalization of Vowels. Journ. of Speech and
Hearing Res., 1956, 21, 218-232.

Hyman, L. The Phonology of Fe Fe. UCLA Ph.D. dissertation to be published as a monograph by
Studies in African Linguistics, 1972.

Jackson, H. On the nature of the duality of the
brain. In J. Taylor (Ed.), Selected Writings
of John Hughlings Jackson. London: Hodder and
Stoughton; 1932.

Kozhevnikov, V.A., Chistovich, L.A., Alyakrinskiy,
Bondarko, L.V., Goluzina, A.G., Klass, Yu A.,
Kuz'min, Yu. I., Lisenko, D.M., Lyublinskaya,
V.V., Fedorova, N.A., Shuplyakov, V.S. and
shuplyakova, R.M. 1965. Rech': Artikulyat-
siya i vospriyatiye, ed. by Kozhevnikov, V.A.
and Chistovich, L.A. Moscow and Leningrad:
Nauka. Trans. as Speech: Articulation and
Perception. Washington: Clearinghouse for
Federal Scientific and Technical Information.
JPRS. 30. 543.

Ladefoged, P. In Ansre, G. (Ed.), The Tones of Ewe
Verbals. ASCILNA 1963, 112-118.

Ladefoged, P. Three Areas of Experimental Phonetics. Oxford Univ. Press, 1967.

Ladefoged, P. Preliminaries to Linguistic Phonetics. Chicago: Univ. of Chicago Press, 1971.

Ladefoged, P. The Three Glottal Features: In
U.C.L.A. Working Papers in Phonetics, 1972, 22.

Ladefoged, P., DeClerk, J., Lindau, M., and Papcun, G. An Auditory-motor theory of speech production. In U.C.L.A. Working Papers in Phonetics, 1972, 22.

Lindau, M., Jacobson, L., and Ladefoged, P. The Feature Advanced Tongue Root. In U.C.L.A. Working Papers in Phonetics, 1972, 22.

Lindbloom, B.E.F. and Sundberg, J. Acoustical Consequences of the Lip, Tongue, Jaw, and Larynx Movement. J. Acoust. Soc. Amer., 1971, 50, 1166-1179.

McRuer, D.T., Hofmann, L.G., Jex, H.R., Moore, G.P., Phatak, A.V., Weir, D.H., and Wolkovitch, J. New Approaches to Human-Pilot/Vehicle Dynamic Analysis, 1968, AFFDL-TR-67-150, Tech. Report. Feb. Airforce Flight Dynamics Lab. Air Force Systems Command, Wright Patterson Air Force Base, Ohio.

Moore, G. Respiratory Controls. (Unpublished MS) 1966.

Ohala, J. The role of physiological and acoustic models in explaining the direction of sound change. Project on Linguistic Analysis (Berkeley: University of California) 1971, 2.15, 25-40.

Perkell, J. Physiology of Speech Production: A preliminary study of two suggested revisions of the features specifying vowels. Quarterly Progress Report. Research Laboratory of Electronics, M.I.T., 1971, 102, 123-139.

Popper, K.R. Quoted in Osiander, A. (Ed.) Conjectures and Refutations, the growth of scientific knowledge. New York. Basic Books, 1965, 98.

Pribram, K. Languages of the brain: experimental paradoxes and principles in neuropsychology. Prentice Hall, N.J. 1971.

Rosenblith, W.A. In Darley,,F.L., Millikan, C.H. (Eds.), Brain Mechanisms Underlying Soeech and Language. N.Y. Grune and Stratton, 1965.

Sapir, E. Language. New York: Harcourt, Brace and World, 1921, 1949.

Sapir, E. Sound Patterns in Language. Language, 1925, 1, 37-51.

Sawashima, M. Laryngeal Research in Experimental Phonetics. In Status Report on Speech Research (Haskins Laboratories) 1970, SR-23, 69-115.

Schuh, R.G. Natural Tone Processes. U.C.L.A. (Unpublished MS), 1972.

Slis, J.H. and Damste, P.H. Transillumination of the glottis during voiced and voiceless consonants. IPO Annual Prog. Report, 1967, 2, 103-109.

Walshe, R.M.R. On the mode of representation of movements in the motor cortex with special reference to "convulsions beginning unilaterally". Brain, 1943, 66, 104-139.

Wickelgren, W.A. Context-Sensitive Coding and Serial vs. Parallel Processing in Speech, 1972 (this volume).

Wickelgren, W.A. Context-sensitive coding, associative memory, and serial order in (speech) behavior. Psych. Rev. 1969(a) 76, 1-15.

Wickelgren, W.A. Context-sensitive coding in speech recognition, articulation, and development. In K.N. Leibovic (Ed.) Information Processing in

the Nervous System. New York: Springer-
Verlag, 1969(b), 85-95.

Chapter 3

ACOUSTICS OF SPEECH

Osamu Fujimura

Research Institute of Logopedics and Phoniatrics
Faculty of Medicine, University of Tokyo
Hongo, Tokyo (113)

INTRODUCTION

The problems I shall discuss in this paper are
those of speech phenomena in more or less direct relation to linguistic units and their functions. Ultimately, our concern will be in understanding of the
essentials of the relation between the linguistic
codes and the acoustical (and related) properties of
speech phenomena, but for this to be achieved, it is
first necessary to outline acoustical theory and facts
that restrict the nature of phenomena we will observe.
I will refer to some problems only as criteria for
our understanding and hypotheses. For obvious reasons, I will have to restrict myself to reorganizing
the vast problem, showing crucial points by concrete
examples, without going into individual details.
    Looking at speech phenomena carefully from an
observational point of view, we find first of all
that they are variable or "noisy" in a broad sense of
the word. Variability and fluctuation, as a matter
of fact, seems to be one of the very essential
characteristics of human performance, particularly
in contrast with what machines do. The signal to be
received being always noisy, a human being is somehow equipped with an effective means of extracting
signals from noise, and of uncovering the code struct-

ure of language, from this limited noisy experience.
This is a remarkable, and indeed intriguing fact not
only for the engineer but also for the speech scient-
ist and the linguist, because it does seem the case
that there is no algorithm which can be written for
duplicating this plain human ability. Even though
I perfectly agree with the Chomskyan thesis that a
rigorous description of the linguistic regularity has
to be based on a totally deductive methodology, it
is at the same time true that, from a heuristic point
of view, our science needs faithful recording of natural phenomena and inductive data processing as much
as is practical. Since we have not yet established,
or even proposed, as a matter of fact, the entire
chain of descriptive levels from syntactic codes down
to acoustic waves, we need to narrow down the domain
of search by whatever means are known.

As is well known, speech phenomena are actualiz-
ations of linguistic codes. It must be emphasized,
however, that not all the information conveyed by
speech waves is related to the linguistic entity. We
can make judgements, for example, about some physical
characteristics of the speaker, whether male or female,
old or young, and probably even tall or short (to
some extent), by merely listening to his voice, which
does not involve much semantic or syntactic idiosync-
racy. Putting aside for a moment the question of
where to place the boundary between linguistic and
non-linguistic aspects of speech, it is perfectly
clear that not all the information contained in the
speech waves can be treated in any structural description of language. In order to discuss characteristics of speech, it is important to know about
these extra-linguistic factors to some extent, even
when our concern is only in understanding of acoustic
correlates of linguistic (phonological) structural
units. This is so because what we observe as natural
phenomena inevitably involves such extra-linguistic
factors, and therefore we shall have to be somehow
prepared to exclude the effects of these irrelevant
factors by some sort of abstraction, or filtering.

This sort of filtering is nothing like any mechanical process commonly known in electronic techniques, but is something intricate, and quite commonplace in the daily mental processes of a human being although still escaping his appreciation.

One and perhaps the only way to cope with the complexity of our problem in an empirical approach, (before having even a tentatively proposed overall outline of structural description) is to try to find a set of observational samples that correspond to different values of a certain dimension under control, and to keep all variables in other dimensions in the "same" condition as parameters, even though we do not know exactly what these may be. This method of minimal contrast, or comparison ceteris paribus as Roman Jakobson puts it, is probably the most practical linguistic advice which one must follow in designing experiments in speech science. In order to do this, however, we still need to have some rough idea at least, about what kinds of control dimensions might come into the picture. In some cases we need exact information about certain relevant (e.g. phonological or phonetic) constraints on combinations of the controlled variable values in different dimensions; if not we may try, for example, to let the subject produce, or identify, phonologically impossible or peculiar forms, which may not exist in his normal language mode.

One particular case of "noise" in the broad sense, is the random variability of human performance in a given linguistically well defined task. In production of a certain sentence, for example, it will not be surprising at all that a speaker does not repeat the same physical utterance twice.* This

---

* Similarly, the auditory image of a listener to the same stimulus, will not be the same, even though the different but redundant signals certainly will lead to the perceptual identification of the same linguistic code.

random variability for the same linguistic material
for the same talker, for example, may be eliminated
from observation only through some kind of statistical processing. In order to make this statistical
process meaningful, however, we need to establish
some, (not necessarily obvious) framework of describing the signal. This often has to be based on
theoretical considerations of the physical production mechanism because we have no other way of understanding the nature of the signal.

By way of illustrating the point of issue, let
us consider an extremely simple case of statistically
processing different utterances of a monosyllabic
word in isolation, which may exist in some language
and be transcribed as [pu].

Suppose we have an impulse-like waveform followed
by a short interval of silence and then a quasi-periodic [u]-sounding waveform. After making sure (by
listening) that we have a sufficiently convincing
sound quality of [pu], let us move the position of
the first impulse-like waveform so as to vary the
duration of the silent interval.

Within a certain range of the duration values, we
will be able to continue hearing good [pu]'s. Let
us make a sufficiently large number of such [pu]-
sounding waveforms that statistically have a normal
distribution around a representative value of the silence duration, and simply add them up as time functions. It will be easy to believe that the resulting
waveform, which is an average of the many [pu]'s,
will sound as a good sample of [Φu] or [fu].

This Gedankenexperiment can be easily reinterpret-
ed as representing a case of analyzing natural speech
samples spoken as [pu]. If we did not know what the
relevant variable is in discussing inherent characteristics of the consonant, and if we blindly dared to
take the statistical average of the observed waveforms for a set of utterances of [pu], obviously we
would reach the wrong conclusion. What we should do
instead, is to measure the relative timings of the
occurrence of the impulse-like wave relative to the

initiation of the vocalic waveform, and take the average for this parameter value separately from others that may be processed similarly. Then a recon-
struction of the "average" waveform will surely sound
as a representative [pu].

How can we know, then, if we are doing the right
thing in each case of exploring the relevant characteristics of speech sounds? Are we simply trying to
give a meaningless answer to a circular problem? It
is quite clear that truly inductive methodology cannot survive if we wish to be logically rigorous in
our research approach. Even seemingly inductive experiments have to be guided by theoretical insights.
There was good reason for scientists in general speech
studies to depend heavily on an acoustic theory of
speech production and on speech synthesis experiments,
although it is true that the invention of the sound
spectrographic technique for speech analysis led us
to a new epoch of speech research in the early 1950's.

ACOUSTIC WAVES

A speech signal, in the physical form of a sound
pressure wave, carries a verbal message from a speaker to a listener. The speaker also monitors the
actualization of his message through this signal as
the final product, as well as through some other
physiological feedback channels. It is important to
recognize, particularly for the engineer designing a
system for processing speech signals, that this
form of signal as the output from the speaker is never the same as the acoustic signal that the listener,
or any receiving device, receives at a far distance
in a room, as in most conversational situations. Acoustic distortion introduced in this process of transmission is not insignificant, and no known device,
however sophisticated, can exactly restore the original signal, even though the distortion is strictly
linear. It is amazing that a human listener can communicate in ordinary rooms, even those in which there
is a high degree of noise. This fact is, by itself,

already strong enough proof that the speech signal as
it comes out of one's speech organs is highly restricted in physical characteristics, viz. that it is
highly redundant as an acoustic signal, and also that
the human process of verbal perception is not something of a simple nature that one can lightly attempt
to simulate by a machine, if a general performance
for a wide range of message material is claimed. I
must emphasize that when I talk about the nature of
speech waves it is strictly speaking about an ideal
situation, where, for example, the sound signal is
picked up by a high quality microphone in an anechoic
chamber. The characteristics of the perceptual process as mentioned above are of an inherently different nature compared with the physical phenomena we
will talk about here. Today we can demonstrate some
machines that can, for example, recognize spoken digits almost perfectly correctly even in a noisy laboratory environment, if the speaker's voice for the
material to be recognized is processed and stored
beforehand. This kind of achievement is certainly
not to be expected from engineering that pays no
attention to the essential characteristics of speech.
On the other side of the coin, the problem of speaker
identification or verification poses similar complex
problems.

ACOUSTICAL THEORY OF SPEECH PRODUCTION

An acoustical theory of the speech production process was developed to practical significance in the
1940's by M.Kajiyama, a physicist, based on his radiographic experiments conducted in cooperation with T.
Chiba, a linguist. The results were reported in a
book which was published in English about thirty
years ago (Chiba and Kajiyama 1941). He applied Web-
ster's horn equation to the acoustic system, (the
vocal tract,) which is formed by the speech organs
extending from the glottis to the lips. Based on
midsagittal dimensions obtained from lateral x-ray
photographs and some other necessary estimations for

112

the cross-sectional shapes of the tract, he derived
(through approximate calculations) the formant frequencies for the five Japanese vowels. In order to
corroborate the validity of the calculations, the
vowel sounds were also acoustically synthesized for
listening evaluations.

Independent of this early work, workers at the
Acoustics Laboratory of MIT, (including Gunner Fant
from Sweden,) took up the same problem and proposed
electrical circuits simulating the acoustic system
(Stevens et al., 1953). Based partly on this simulation experiment and partly on numerical calculations
of the acoustic tube, (by the same physical principle
as in the Kajiyama work and supported by network
theory considerations,) Fant completed a substantial
and well developed work comprising a new approximation theory for vowels and theoretical and experimental materials for different kinds of consonants.
This work was published in 1960 as the first comprehensive treatise of speech acoustics (Fant 1960).

The starting point of the modern theory of speech
production is to regard the vocal tract as a linear
acoustic transfer system (four-terminal). It means
at the same time assuming no coupling between the
source generator and the transfer system, which is
not really true but in practice quite workable in
most cases with which we are concerned. The plane
wave propagation, - the rigid walls (with dissip-
ation) and a tilted flat spectrum envelope for the
voice source spectrum, - all these commonly held assumptions are not exactly true from a rigorous point
of view. Nevertheless they work well for many purposes, and we can appreciate the merit of these assumptions by reflecting what would have happened if
we did not adopt them to start with. We have learnt
in many fields of physics that even a grossly approximate but at the same time comprehensive basic framework for data interpretations and discussions is
something indispensable to scientific progress.

Spectral and Temporal Aspects

The acoustic speech signal is characterized in two aspects, viz. in temporal and frequency domains. Individual vowels in terms of their acoustic correlates are more strongly characterized in the frequency domain by their inherent spectral properties, whereas consonants often cannot be characterized without specification of temporal patterns. As is well known, the sound-spectrographic technique of speech signal analysis has made it possible to represent and record the temporally changing spectral patterns in a form of two-dimensionally distributed blackness display for visual inspection of the signal characteristics. In principle there is an inherent uncertainty about simultaneous specifications of both temporal and spectral structures of a given signal, and one of the salient successes in the design of the spectrograph for speech analysis was the adoption of a rather loose frequency resolution, viz. 300 Hz for the filter bandwidth (Potter et al. 1966).

In treating the general problem mathematically, it is handy and comprehensible to represent the characteristics of the signal and those of the system by Laplace transforms of the time functions; time serving as a relatively slowly changing parameter after the transformation. By doing so, the output signal from the articulatory system can be represented simply as a numerical product of two functions representing the source signal and the transfer function of the vocal tract, respectively. Thus, in such a quasi-static representation, we can relate the sound pressure picked up at a certain distance from the mouth $p(s)$ to the product of three terms: the volume velocity at the glottis $u_g(s)$, the transfer function of the vocal tract $T(s)$ defined as the ratio of the output volume velocity to the input volume velocity, and the radiation characteristics $R(s)$, as follows (s represents frequency in the complex number domain):

$$p(s) = R(s) \cdot T(s) \cdot u_g(s) \qquad (1)$$

Among the three terms, $T(s)$ is the determinant fact-
or for phonetic values.

The Vocal Tract

In the case of vowels, we assume that the vocal
tract is an acoustic tube with no branching and with
the sole excitation applied at its closed glottal
end. According to Fant's theory (Fant 1960, 1956,
1968), the transfer function $T(s)$ can be decomposed
into separate formant terms $F_i(s)$, each representing
a simple-tuned resonance:

$$T(s) = \prod_{i=1}^{n} F_i(s) \qquad (2)$$

where n is supposed to be sufficiently high, or otherwise the expansion can be truncated at a certain
point beyond which a so-called higher pole correction
term represents the effects of the rest. Each term
$F_i(s)$ for the i-th formant can be represented as

$$F_i(s) = \frac{s_i \cdot s_i^*}{(s - s_i)(s - s_i^*)} \qquad (3)$$

where, in general, s_i^* denotes the conjugate complex
of s_i, and s_i represents the formant frequency and
the damping factor. This s_i (and s_i^*) represents a
"pole" of the transfer function in circuit theory
terminology.

In the case of consonants, inherently transient
characteristics have to be treated as temporally
changing phenomena, and the treatment of vowels above
provides the basis of the notion of formant transition. Namely, the set of formant frequencies,
(which may be called the F-pattern after Fant, including let us say up to the third formant considering
its direct perceptual effect,) changes in time in a

manner that is characteristic of the phonetic segmental sequence. For a more or less stationary time
segment that is pertinent to a consonant in the acoustic signal, we can generalize the expression of
T(s) as (apart from a numerical multiplication
factor):

$$T(s) = \prod_i F_i(s) \cdot \prod_j A_j(s), \quad (4)$$

where $A_j(s)$ has an inverse characteristic of $F_i(s)$,
viz.:

$$A_j(s) = (s - s_j)(s - s_j^*) / s_j \cdot s_j^* \quad (5)$$

This term characterized by the zero s_j of the transfer function considered for the speech production
mechanism may be called the antiformant (Hattori
et al. 1958). An antiformant can be observed as a
valley in the speech spectrum and represents a spectrographic consequence of a consonantal feature that
is characterized by a particular way of deviating
from the acoustic conditions for vowels, i.e. either
branching of the vocal tract or location of the excitation source somewhere midway along the tract.
Usually it does not appeal to direct perceptual effects, but is important as a structural determinant
of the entire spectral shape of the output sound.
A vowel formant can be annihilated by an antiformant
in some cases such as nasalization, giving perceptual effect of deviation from the vowel-like quality
(Fujimura and Lindqvist 1971). An introduction of
an antiformant caused by a topological change (switch-
ing of relevant channels) in the acoustic system of
speech production in cases such as [mi], [si], and
perhaps [li], too, sometimes causes an apparent
spectrographic discontinuity (Hattori et al. 1958).
    The pole-zero locations of the vocal tract trans-
fer function can be calculated if the cross-sectional
area of the vocal tract is given as a function of the
position along its longitudinal axis (the area func-

tion), except that it is hard to give exact estimations of the damping factors (real parts of poles
and zeros) and also the exact distribution and nature of the turbulent noise sources, with our present-
ly available physical data.

Direct Measurement of the Transfer Characteristics

Fant's theory of the transfer function for vowels was proposed early in the 1950's, and its validity has been attested through synthesis experiments. Theory predicted that a series connection of
simple-tuned resonance circuits, in accordance with
the formulae above, would provide us with complete
control of the phonetic value in the entire range of
vowel qualities, and experiments corroborated that
natural-sounding vowels of clear phonetic values
could be produced by controlling only the lowest
three formant frequencies, all parametric conditions
being left constant.

More recently, an acoustic measurement of the
vocal tract characteristics gave further experimental
support to the theory (Fujimura and Lindqvist 1971).
The point of this study is that in making observations of the speech signal we always have data which
reflect an inseparable combination of the source and
transfer characteristics. When both factors have to
be hypothesized, (while on the other hand our theory
prescribes a clear-cut separation) one wishes that
at least one of these factors could be substantiated
independently from the other through direct observations.

An artificial sound source, in a form of sweeptone, was applied to the vocal tract just above the
closed glottis of a normal subject, through the thin
wall of the anterior portion of the neck. Assuming
that the transfer characteristic through the neck
wall did not change from one vowel articulation to
another within a series of measurements in a short
experimental session, we then compared frequency re-

sponse curves of different articulations quantitatively, and tried to see if the difference could be
interpreted as due only to different F-patterns, in
conformity with the theory.

Even though, in this method of study, there is
still an unknown factor that is included in the data
we can measure, all we need as the relevant assumption is independent of a similar one for the voice
source which could be claimed in the case of comparing speech waves for different articulations of the
same subject. Also, in this case of sweeptone excitation, we obtain accurate frequency response curves
rather than only a set of frequency sampled values,
the latter being the case when we observe the sound
spectrum with harmonic structure due to periodic excitation.

The actual procedure for quantitative interpretation of the data curves was as follows. Let us
denote the sound pressure amplitude of the sinusoidal wave picked up in front of the subject's mouth
orifice by $D(f)$ as a function of frequency f. This
function is assumed to be decomposed into the product of the formant functions F_i, with the formant
frequency f_i and the formant bandwidth b_i as parameters, multiplied by a common fixed frequency function $C(f)$, viz.

$$D(f) = C(f) \cdot \prod_i F_i(f; f_i, b_i). \qquad (6)$$

For each of the frequency response curves recorded
for different articulations, the second function on
the right (the product form) was actualized by a
series connection of simple-tuned circuits, their
parameters f_i's and b_i's being controlled for the
best match between both sides (6), using ad hoc but
fixed function $C(f)$. When a satisfactory match was
obtained, the parameter values were recorded as the
estimated formant data for the observed articulations.
The function $C(f)$ was determined by a successive
approximation, starting from a first guess and re-

118

touching it to minimize the average mismatch for all
the data curves in a set of measurements for which
it is supposed to remain fixed, in a course of repeated matching processes. This process of interpretation as a deductive technique of analytic measurement is called "analysis by synthesis", proposed by
K.N. Stevens and Morris Halle (Halle and Stevens 1962,
Stevens 1960) for spectral analyses of speech sounds,
with the intention that it serves as a model of human speech perception. In a series of experiments
conducted at MIT, data have been derived for spectral
structures of vowels, nasal murmurs etc., applying
this method by use of an interactive computer (Bell
et al. 1961, Fujimura 1962, Paul et al. 1964). The
sweeptone measurements, as described above, represented another study in the same vein, and provided
us with accurate estimates of the formant bandwidth
values for vowels, which revealed the fact, contrary
to what had been said, that typical bandwidth values
for the first formant are larger when the first
formant frequency is low than when it is in the middle
range. This finding constituted further experimental
evidence for the acoustical significance of compliance
of the vocal tract walls, which had been inferred by
Fant and Sonesson from analyses of speech in high
pressure environments (Fant and Sonesson 1964). At
the same time, by empirically deriving the fixed
function $C(f)$ for the particular measurement conditions through vowel samples, we also estimated unknown frequency characteristics of the articulatory
system for some consonantal (stationary) gestures.
Resonance frequencies of the vocal tract during complete closure conditions for different stop consonants
were also derived, and the theory of nasalization
and nasal murmurs (Hattori et al. 1958, Fujimura 1961,
1962) was supplemented with new quantitative data.

The Sources

In the case of vowels, liquids, nasals and
semi-vowels, the source of acoustic excitation of the

119

vocal tract is primarily the glottal modulation of
the air flow through the vibrating vocal cords.
When there is a narrow constriction somewhere along
the vocal tract, as the air flows through, turbulence is produced and serves as an excitation source.
The location of this source varies according to the
place of articulation, and the spectral shape of the
output signal varies depending on this location even
if the turbulence itself has the same spectrum. In
general, if the vocal tract shape is kept the same,
the formants are located in the frequency domain at
the same positions regardless of the place of excitation, but antiformants vary, and so does the resultant spectrum.

The turbulence noise as the excitation source,
typically in the case of voiceless fricatives, is
called frication. An explosion of the stop consonant is quite often accompanied by short frication,
immediately after the impulse-like transient waveform
introduced to the measured sound pressure signal by
a sudden release of the articulatory closure. When
the constriction is opened up to a certain cross-
sectional area in the articulatory movement, (for
example, towards the following vowel after the voiceless stop,) and if the glottis remains appreciably
open without having the vocal cords set in vibration,
a fair amount of direct-current air flow passes
through the glottis, and some turbulence noise is
produced there. This excites the acoustic system
and produces an h-like sound, produces an effect
called aspiration. The transition between frication
and aspiration is not necessarily clearcut; it is
presumably an automatic consequence of the articulatory movement, when, for example, a vowel articulation follows a voiceless aspirated stop. The laryngeal (and pulmonic) gestures determine the extent
of aspiration, i.e. when the glottis is narrowed and
voice onset takes place.

It has been said sometimes that [h] is characterized by an inherent narrow glottal constriction,
thereby producing turbulence noise. According to

120

recent findings by direct observations of the glottal images during consonantal articulations this does not seem to be the case. In [h] the vocal cords tend to maintain vibration presumably in spite of distinctly abducted vocal cords, at least partially, because of the larger value of the air flow rate. The glottis is often wider than that for [s], for example, in the same environment (Sawashima 1968).

In Japanese, it has been proposed that the phoneme /h/ is manifested as [h] when followed by the vowel /e/, for example, as [ç] when followed by /i/, and as [Φ] when followed by /u/ (cf. Hattori 1951). Even though this is apparently true phonetically, it is still questionable whether this allophonic variation should be interpreted as a consequence of context sensitive phonological rules of Japanese. In other words, it seems possible that we can interpret this phenomenon as a consequence of physical rules assuming the same control gesture for /h/, except that the articulatory conditions are left unspecified by this segment but are conformed with the gestures for the following vowel. The main source of turbulence noise might be located at the place of the articulatory constriction or at the glottis, or perhaps along an extended region of the vocal tract, depending on which constriction is aerodynamically the most favorable for the turbulence to take place. If this view is factually correct, then the next question will be "what happens in the case of English?" for example, where /hi/ is often described as [hi]. Whether the wider articulatory constriction should account for the difference between the two languages, and whether there should be differenct temporal characterizations either for the particular segments or consonants in general, in terms of, e.g. some time constant, has to be determined.

Vocal Cord Vibration

Recent research effort has been concentrated on clarification of the vocal cord vibration mechanism.

Van den Berg first proposed a myoeleastic-aerodynamic theory (van den Berg 1958), which set a physical
interpretation that is now considered standard.   J.L.
Flanagan, K.N. Stevens, and K. Ishizaka contributed
improvements and data as well as deeper insights into
the mechanism and its linguistic implications (Flanigan 1965; Flanagan and Cherry 1969; Ishizaka and
Matsudaira 1968; Stevens, to be published).
      The main point of interest is to see which part
of the voice modulation in speech can be attributed
to laryngeal control gestures and which to a more
physical sort of effect caused by other kinds of control, such as articulatory closure. The role of the
pulmonary contraction gestures in relation to segmental and non-segmental properties is also not understood though there have been warm disputes about
it.
      Recent fiberscopic observations of the larynx
during speech utterances, have indicated that tense
or voiceless stops in Japanese and English exhibit
laryngeal gestures that widely vary depending on the
phonological environment (Sawashima 1968, 1970; Sawashima et al. 1970; Fujimura and Sawashima 1971).
Even though the glottis is kept wide open during the
closure period for these consonants, typically in absolute initial prestress position, the same consonant
is actualized by an almost closed glottis in word
medial position. In the latter case, the slit is
considerably wider for voiceless fricatives in the
same environment. This may be interpreted as a purely physical or perhaps partially physiological (feedback dependent) consequence of the same laryngeal
control and different flow conditions for the two different classes of consonants, or perhaps as inherently different motor specifications depending on whether
the consonant is a stop or a fricative.
      Linguistic studies of languages do not tell us
definitively, on independent grounds, what the phonological units are, and their possible values, for
example, whether there is one dimension or more for
the glottal constrictive gestures, when we do not

122

know the phonetic fact precisely. Stevens and Halle discussed the possible relevance of a particular physical dimension - the coupling constant for two masses in Ishizaka's vocal cord model - to this important question in phonological theory (Halle and Stevens 1971). Ishizaka's two-mass model for a computer simulation of the myoeleastic-aerodynamic vibration system was proposed as a technical improvement over Flanigan's similar work with use of one vibrating mass for the vocal cord (Flanagan 1965, Ishizaka 1968). But from Stevens-Halle's point of view, the additional degree of parametric conditioning of vocal cord vibration could be crucial for phonetic interpretation of the linguistic sound system. Whether this particular proposal is true or not, is not known, but it will not be difficult to see that this is a physical or physiological matter that interacts with fundamental phonological interests. In a sense, a physical or physiological model can be gross or must be detailed, depending on whether the detail is used in language for a functional distinction. What kind of details can be utilized? Or let us say, what are details and what are gross differences - a fundamental and non-trivial biological question that points to the essential nature of human cognitive behaviors. K.N. Stevens points out a possible principle as a criterion of this issue: physical correlates at the consequent signal level must be little affected by deviations from the standard in motor gestures, for the latter to be used in language as physiological correlates of a phonological unit. He suggests that this stability principle works well, particularly when the mapping between the control and output levels is non-linear (Stevens 1971 and to be published).

Pitch and Intensity

In the case of voiced sounds, typically vowels, the acoustic waveform is quasi-periodic, and the fundamental period is determined by the rate of vibration of the vocal cords. The fundamental frequency

observed in the harmonic structure of the spectrum
generally changes during an utterance, and the changing pattern reflects physiological control as well as
natural tendency as a consequence of, for example,
the decaying pulmonic overpressure towards the end of
a stretch of voicing. Both the so-called subglottal
pressure (which reflects that pulmonary state and
pertinent respiratory efforts,) and the laryngeal
gestures, affect the voice fundamental frequency or
pitch. Which physiological control dimension corresponds to which linguistic or non-linguistic feature
is an important and largely unanswered question, except some few well-established functional aspects of
the laryngeal muscles, in particular the cricothyroid,
in relation to the accent patterns of Japanese and
Swedish (Öhman et al. 1967; Gårding et al. 1970;
Simada and Hirose 1970, 1971).

Some characteristics of the pitch contour are
used for identification of various phonological units,
i.e. they manifest sentence types (intonations), phonological phrase boundaries (the configurational features in Jakobson et al. 1951), prosodic (suprasegmental distinctive) features, and also inherent (segmental) features. For the last aspect, which is perhaps less well recognized (apart from the problem
of syllabic tones in e.g. Chinese), there is for instance experimental evidence that the pitch inflection pattern near the stop release in a stop-vowel
syllable serves as a secondary cue, in a certain
reasonable sense of the word, for the perception of
the tense-lax or voiceless-voiced distinction of the
consonant, while the voice onset time in reference
to the explosion plays the role of the primary cue
(Fujimura 1971). In analyses of natural utterances,
too, this effect of consonants on the pitch contour
cannot be ignored, when we wish to account for the
actual time course quantitatively, (described below).

Correlation between the voice intensity and
fundamental frequency is an intriguing question.*
Traditionally, it was held that English is a "stress
language" whereas Japanese is a "pitch language".

124

This is incorrect at least in the sense that one can produce rather natural sounding synthetic speech in English without distinctive use of intensity at all. The "stress" referring to (necessarily subjective) intensity as distinct from "pitch", is a dubious notion itself, even though it may sound physically simple and clearcut. The physically defined intensity of the speech wave is certainly clearcut, but the output intensity is so severely affected by the articulatory condition, that it can scarcely be correlated with the so-called stress. The source intensity for voiced segments ignoring some effects of the vocal tract-source interaction makes sense, but this quantity is not easily measured from speech waves. We seem to lack, at the moment, reliable data about the correlation between intensity and pitch.

Extraction of the fundamental frequency is not technically simple either, and in connection with the necessity in vocoder systems, this problem has been intensively studied for a long time.* This is one of those typical cases in speech research where a problem looks simple but is technically extremely difficult. At present we have only a few sophisticated methods to solve the difficulty. For phonetic studies the most effective method is probably the (narrow-band) spectrographic examination.

OBSERVATIONS OF THE NATURAL PROCESS OF PRODUCTION

As the basis of hypothesizing a working model of the human speech production process and also for offering the quantitative data that we may match against the consequences of the hypothesized model for its evaluation, we need an extensive body of accurate data on natural articulatory movements and laryngeal gestures. For these purposes we have several new techniques which are worth mentioning.

---

* See Flanagan (1965) for a brief review.

Articulatory Movements

In the classical works of phonetics, descriptions of the phonetic values in general were given almost exclusively in terms of articulatory conditions. After intensive studies of the acoustical structure of speech signals for ten to twently years, our attention is now drawn back to the old topics, but this time for more accurate and quantitative measurements with use of an extensive data material, rather than occasional qualitative and subjective observations.

Optical Observations

The visual observation of the articulatory movements has been, perhaps next to auditory evaluation, the most trivial and common technique of phonetics, even though quite often it was not mentioned explicitly in literature. It is still one of the most useful research techniques particularly when equipped with modern devices such as high speed motion pictures, fiberoptics, high sensitivity photo-multipliers, etc., and perhaps more so when used in combination with an interactive computer for data processing.

It seemed that the effective use of high speed photography had been somehow ignored until about twelve years ago, when I designed an experiment at MIT specifically for collecting quantitative data of speech dynamics of the lips and the mandible (Fujimura 1961(a); 1961(b)). A particular interest was directed to the separation of the physiologically controlled gestures from the uncontrolled movements. For example, it has been found that there is an uncontrolled component in the motion of the lips immediately after the explosion of an initial stop consonant, in the form of a so-called ballistic motion. In connection with this, the labial movement in this kind of environment was found to be so fast that there would be no meaning in expecting direct perceptual effects of formant transitions as such in

126

the initial part of the consonant-vowel transition.
A moderately high frame-rate, i.e. a few hundred fps, combined with the use of fast stroboscopic
techniques, is sufficient for the purpose of such
studies. Since optical measurements give accurate
data without interfering with articulatory actions,
it is substantially superior to other techniques of
mechanical measurements. The main weakness of this
approach, apart from the obvious point that we cannot
observe the hidden articulatory organs such as the
tongue, is that it requires a tedious and time-con-
suming work for data processing. Some techniques
have been devised in order to record the data directly as curves representing important articulatory
variables but, in general, direct observations of the
body surface is not only more informative but also
quite often necessary in order to avoid gross errors
in measurement. Moreover, it is very useful for
gaining insights in the first stage of the explor-
ation as to what are the most relevant factors to be
detected and measured by processing the optical data.
Computer processing of optical images with advanced
techniques of pattern recognition, or computer controlled object search techniques, may be the best
solution (cf. the radiographic technique, infra).

Radiography

For a long time, radiography of various sorts,
including in particular high speed cineradiography,
has been the major source of objective information
about the articulatory conditions of the tongue.
Unfortunately, the hazardous effects of radiation
on the subject restrain us when we wish to use these
methods extensively, and, as a result, the data body
is always unsatisfactory in size from the point of
view discussed above (cf. Introduction). Data processing from cineradiographic images, in addition,
is not only tedious, as in the case of optical images,
but also simply not feasible by any automatic means,
and often not possible by visual inspection.

A new technique is being developed at our laboratory in order to solve both problems at the same
time. It employs a computer to control the direction
of a fine x-ray beam, which after passing through
the object is detected by a high-sensitivity scint-
illation counter. The radiopacity at the selected
point (about 1 mm in diameter) in the object is thus
estimated and read into the central processor in dig
ital forms. This method, when technically well developed, will provide us with means to obtain useful
information about the tongue movements as physiological correlates of different kinds of phonological
units. As present, however, a device exists only for
pilot studies of the new method itself. Even though
preliminary results have been very successful (Kiritani and Fujimura 1970; Kiritani 1971), actual data
acquisition in speech research remains constrained
until the completion of a larger x-ray device (Fujimura et al. 1968; and to be published). One modest
exception is its use in actual real-time monitoring of
the tip of the fiberscope which is inserted into the
pharynx for observation of the glottis during speech
utterances. Fig. 1 illustrates an example of the
automatically located fiberscope, the points of x-ray
exposures for the automatic identification and tracking, and a track of movement during velum articulations.

Another limitation of the measurements in the
form of lateral cineradiography is that it is hard
to estimate the three-dimensional shape of the organs that surround the vocal tract. As a consequence
we need some guess work in estimating the cross-
sectional areas at different points along the vocal
tract axis, such information is needed for calculat-
ing acoustic consequences, such as formant frequencies. Also, for physiological considerations which
can be crucial for determining what the effective
physical dimensions are for the dynamic characteristics of the articulatory movements, (particularly of
the tongue,) we quite often wish to determine the
movements of specific points fixed on the tongue

128

rather than its surface contour. This information can be obtained by placing small metal pellets on the tongue surface, which at the same time makes it feasible to measure the tongue position accurately in each frame. It can be advantageous, to some extent, also in estimating the three-dimensional shape of the tongue. For these reasons, this pellet technique has been employed in some recent representative cineradiographic studies (Houde 1968(a), 1968(b); Perkell 1969; Kent unpublished dissertation), and will be used for the computer-controlled microbeam method. Tomographic methods of various kinds can be employed for some specific problems (Hollien 1965). This, however, suffers from the limitation in the available dosage even more seriously than the regular cineradiography.

Palatography

Palatography is an old technique used in experimental phonetics which should be mentioned here. Its obvious shortcoming is that the palatogram records the total area of palato-lingual contact during any part of the entire time course of the test sample, and no information can be obtained concerning movements of the tongue. Recent techniques developed independently by a few groups in different parts of the world have more or less similar effects of recording the temporal change of the contact by use of electric conduction through the tongue surface (Rome 1964; Kozhevnikov and Chistovich 1965; Shibata 1968; Hardcastle 1969). The dynamic palatography developed in our laboratory employs typically 64 sample points on a thin artificial palate, manufactured for the particular subject, and the data can be recorded in different forms. One output form is the "palatospectrogram" which displays, together with part of the regular sound spectrogram, time varying on-off traces of the palato-lingual contact for each of the 64 electrode positions, which are assigned 64 different frequencies (Shibata 1968). This is a convenient way

of recording the data for visual inspection. The
other form of output is the computer mediated oscil-
loscope display in the form of slow-motion movies of
the palatal pattern frames (Fujii et al., 1971; Fujimura et al., 1972). Fig. 2 illustrates an example
of this display, which includes a curve representing
the speech amplitude. The time of the pertinent frame
can be identified as a brightened dot on the speech
amplitude curve. Both the palatal (automatically di-
chotomized) signals and the (analog) speech signal
can be stored in real time on magnetic tape by a special analog-digital hybrid recorder (Ishida 1969).
This method is particularly suitable for automatic
digital processing of the palatal data by a computer,
since palatography causes no problem of biological
disturbances and it is practical to record a very
large data body which has sufficient statistical significance. Variability of speech utterances in different senses can be quantitatively estimated by this
technique, and some of the results are being published (Fujimura et al., 1972).

Even though the palatal contact patterns as time
series do not provide us with complete information
about tongue movement, the data in this form will be
particularly useful in complementing the radiographic
data, which would not be complete by itself. For example, the variability observed among repeated utterances of the same word or sentence has rarely been
studied quantitatively in most aspects of speech production (but see Malecot 1968; Lubker and Parris
1970). Variability in respect to the phonological
context or speech environment is, needless to say, a
point of common interest for both basic research and
applications, and still for obvious reasons past
treatment (even on an acoustic level) tended to be
largely restricted in terms of the size of available
or rather processable material. This kind of basic
data, particularly at the level of articulatory movements, will be important in making a substantial step
forward in automatic speech recognition or speaker
identification research.

Laryngeal Gestures

One of the least understood topics in experimental phonetics is how one controls the laryngeal conditions in speech, particularly in connection with the production of various consonants. For example a gross qualitative statement as to whether the glottis is open or closed during the articulatory closure of the non-aspirated stops in French and many other languages used to be simply a matter of conjecture. Observation of the glottis during real utterances with an actual stop of air flow, which used to be impossible for the regular laryngoscopic techniques, is necessary to understand the essential characteristics of the manner distinctions (e.g. /p/ vs. /b/b) in different languages. The interaction between laryngeal and vocal-tract conditions during the aerodynamic process is so strong that we cannot simulate the real situation during an articulatory closure with air passage of the vocal tract left open. Radiographic studies have also been attempted in this area, although the dosage problem is a handicap. In particular, when one attempts to take frontal views of the larynx for studying the glottal adduction-abduction process, we cannot avoid including the radiosensitive vertebrae in the image field. Also, the structures forming the glottis are not favorably radiopaque, and any effort to reinforce the radiopacity artificially, tends to disturb the mechanically and sensorily delicate glottal actions in natural utterances. Within these limitations, however, there has been some interesting work of linguistic relevance. For example, Kim in his studies of Korean stops, presented an account of the degrees of aspiration in terms of the glottal conditions at the moment of articulatory release (Kim 1970). Other studies have been concerned with the role of the pharyngeal conditions in relation to the source or tenseness feature. Perkell, for example, concluded in his study of lateral cineradiographic images that English lax stops were characterized by more yielding pharyngeal walls than

131

tense stops. Whether this effect is caused by the
air pressure against a passively compliant tongue
surface, the compliance being dependent on the muscular states, or is the result of some motor control
for active enlargement of the cavity for facilitating
the vocal cord vibration is a matter of future studies (Perkell 1969).

Recently, the gap in our knowledge with respect
to glottal conditions is being filled by data obtained with a new optical method (Sawashima and Hirose 1968; Sawashima and Ushijima 1971), i.e. the use
of a fiberscope, especially designed for laryngeal
observations. A flexible cable, 4 to 6 mm in diameter contains two bundles of glass fibers; one is a
coherently arranged fiberoptic bundle for image conduction, and the other for conducting light for il-
lumination. The cable, the tip of which houses an
objective lens, is inserted through the nasal passage down to the middle pharynx, and the image of the
glottis is viewed or photographed through an eye piece
attached to the outside end of the cable. With an appropriate light source connected to another branch of
the cable, a color movie can be readily made typically with a rate of 60 frames/sec. In this way, the
overall laryngeal state in segmental articulations
can be directly viewed and recorded. The pitch control gestures can also be studied by examining the
qualitative change of apparent vocal cords in vibration, and also some consistent up and down movements
of the larynx associated with pitch changes in speech
utterances have been observed (see infra).

For laryngeal gestures in connection with the
problem of manner distinctions or their relevant
source features, a particularly interesting case exists in Korean stops. It has been suspected, from
some cross-language studies on the so-called voice-
onset time (referring to the articulatory explosion),
that the phonetically significant physical dimensions,
or the corresponding physiological correlates, might
be substantially different from many other languages
(see Lisker and Abramson 1964). Some preliminary re-

sults of fiberscopic studies have indicated very interesting facts about this problem (Kagaya 1971).
Some examples of the laryngeal images for the three
manners of the dental stop are illustrated in Fig. 3.

Among the three types of dental stops, desig-
nated by /T/, /t/, and /t^h/ in Fig. 3, respectively,
the first is called the forced type, or the tense
non-aspirated, and it is known to be always voiceless during the articulatory closure.* The "tenseness" of this type of articulatory manner (Kim 1965)
may be related to the following observation peculiar-
ities in the case of isolated /CV/ syllables (Kagaya
ibid.): (1) The vocal cords, particularly the vocal
processes, become closed more than 100 msec prior to
the voice onset, which takes place at the time of articulatory explosion, (2) The closing action of the
vocal cords is quite rapid, (3) The larynx is sharply
lowered at the same time as the glottal adduction.
The voice pitch at time of onset, however, is marked-
ly high compared to the other two types in the same
environment, which show apparently higher laryngeal
positions. This is in contrast to the usual correspondence between a higher pitch and a higher laryngeal
position (see supra).

The "lax" stop, /t/ in Fig. 3, shows a slow
closing action of the vocal cords, and voice onset is
slightly later than the articulatory closure, leaving
some short length of aspiration. Even after the
voice onset, in this case as well as in the heavily
aspirated type /t^h/, the glottis at the vocal processes is still slightly open. The lax /t/, incidentally,
becomes voiced throughout articulatory closure when
the consonant is in word medial inter-vocalic position.

Even though it is too early to draw conclusions

---

* For some relevant studies of the Korean stops, see,
among other studies, the following works of acoustical analyses: Umeda and Umeda 1965; Kim 1965; and
Han and Wietzman 1970.

from the limited data of one subject,* it may be
worth while to hypothesize the following accounts.
In the case of the lax articulation, the vocal cords
are loosely set to a position ready for vibration
with a slack gesture (Halle and Stevens 1967) somewhat preceding to the articulatory explosion. As
soon as the air flow builds up beyond a threshold
value after the release of the articulatory stop, the
cords start vibrating. The forced type, in contrast,
has a positive adductive gesture well preceding the
explosion. The pressure difference across the glottis, which is necessary for vibration, is created by
a positive lowering action of the larynx, expanding
the supraglottal cavity (Fischer-Jorgensen 1963;
1968). The vocal cords are tightly closed, and
block the air flow up to a certain value of transglottal pressure differences, and this blockage is
broken immediately preceding the explosion. There
may be an appreciable amount of acoustic interaction
between the articulatory stop release and initiation
of vibration of the stiff vocal cords. The stiffened
vocal cords and the transient transglottal pressure
cause the observed high pitch. The third type, (i.e.
heavily aspirated,) is characterized by a wide opening of the glottis which is maintained well into the
moment of articulatory stop release, thus confirming
Kim's account (Kim 1970). The vocal cords may be
stiff or slack, and when they are drawn together for
the succeeding vowel gesture they are ready to vib-
rate even before the adduction of the arytenoidal
cartilages has been completed, because the air flow
rate is already high (Stevens, to be published).
    If these hypothetical characterizations of the
source features for the Korean stops are correct, we
should be able to observe a marked transient drop of
supraglottal pressure immediately before the explosion of the forced type stop, and perhaps its reflection on the manner of movement of the articulator,
e.g. the external shape of the lips for /P/, as was
observed in studies of American English stops in contrast to /m/ (Fujimura 1961(b)). The forced stop is

also expected to show a marked activity of the vocalis muscle.* We should be able to simulate the characteristic transient phenomena of these different manners of production by an appropriate computational
model, if we couple the already available vocal tract
simulation (Flanagan and Cherry 1969; Flanagan et al.
1970).

We may go a step further and hypothesize about
abstract phonological specifications for the Korean
stops, in conformity with the above-mentioned tentative account of the phonetic facts. Let us assume
that there are distinctive features in respect to
the laryngeal gestures, adduction-abduction and stiff-
slack, roughly along the line Halle and Stevens propose (Halle and Stevens 1971). For the time being,
the two features will be assumed to be binary. Let
us also assume that when a feature value is not specified in the abstract level, then it is later determined by some context sensitive (assimilation) rule,
(see Chomsky and Halle, 1968). Let us assume that
the lax stop is assigned no specification for adduction or abduction, but a specification of the non-
stiffness is. When there is a certain kind of boundary preceding the pertinent consonant segment, then
this segment will be given a status abducted. In
other words, the boundary as a phonological unit may
be considered to have an assignment of abduction status, and an assimilation (redundancy) rule will assign
an abducted status to the consonantal segment that is
non-specified in respect to this feature. There is
some experimental indication in the data referred to
above, however, that the closing action toward the
lax voiceless stop is loose and unstable. This may
be taken as an indication that the assignment of the
abducted status for the stop segment is not of a dis-

---

* Marked electromyographic activities of the vocalis
muscle in connection with glottal stops and also some
other related problems of source control are discussed
elsewhere (Gårding et al. 1970)

crete nature, but the non-specified status is carried down to the phonetic level at which coarticulatory rules process continuous time functions of a physical nature.

The case of Korean, of course, has important bearings on general phonetic theory as a crucial special case, and the hypothesis proposed above does not agree with the account proposed by Chomsky and Halle (1968) or a later tentative theory by Halle and Stevens (1971).

As another interesting topic of studies using the fiberscope, Sawashima and his coworkers have clarified the characteristics of the vowel devoicing phenomena in Japanese (Sawashima 1971; Sawashima et al. 1971). Comparing, among other things, a set of words like /sekikei/ and seQkei/, which are actualized as [sekikie:] and [sekke:], respectively, he measured the width of the glottal opening both at the vocal processes of the arytenoids and the membranous portion of the cords as functions of time. He found that the word medial sequences [kik] and [kit] had a significantly larger glottal opening than the geminate consonant [kk] and [tt] (Fig. 4) even though the durations of these two kinds of segment sequence were approximately the same. It was concluded, based on this finding, that the glottal maneuver for devoicing of the vowel is not a mere skipping of the phonatory adjustment for the vowel, but a positive gesture of glottal abduction for the devoiced vowel, even though this devoicing is not phonemically distinct. Supporting EMG data have been discussed elsewhere by Hirose (1971). This is probably one of the many allophonic rules that assign specific feature values depending on the context prior to the application of a coarticulatory rule of a physical sort.

The fact that voiced consonants are usually associated with a lower pitch, as discussed in § 1. 3. 2., possibly could be a result of a particular laryngeal gesture for voiced consonants, in distinction to vowels (Chomsky and Halle 1968). But this suspicion is at present a matter of conjecture. Pitch control

is usually associated with some change in the height
of the larynx, at least for the accent pattern in
Japanese* and the tone in Chinese (Chuang, 1971).
In the case of Japanese, the pitch control can be observed in respect to this physiological correlate,
even in devoiced vowel segments (Fujimura, 1971(j)).
Correlation between the laryngeal and pulmonic
gestures in relation to different linguistic functions
is an interesting, fundamental, and yet a controv-
ersial and confused issue. We simply need crucial
experimental evidence to separate the contributions by
the two physiologically distinct factors.

FUNCTIONAL MODELS

An ideal methodology for studying the production
mechanism might be as follows. Data be derived for
natural utterences at different levels of production,
such as cerebral motor commands, neuromuscular activities, mechanomuscular states, proprioceptive and
other sensory afferent neural feedback, states
(shapes) and movements of the speech organs, vocal
antiformant frequencies. Similar specifications would
have to be obtained for source characterization such
as laryngeal gestures and pulmonic conditions, and
aerodynamic states near and above the glottis. All
these combined would allow a description of the entire
course of transfiguration from linguistic code specifications to the sound wave, by proposing theory and
models for the relation between each pair of consecutive levels, checking with observed data of natural
utterances level by level. Obviously, reality is far
from this ideal case.
As we have seen above, the experimental techniques for observation and measurements of the natural

---

* The Larynx in Speech Utterance, Research Institute
of Logopedics and Phoniatrics, Faculty of Medicine,
University of Tokyo (demonstration movie, 16 mm in
color).

processes of speech production are often very new, and
we are expecting most results and data to come out of
experiments in the near future. No doubt these contributions will enhance our knowledge of the speech
production mechanism at some levels of the heirarchic-
al process. Yet in view of the inherent complexity
and variability of the phenomena as discussed in the
introduction, it is to be doubtful whether these empirical observations alone would lead us to usefully
organized, comprehensive descriptions, of the natural
processes. Even though the physical constraints of
the production mechanism are the only solid basis for
us in disambiguating the complex phenomena, the anatomical structure of the speech organs is formidably
complex. The physiological role of no single organ,
not the tongue, nor the lips nor the mandible, is
thoroughly known, in intricate speech gestures. Rather than go into details of what is known about these
problems, which I understand will be discussed in
another paper of this symposium, I would like here to
describe briefly the kinds of problems we have to face
in relating the mechano-physiological findings to acoustic phenomena.

Since we do not have sufficient knowledge of
any of the higher levels that constitute the speech
production mechanism, we should try to compensate
for the gaps of data by constructing a model for the
lower levels and piece together fragmental data at
different levels in order to check the adequacy of
the hypothesized model. From this point of view, our
theory and observational data are by and large solid
for acoustic phenomena, and the main point of issue
in the present research efforts is in constructing a
workable dynamic model of the mechano-physiological
articulatory system, which would take some input specifications that are more or less directly interpretable in terms of discrete linguistic codes.

Specification of Area Functions

One level of description we would have to work

138

out within this framework is the quantitative specification of the area function. This will be determined by the states and movements of the speech organ, and will derive the acoustic measures of the
speech phenomena. Some early works offered simple
and effective approximations of the area functions
in the form of a family of simple mathematical functions that are characterized through a set of three
"articulatory" variables, which represented roughly
the place of the main lingual contriction, the extent of the lingual constriction, and an acoustically
effective measure of the labial contriction (Stevens and House 1955; 1956; Fant 1960). Based on this
descriptive framework of the area function, some
useful charts were provided by these workers relating
these kind of articulatory variables to the consequent
formant frequencies. Considerable non-linearity in
the relation was apparent, which carried important
implications for succeeding work.

In order to substantiate the validity of this
kind of parametric specification of the area functions, we need some data of actual area functions for
natural utterances. Unfortunately there has been no
success in estimating the area function by direct
measurements.* Radiographic studies, which are pertinent to the shape of speech organs, a higher level
description, are at present the only source of infor-

---

* There is still a hope to measure the acoustic impedance looking into the vocal tract at the mouth opening, which in addition to the series of formant frequencies, gives another series of characteristic values, viz. the zeros of admittance. These would serve
as the mathematically required information for determining the acoustically effective area function (see
infra). Technical problems have not been solved for
useful acoustic measurements at the moment (Shroeder
1967; Sondhi and Gopinath 1971).

mation for deriving the area function. A difficulty
arises, from this point of view, in relating what we
can obtain by radiographic measurements to the area
function.

Let us assume, to be concrete, that we have good
and accurate estimates of the midsagittal contour of
the tongue surface obtained from the lateral x-ray
frames. At the same time, we would have good simultaneous sound recording for the utterances. As discussed above we have for most purposes solid enough
theoretical means to numerically derive formant frequencies for the given area function. On the other
hand, we have reliable means to derive formant frequencies from the speech waveform, i.e. the formant
extraction techniques (Flanaga 1965; Schafer and Rabiner 1970; Olive 1971).

Thus we would be able to test the adequacy of
our theory and the reliability of measurements by comparing the data that are obtained for the same utterance at two distinct levels, i.e. the x-ray measurement and the acoustic waves, separately, and evaluate the acceptability of match between the sets of
data at the level of formant frequencies.

The main problem concerns the conversion from
the midsagittal cross-dimensions to the acoustically
effective cross-sectional areas for the formant calculation. Research workers have been concerned with
this problem for the past several years (Fant 1960;
Heinz and Stevens 1965; Sundberg 1969). Obviously,
we need a simplification in the form of a three-dimensional model of the deformable speech apparata.
Simplified parametric descriptions and related computations tend to be still quite complex, but appropriate techniques of analysis-by-synthesis seem to
work effectively. Consistent and plausible descriptions of the articulatory conditions seem to be derived for some simultaneously recorded cineradiographic and acoustic data of vowels (Maeda 1971).

It will be worth while at this point in the discussion to raise a question as to whether a more
straightforward approach can be applied to the prob-

lem at hand. If we could make an inverse calculation
deriving the area function directly from the formant
frequencies, or any other extractable information in
the acoustic speech signal, then we would have for
comparison the x-ray measurements of the midsagittal
vocal tract dimensions on the one hand and the area
function thus derived on the other. By accumulating
data for different articulatory conditions (let us
say for the same subject), we should be able to find
quantitative relations between the midsagittal linear
dimensions and the areas for different cross sections
along the vocal tract, without any indirect analysis
by synthesis. Many efforts have been invested to
clarify the problems pertinent to this issue, and
very interesting results have been provided through
theory and computations (Mermelstein 1967; Schroeder
1967). The particular point at issue, however, has
been concluded negatively, in my opinion. If we consider a loss-less acoustic system for the inverse calculation from formant frequencies to area function
as a general problem, we can show theoretically that
the solution is infinitely ambiguous. In other words,
the set of formant frequencies simply does not provide
us with sufficient information to determine the area
function.

The acoustic theory and synthesis experiments
based thereon tell us that a specification of three
formant frequencies suffices for determination of the
perceptual phonetic quality of any vowel (Delattre
et al. 1952; Fujimura 1967). It could be said,
therefore, that there are only three degrees of freedom for the independent variables to describe the overall articulatory conditions of vowels. Then we
should be able to determine these articulatory parameters, instead of the area function with too many
unknown variables, from measured formant frequencies.

If we consider human physiological capability in
a universal phonetic sense, we may will assume that
there are more than three muscles which can be controlled independently for the articulation of different vowels. Even for the labial gestures alone, it is

141

actually observed that protrusion with rounding is
unnecessary for some marked labial constriction, as
seen in the distinction between /ʉ/ and /y/ in
Swedish. Whether these two vowels represent a phonetic minimal distinction in this respect may be somewhat unclear (Fant 1971), but in any case it seems
hard to argue with our present pertinent knowledge of
physiology that this labial distinction has to be
necessarily coupled with some difference in the lingual gesture. The situation is not essentially different for the lingual gestures proper. It will be
reasonable to assume that for any commonly known language the number of independent muscular controls for
the lingual states that are utilized in vowel articulation is more than three (e.g. the anterior and
posterior portions of the genioglossus, the stylo-
glossus, and at least one more for the mandible pos-
iton).

While the anatomical constraints of the human
speech apparatus restrict the set of possible area
functions for the vocal tract, it is at the same time
likely that not all the physiologically independent
muscular controls are effectively independent in
determining the acoustically relevant specification
of area function. The labial articulations in Swedish vowels exemplify the case. Whatever the articulatory features may be, the acoustical effect of labial constrictions can be approximated by a lumped
mass of the air at the orifice and can be represented
by a single measure, viz. the effective opening area
divided by the effective length of the orifice. The
point is then not really in the number of independent
variables in articulatory control of vowel quality,
but in the lack of correspondence between the articulatory and acoustical levels. What, then, are the
most effective articulatory dimensions as physiologically controlled, and linguistically relevent variables? In inquiring into this, it turns out that we
have to consider not only static articulations of
vowels, but also the dynamic aspects of speech production, the temporal organization.

The Cylinder Model of the Tongue

The midsagittal outline of the tongue in various vowel articulations can be roughly represented for its main portion by a circle with a fixed radius but movable in the two dimensional position - front-back and open-close - relative to another circular fixed wall which represents the palate and the back pharyngeal wall. The gap between the two circles (with a straight portion appended near the glottal end), together with an adjoining lip section, forms the vocal tract. I proposed this rough static model and informally tested it by use of an electrical vocal tract analog at MIT in 1959, and my intention at that time was to see how we should relate the dichotomous distinctive-feature specifications of vowels to articulatory specifications and then automatically to acoustic signals. Selecting appropriate values for the radii of the circles and also adopting non-orthogonal geometrical axes for the two articulatory dimensions, open-close and front-back, it seemed to be grossly workable even with a crude assumption of a proportionality between the gap dimension and the cross-sectional area. Later at Bell Labs, Cecil Coker adopted this model and elaborated it into a new dynamic model with many novel and interesting features, some of which seem to point to the very essential characteristics of the temporal organization of the speech phenomena (Coker and Fujimura 1964; Coker 1968; Flanagan et al. 1970). The model which has been implemented as a computer simulation program in combination with a hardware terminal analog synthesizer, is available for a rather large-scaled experiment of synthesis-by-rule, and Coker jointly with Mrs. Noriko Umeda, a linguist, developed an elaborate and in a sense amazingly complete system which approximates the entire chain of processes from linguistic codes to the sound waves.

Some workers recently have forwarded more physiologically motivated and still practical models, particularly in explicit references to the role of

the mandible in determining both the lingual and
the labial constrictions (Lindblom 1965; Mermelstein
et al. 1970). Lindblom and Sundberg in their comprehensive report (1971) also discussed the old problem of acoustical interpretation of the articulatory
variables anew based on this descriptive model. The
classical notion of the height of the tongue is formally analysed into two essentially different components, one due to the mandible position and the other
reflecting the lingual muscular efforts based on the
mandible. The same effect is claimed by Mermelstein
and his coworkers, who proposed a mathematically par-
ameterized tongue shape specification in reference
to the mandible base. Both of these models, as well
as the cylinder model, try to represent the apparent
restriction imposed on the laterally observed tongue
surface contours for different vowels, which was discussed in some detail also by Kent in his cineradiographic studies (Kent 1970(a), (b)). These models
take note of the fact that the vocal tract is bent,
which is essential in consideration of the occurence
of articulatory constrictions caused by different
locations of the tongue body, though not relevant in
acoustical considerations.

Temporal Organization

Coker's model is effective as a research tool
particularly since the transitional characteristics
can be more simply described at the articulatory level than at the acoustic level, presumably due to the
fact that speech dynamics are essentially determined
by articulatory physiology rather than auditory physiology. It has long been known that different physiological variables, (or their pertinent mechanical
subsystems,) not only have different time constants
of their own, but also are often apparently out of
synchrony (Fujimura 1961(a)). This makes it difficult to fully discuss the temporal structure of speech
by examining the acoustic phenomena alone, even
though it is true that many valuable findings have

144

been made at this level of the speech event (e.g. Delattre et al. 1955; Lindblom 1963; Ohman 1966; Stevens et al. 1966). The effects of controls in all of these dimensions are collapsed into one and the same acoustic variable, sound pressure, even through the highly non-linear mapping as mentioned above.

We may assume a feature matrix model for the sequence of codes that specify speech gestures for a given utterance unit (Fant 1962, 1971; Chomsky and Halle 1968). This model is basically segmental in the sense that all temporal information is represented by a horizontal arrangement of columns, each of which correspond to, roughly speaking, the phoneme. Details of temporal organization for phonetic degrees of freedom are specified through the mechanism comprised of phonological rules and phonetic actualization processes. The input of this interpretive transducer may be taken as the syntactic surface structure of a sentence (or some other linguistic form). The output will be the phonetic event, as represented at some level of physical or physiological description of the speech production process (Fujimura 1967(J)). The information carried by the output, however, does not correspond exactly to that at the input level. Extra-linguistic information such as expressive features (Jakobson et al. 1951), voice characteristics etc. must be added to account for actual human speech phenomena. Also, some additional modifications will have to be treated as random factors.

Within the realm of linguistic problems, we still need some phonetic actualization procedure, in order to complete our theory of sound shape up to the level of empirical tests. Just like the notion of kernel sentences in the earlier formulation of transformational syntactic theory (Chomsky 1957), we may propose a minimal phonetic actualization procedure in order to derive a "standard" phonetic event for a given linguistic specification of an utterance. This process of producing "kernel utterances" may be materialized in the form of synthesis by rule experiments, where one actually tries to execute all the phonolog-

145

ical and phonetic processes by logical computations
and computer-controlled hard- and/or software simulation of the physical sound production process
(Holmes et al. 1964; Mattingly 1966; Rabiner 1968;
Allen 1968; Lee 1968; Umeda et al. 1968; Teranishi
and Umeda 1968; Coker 1968; Flanagan et al. 1970).
    The principle of generating time functions for
individual constituent features will involve the notions of target, coarticulation, undershoot, reduction
etc., in terms of articulatory states and movements
probably being supplemented by a matching with norms
at the acoustic level. The overall process may be
roughly characterized as follows:
    (1) A table of inherent (target) values for in-
        dividual phonological units are given
    (2) Specification of complex (i.e. multi-dimen-
        sional) sequence of phonological segments
        is given for the linguistic form to be ut-
        tered.
    (3) According to the partially universal and
        partially language dependent phonological
        rule system, logical interpretations of val-
        ues of phonological units for individual
        feature-segment cells in the matrix are
        performed.
    (4) Partially overlapping this logical process,
        physical interpretations are given by par-
        tially universal, partially language depen-
        dent, and partially idiosyncratic phonetic
        actualization rules. This process is affect-
        ed by random variations as well as system-
        atic extralinguistic variations.

    The interpretive process, more concretely, will
be described in reference to segments of various sizes
as well as phonological boundary symbols of various
kinds. Inherent values may be specified for not only
stationary target values, but also for transitional
characteristics. Information that is utilized in the
interpretive process is generally divided into a few
categories: first, that inherent in the lexicon, per-

haps including probabilistic characteristics of words;
second, that for specifying syntactic (surface) structure including grammatical formatives; third, surface
proper characterization which are often suprasenten-
tially context dependent, such as emphasis and contrast of different kinds, focus-presupposition status
etc. (Chomsky 1970; Takahasi et al. to be published).
Some synthesis by rule experiments employ novel principles for determining durational pitch quantities
(in this connection) (Coker and Umeda 1969; Umeda and
Coker 1971). As for prosodic features that are specified in the lexicon, accent type specification and
the related process of actualization have been quantitatively discussed; Ohman (1968) proposed an attractive unified theory for Scandinavian dialects, and
Fujisaki and Sudo (1971) made an elegant step further
in modeling the actualization transducer for Japanese
pitch contours.
    The temporal structure of articulatory movements
of speech organs is one of the central topics of recent speech research. Through suudies of cineradiographic data, Öhman introduced a basic principle,
(beyond the traditional notion of segment sequence
and smoothing,) that consonantal gestures can be considered as an articulatory perturbation superimposed
upon the basic time course for concatenated syllable
nuclei (Öhman 1967). This notion seems to be justified by other cineradiographic observations of tongue
movements (Houde 1968(a), (b)). Houde, in particular,
suggested an account for the inherent vertical movement of the tongue for palatal/velar stops that may
explain the so called allophonic variations of the
consonant as the physical superimposed vowel gestures.
We may speculate further that the consonant gestures
are given through particular muscular mechanisms that
are separate from those for vowel gestures. Thus the
raising of the tongue hump for [g] may be performed
through an essentially different muscular mechanism
than the apparently similar gesture for [u]. There
are still some factors that complicate the actual
trajectory of the tongue movements. Further exper-

imental studies will have to clarify this point of
basic interest.

Coker and his coworkers simulated this kind of
complex tongue movement in their synthesis experim-
e ts and also introduced an important notion in quant-
ifying the coarticulatory processes. It is what they
call "priority strategy" (Flanagan et al. 1970),
through which they implement hierarchical treatment
of articulatory features in respect to the actualization timing of selected variables. Thus a labial
stop, for example, is characterized by the feature of
labial constriction, and this has to be actualized, if
necessary, in a form of invasion into the adjacent
(or even further) time segment for triggering the pertinent gesture. Two components with substantially
different temporal characteristics of labial articulation are reported to be necessary by these authors,
lip protrusion particularly for vowels and the semi-
vowel /w/, and lip opening (constriction) primarily
for consonants (Flanagan et al. 1970).

In short, our question is: what are controlled
and what are physiological and physical constraints?
Our present knowledge is obviously too poor to answer
this question. We may say, reviewing the works mentioned above, that we have some fragmented observations and even partial answers that narrow down the
domain for future search.

The study of speech phenomena, as we have seen
above, is also characterized by an inherently inter-
disciplinary kind of approach. This is not surprising, since we are to deal with the most intricate aspect of human mental activities as reflected in complex physical phenomena.

References

Allen, J. Machine-to-Man Communication by Speech, Part II: Synthesis of Prosodic Features of Speech by Rule. Spring Joint Computer Conference (1968), 1968, 339-344.

Bell, C.G., Fujisaki, H., Stevens, K.N., and House, A.S. Reduction of speech spectra by analysis-by synthesis techniques. J. Acoust. Soc. Amer., 1961, 33, 1725-1736.

Chiba, T., and Kajiyama, M. The Vowel, its Nature and Structure. Tokyo: Tokyo-Karseikan, 1941.

Chomsky, N. Syntactic Structures. The Hague: Mouton, 1957.

Chomsky, N., and Halle, M. The Sound Pattern of English. New York: Harper and Row, 1968.

Chomsky, N. Deep Structure, surface structure and semantic interpretation. In R. Jakobson and S. Kawamoto (Eds.) Studies in General and Oriental Linguistics. Tokyo: TEC Co., Ltd., 1970, 52-91.

Chuang, C.K., Hiki, S., Sone, T., and Nimura, T. The acoustical features and perceptual cues of the four tones of standard colloquial Chinese. Proc. of the 7th International Congress on Acoustics, 1971, 3, 297-300.

Coker, C.H., and Fujimura, O. Model for specification of the vocal tract area function. J. Acoust. Soc. Amer., 1966, 40, 1271.

Coker, C.H. Speech synthesis with a parametric artic- ulatory model. Preprints: Speech Symposium, Kyoto, 1968, A-4-1 - A-4-6.

Coker, C.H., and Umeda, N. Acoustical properties of word boundaries in English. J. Acoust. Soc. Amer., 1970, 47, 94.

Delattre, P.C., Liberman, A.M., Cooper, F.S., and Gerstman, L. An Experimental Study of the Acoustic Determinants of Vowel Color: Observ- ations on One-and Two-Formant Vowels Synthes- ized from Spectrographic Patterns. Word, 1952, 8, 195-210.

Delattre, P.C., Liberman, A.M., and Cooper, F.S. Acoustic loci and transitional cues for conson- ants. J. Acoust. Soc. Amer., 1955, 27, 769-773.

Fant, G. On the Predictibility of Formants Levels and Spectrum Envelopes from Formant Frequencies. For Roman Jakobson, The Hague: Mouton et Co., 1956, 109-120.

Fant, G. Acoustic Theory of Speech Production. The Hague: Mouton and Co.

Fant, G. Descriptive analysis of the acoustic aspects of speech. Logos, 1962, 5, 3-17.

Fant, G., and Sonesson, B. Speech at high ambient air-pressure. Quarterly Progress and Status Report, Speech Transmission Laboratory, KTH, Stockholm, 1964, 2, 9-21.

Fant, G. Analysis and Synthesis of Speech Processes. In B. Malmberg (Ed.) Manual of Phonetics. Am- sterdam: North-Holland, 1968, 173-277.

Fant, G. Distinctive Features and Phonetic Dimen-
    sions. In G.E. Perren and J.L.M. Trim (Eds.)
    Applications of Linguistics. Cambridge: Cambs.
    Univ. Press, 1971, 219-239.

Fischer-Jørgensen, E. Beobachtungen über den Zusam-
    menhang zwischen Stimmhaftigkeit und intraoral-
    em Luftdruck. Z. für Phonetick, 1963, Band
    16, Heft 1-3, 19-36.

Fischer-Jørgensen, E. Voicing, tenseness and as-
    piration in stop consonants, with special ref-
    erence to French and Danish. Annual Report,
    Institute of Phonetics, University of Copenhagen,
    1968, 3, 63-114.

Flanagan, J.L. Speech Analysis, Synthesis and Per-
    ception. Berlin: Springer-Verlag, 1965.

Flanagan, J.L. and Cherry, L. Excitation of vocal
    tract synthesizers. J. Acoust. Soc. Amer.,
    1969, 45, 764-769.

Flanagan, J.L., Coker, C.H., Rabiner, L.R., Schafer,
    R.N., and Umeda, N. Synthetic voices for com-
    puters. Spectrum, 1970, 7, 10, 22-45.

Fujii, I, Fujimura, O., and Kagama, R. Dynamic
    palatography by use of a computer and an oscil-
    loscope. Proc. 7th International Congress on
    Acoustics, 1971, 3, 113-116.

Fujimura, O. Motion-picture studies of articulator
    movements. Quarterly Progress Report, Research
    Laboratory of Electronics, M.I.T., 1961(a), 62,
    197-202.

Fujimura, O. Bilabial stop and nasal consonants:
    A motion picture study and its acoustical im-
    plications. J. Speech Hearing Res., 1961(b), 4,
    232-247.

Fujimura, O. Analysis of nasal consonants. J. Acoust. Soc. Amer., 1962, 34, 1865-1875.

Fujimura, O. On the second spectral peak of front
vowels: A perceptual study of the role of the
second and third formants. Language and Speech,
1967, 10, 3, 181-193.

Fujimura, O. Nihongo-no Onsè. Soritsu Zo-nen Kin-
enronbunshu. Tokyo: NHK, Radio and Television
Culture Research Institute, 1967, 363-404.

Fujimura, O., Ishida, H., and Kiritani, S. Computer controlled dynamic cineradiography. Annual Bulletin, Research Institute of Logopedics
and Phoniatrics, University of Tokyo, 1968, 2,
6-10.

Fujimura, O. Current issues in experimental phonet-
ics. In R. Jakobson and S. Kawamoto (Eds.)
Studies in General and Oriental Linguistics,
Tokyo: TEC Co., Ltd., 1970, 109-130.

Fujimura, O. Remarks on stop consonants - synth-
esis experiments and acoustic cues. In L.L.
Hammench, R. Jakobson and E. Zwimer (Eds.)
Form and Substance. Akademisk Forlag, 1971.

Fujimura, O., and Lindqvist, J. Sweep tone measurements of vocal-tract characteristics. J. Acoust. Soc. Amer., 1971, 49, 541-588.

Fujimura, O., and Sawashima, M. Consonant sequences
and laryngeal control. Annual Bulletin, Research Institute of Logopedics and Phoniatrics,
University of Tokyo, 1971, 5, 1-6.

Fujimura, O., Fujii, I., and Kagaya, R. Computational processing of palatographic patterns.
Second International Conference on Speech

Communication and Processing, Boston, 1972,
April 24-26.

Fujimura, O., Kintani, S., and Ishida, H. Computer
Controlled Radiography for Observation of
Movements of Articulatory and Other Human
Organs (to appear).

Fujisaki, H., and Sudo, H. Synthesis by rule of
prosodic features of connected Japanese. Proc.
7th International Congress on Acoustics, 1971,
3, 133-136.

Gårding, E., Fujimura, O., and Hirose, H. Laryngeal control of Swedish word tone - A preliminary report on an EMG study. Annual Bulletin,
Research Institute of Logopedics and Phoniatrics, University of Tokyo, 1970, 4, 45-54.

Halle, M., and Stevens, K.N. Speech recognition:
A model and a program for research. IRE Trans-
actions of the Professional Group on Information
Theory. IT-8, 1962, 2, 155-159.

Halle, M., and Stevens, K.N. On the mechanism of
glottal vibration for vowels and consonants.
Quarterly Progress Report.Research Laboratory
of Electronics, M.I.T., 1967, 85, 267-271.

Halle, M., and Stevens, K.N. A note on laryngeal
features. Quarterly Progress Report. Research
Laboratory of Electronics, M.I.T. 1971, 101,
198-213.

Han, M.S., and Wietzman, R.S. Acoustic features of
Korean /P,T,K/, /p,t,k/ and /p^h,t^h,k^h/.
Phonetica, 1970, 22, 112-128.

Hardcastle, W. A system of dynamic palatography.
Work in Progress, Dept. of Phonetics and Linguistics, University of Edinburgh, 1969, 3, 47-52.

Hattori, S. Onseigaku ("Phonetics") Tokyo: Iwan-
amishoten, 1951. (In Japanese).

Hattori, S., Yamamoto, K., and Fujimura, O. Nasalization of vowels in relation to nasals. J.
Acoust. Soc. Amer., 1958, 30, 267-274.

Heinz, J.M., and Stevens, K.N. On the relations
between lateral cineradiographs, area functions,
and acoustic spectra of speech. 5e Congrès
International D'Acoustique, 1965, A44.

Hirose, H. The activity of the adductor laryngeal
muscles in respect to vowel devoicing in Japanese. Phonetica, 1971, 23, 156-170.

Hollien, H. Stroboscopic lanunagraphy of the vocal
folds. Proc. 5th International Congress of
Phonetic Sciences, 1965, 362-364.

Holmes, J.N., Mattingly, I.G., and Shearme, J.N.
Speech synthesis by rule. Language and Speech,
1964, 7, 3, 27-143.

Houde, R.A. Perturbation in the articulatory motion
of the tongue body. 6th International Congress
on Acoustics, 1968(a), II, B-13 - B-16.

Houde, R.A. A study of tongue body motion during
selected speech sounds. SCRL MONOGRAPH #2,
Speech Communications Research Laboratory, Inc.,
Santa Barbara, 1968(b).

Ishida, H. An audio-digital hybrid magnetic tape
transport. Annual Bulletin, Research Institute
of Logopedics and Phoniatrics, Univ. of Tokyo,
1969, 3, 67-78.

Jakobson, R., Fant, G., and Halle, M. Preliminaries
to Speech Analysis: The Distinctive Features
and Their Conclates. Acoustics Laboratory,

M.I.T., 1951, Report #13.

Kagaya, R. Laryngeal gestures in Korean stop consonants. Annual Bulletin, Research Institute of Logopedics and Phoniatrics, University of Tokyo, 1971, 5, 15-23.

Kent, R. A Cinefluorographic-Spectrographic investigation of the component gestures in lingual articulation. Ph.D. Dissertation, University of Iowa, 1970(a).

Kent, R. A Cinefluorographic-Spectrographic investigation of the component gestures in lingual articulation. Newsletter, Department of Speech Pathology and Audiology, University of Iowa, 1970(b), 3.

Kim, C.W. On the autonomy of the tensity feature in stop classification (with Special Reference to Korean Stops). Word, 1965, 21, 339-359.

Kim, C.W. A theory of aspiration. Phonetica, 1970, 21, 107-116.

Kiritani, S., and Fujimura, O. A preliminary experiment of the observation of the hyoid bone by means of digitally controlled dynamic radiography. Annual Bulletin, Research Institute of Logopedics and Phoniatrics, University of Tokyo, 1970, 4, 1-7.

Kiritani, S. X-Ray monitoring of the position of the fiberscope by means of computer controlled radiography. Annual Bulletin, Research Institute of Logopedics and Phoniatrics, University of Tokyo, 1971, 5, 35-39.

Kozhevnikov, V.A., and Chistovich, L.A. Rech: Artikulyatsiy i Vospriyatiye. Chapter II. Moscow: Leningrad, 1965.

Lee, F.F. Machine-to-Man Communication by Speech, Part I: Generation of Segmental Phonemes from Text. Spring Joint Computer Conference, 1968, 333-338.

Lehist, I. Suprasegmentals. Cambridge, Mass.: M.I.T. Press, 1970.

Lindblom, B. Spectrographic study of vowel reduction. J. Acoust. Soc. Amer., 1963, 35, 1773-1781.

Lindblom, B. Jaw-dependence of labial parameters and a measure of labialization. Quarterly Progress and Status Report, Speech Transmission Laboratory, KTH, Stockholm, 1965, 3, 12-15.

Lindblom, B., and Sundberg, J. Acoustical consequences of lip, tongue, jaw and larynx movement. J. Acoust. Soc. Amer., 50, 1166-1179.

Lisker, L., and Abramson, A.S. A cross-language study of voicing in initial stops: Acoustical Measurements. Word, 1964, 20, 384-422.

Lubker, J.F., and Parris, P.J. Simultaneous measurements of intraoral pressure, force of labial contact, and labial electromyographic activity during production of the stop consonant cognates /P/ and /b/. J. Acoust. Soc. Amer., 1970, 47, 625-633.

Maeda, S. Conversion of Midsagittal Dimensions to Vocal Tract Area Function. Paper presented at the 82nd. Meeting of the Acoustical Society of America, 1971.

Malécot, A. The Force of articulation of American stops and fricatures as a function of position. Phonetica, 1968, 18, 95-102.

Matsui, E., Suzuki, T., Umeda, N., and Omura, H.
     Synthesis of fairy tales using an analog vocal
     tract. 6th International Congress on Acoustics,
     1968, II, B-159 - B-162.

Mattingly, I.G. Synthesis by rule of prosodic feat-
     ures. Language and Speech, 1966, 9, I, 1-13.

Mermelstein, P. Determination of the vocal-tract
     shape from measured formant frequencies. J.
     Acoust. Soc. Amer., 1967, 41, 1283-1294.

Mermelstein, P., Maeda, S., and Fujimura, O. Des-
     cription of tongue and lip movements in a jaw
     based coordinate system. J. Acoust. Soc. Amer.,
     1971, 49, 104.

Öhman, S. Coarticulation in VCV utterances: spectro-
     graphic measurements. J. Acoust. Soc. Amer.,
     1966, 39, 151-168.

Öhman, S. Numerical model of coarticulation. J. Ac-
     out. Soc. Amer., 1967, 41, 310-320.

Öhman, S., Mårtensson, A., Leanderson, R., and Persson,
     A. Inco-thyroid and vocalis muscle activity in
     the production of Swedish tonal accents: A
     pilot study. Quarterly Progress and Status Rep-
     ort, Speech Transmission Laboratory, KTH, Stock-
     holm, 1967, 2-3, 55-57.

Öhman, S. A model of word and sentence intonation.
     Quarterly Progress and Status Report. Speech
     Transmission Laboratory, KTH, Stockholm, 1968,
     2-3, 6-11.

Olive, J.P. Automatic formant tracking by a Newton-
     Raphson Technique. J. Acoust. Soc. Amer., 1971,
     50, 661-670.

Paul, A.P., House, A.S., and Stevens, K.N. Automatic

reduction of vowel spectra: an analysis-by-synthesis method and its evaluation. J. Acoust.
Soc. Amer., 1964, 36, 303-308.

Perkell, J.S. Physiology of Speech Production: Results and Implications of a Quantitative Cineradiographic Study. Research Monograph #53.
Cambridge, Mass.: M.I.T. Press.

Potter, R.K., Kopp, G.A., and Kopp, H.G. Visible
Speech. New York: Dover, 1966.

Rabiner, L. Speech synthesis by rule: An acoustic
domain approach. The Bell System Technical
Journal., 1968, 47, 1, 17-37.

Rome, J.A. An artificial palate for continuous analysis of speech. Quarterly Progress Report,
Research Laboratory of Electronics, M.I.T., 1964,
74, 190-191.

Sawashima, M. Movements of the larynx in articulation
of Japanese consonants. Annual Bulletin, Research Institute of Logopedics and Phoniatrics,
University of Tokyo, 1968, 2, 11-20.

Sawashima, M., and Hirose, H. New laryngoscopic
technique by use of fiber optics. J. Acoust.
Soc. Amer., 1968, 43, 168-169.

Sawashima, M. Glottal adjustments for English obstruents. In Status Report on Speech Research
(Haskins Laboratories) 1970, SR-21/22, 187-200.

Sawashima, M., Abramson, A.S., Cooper, F.S., and
Lisker, L. Observing laryngeal adjustments during running speech by use of a fiberoptics system. Phonetica, 1970, 22, 193-201.

Sawashima, M. Devoicing of vowels. Annual Bulletin,
Research Institute of Logopedics and Phoniatrics,

University of Tokyo, 1971, 5, 25-34.

Sawashima, M., and Ushijima, T. Use of the fiberscope in speech research. Annual Bulletin, Research Institute of Logopedics and Phoniatrics, University of Tokyo, 1971, 5, 25-34.

Sawashima, M., Hirose, H., Ushijima, T., and Fujimura, O. Devoicing of vowels. Proc. 7th International Congress on Acoustics, 1971, 3, 109-112.

Schafer, R.N., and Rabiner, L.R. System for automatic formant analysis of voiced speech. J. Acoust. Soc. Amer., 1970, 47, 634-648.

Schroeder, M.R. Determination of the geometry of the human vocal tract by acoustic measurements. J. Acoust. Soc. Amer., 1967, 41, 1002-1010.

Shibata, S. A study of dynamic palatography. Annual Bulletin, Reserch Institute of Logopedics and Phoniatrics, University of Tokyo, 1968, 2, 28-36.

Simada, Z., and Hirose, H. The function of the laryngeal muscles in respect to word accent distinction. Annual Bulletin, Research Institute of Logopedics and Phoniatrics, University of Tokyo, 1970, 4, 27-40.

Simada, Z., and Hirose, H. Physiological correlates of Japanese accent patterns. Annual Bulletin, Research Institute of Logopedics and Phoniatrics, University of Tokyo, 1971, 5, 41-49.

Sondhi, M.M., and Gopinath, B. Determination of vocal-tract shape from impulse response at the lips. J. Acoust. Soc. Amer., 1971, 49, 1867-1873.

Stevens, K.N., Kasonski, S., Fant, G. An electrical analog of the vocal tract. J. Acoust. Soc. Amer., 1953, 25, 734-742.

Stevens, K.N., and House, A.S. Development of a quantitative description of vowel articulation. J. Acoust. Soc. Amer., 1955, 27, 484-493.

Stevens, K.N., and House, A.S. Studies of formant transitions using a vocal tract analog. J. Acoust. Soc. Amer., 1956, 28, 578-585.

Stevens, K.N. Toward a model for speech recognition. J. Acoust. Soc. Amer., 1960, 32, 47-55.

Stevens, K.N., House, A.S., and Paul, A.P. Acoustical description of syllabic nuclei: an interpretation in terms of a dynamic model of articulation. J. Acoust. Soc. Amer., 1966, 40, 123-132.

Stevens, K.L. Linguistic factors in communications engineers. In G.E. Perren and J.L.M. Trim (Eds.) Applications of Linguistics, Cambridge: Cambridge Univ. Press., 1971, 101-112.

Stevens, K.N. The quantal nature of speech evidence from articulatory-acoustic data. In E.E. David, Jr., and P.B. Denes (Eds.) Human Communication, A Unified View (to appear).

Sundberg, J. Articulatory differences between spoken and sung vowels in singers. Quarterly Progress and Status Report, Speech Transmission Laboratory, KTH, Stockholm, 1969, 1, 33-42.

Takahasi, H., Fujimura, O., and Kameda, H. Behavioral characterization of topicalization: what is topicalization from a computer system point of view. Proc. 1971 International meeting on Computational Linguistics (to appear).

Teranishi, R., and Umeda, N. Use of pronouncing dictionary in speech synthesis experiments. 6th International Congress on Acoustics, 1968, II,

B-155 - B-158.

Umeda, H., and Umeda, N. Acoustical features of Korean "forced" consonants. J. Ling. Soc. Japan, 1965, 48, 23-33 (in Japanese).

Umeda, N., and Coker, C.H. Some prosodic details of American English. J. Acoust. Soc. Amer., 1971, 49, 123.

van den Berg, J. Myoelastic-aerodynamic theory of voice production. J. Speech Hearing Res., 1958, 1, 227-244.

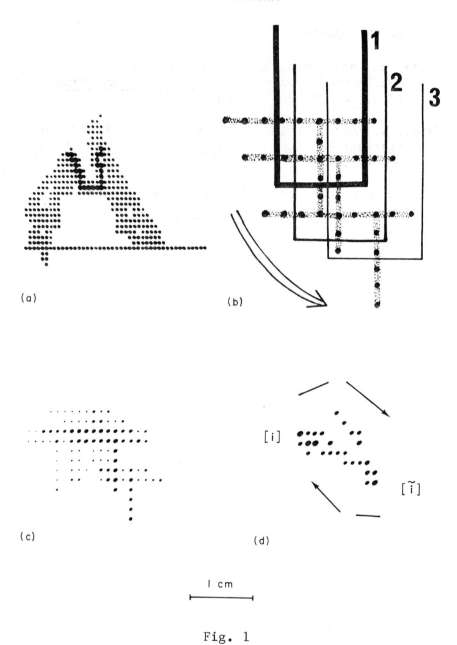

(a)

(b)

(c)

(d)

[i]

[ĩ]

1 cm

Fig. 1

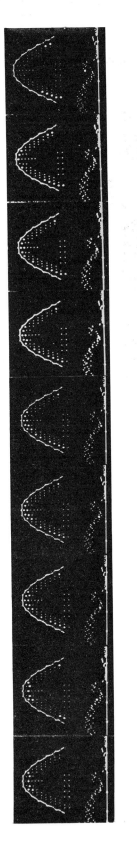

Fig. 2

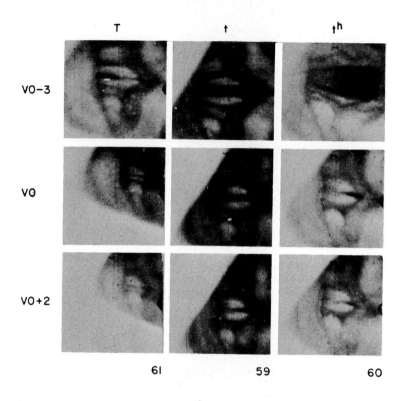

Fig. 3

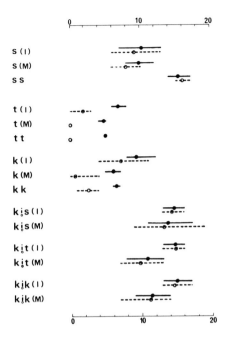

Fig. 4

165

Chapter 4

DISCUSSION PAPER ON ACOUSTICS OF SPEECH

Arthur S. House

Institute for Defense Analysis
Princeton, N.J.

It has never been very clear to me what the role
of discussant should be in a symposium like this one.
Among the various alternatives it is possible to analyze the paper presented with devilish thoroughness
and critical insight. Unfortunately for me - and,
perhaps, fortunately for you - I have neither the
temperament nor the perspicacity to elect such an alternative. Furthermore, I fully recognize the fut-
ility of such a course in discussing Professor Fujimura's remarks. I always have learned from listening to him and today has been no exception.

It is probably no accident that Professor Fujimura discusses various aspects of articulation -
vocal-tract deformations, models for vocal-tract activity, muscle actions, control signals, etc. - as a
major part of his survey of speech acoustics. The
need to do this stems, in part at least, from the
lack of isomorphism among our acoustic, articulatory,
perceptual, neural, etc., representations of speech
activity, a fact well known to most here (since many
present have contributed significantly to our understanding of this lack). It seems proper to say that
the acoustic patterns - as well as the articulatory
configurations - that generally are taken as characteristic of the various speech sounds are descriptions that are based heavily on samples spoken in
isolation, or at best, in simple contexts under

stated conditions, and bear only a loose relationship to the acoustic events that define continuous informal conversational utterances. At any given moment the rapidly changing acoustic patterns of connected speech probably represent configurations that result from, among other things, the differential rates of response of portions of the speech musculature to a variety of instructions, some of which may be graded by linguistic as well as physical considerations. As such, these patterns - and the configurations underlying them - at a given moment of time are not strictly assignable to a given speech sound. The decoding that is done by the human ear/brain becomes more and more remarkable as our descriptions of speech articulations and acoustics become more sophisticated. Professor Fujimura's closing question - "What are controlled and what are physiological and physical constraints?" - is one of the major questions asked by today's experimental phoneticians. His answer that our present knowledge cannot answer this question, reluctantly must be accepted at this time.

It seems to me that among the exciting developments in acoustic research that are embedded intrinsically in the account we have heard are (1) the renascence of interest in consonantal sound production (as evidenced by Steven's recent work), (2) the rapid development of sophisticated time-domain methods using digital techniques (as evidenced by recent work by Itakura and Saito, by Atal, and by Markel and others), and (3) the increased analysis of continuous speech materials, made possible by modern technology. Of course, these developments are not limited to acoustic research as such, but rather are reflected into every aspect of speech research activities - analysis, synthesis, perception, etc.

If it isn't completely out of order at this time, rather than discuss a specific portion of Professor Fujimura's presentation, I'd like to digress a bit and describe some work that dealt with some problems of speech control. The work was done by Dr. Robert A. Prosek who currently is in military service.

Briefly, measures of duration and intraoral air pressure were taken during the production of various speech samples containing stops and fricatives - using words with verb/noun stress alternatives in isolation, these same words in sentences, and sentences containing a large number of allophonic variants of some of the phonemes under study - by normal talkers and by the same talkers deprived of oral sensation by a series of mandibualr, infraorbital, and palatal injections of anesthesia (2% Xylocaine with 10^{-5} parts epinepherine). In addition, the talkers scaled the effort used to produce simple stop-vowel syllables, both with and without anesthesia.

The results of such a study have at least two reasons for being mentioned here. On the one hand, they constitute, in part at least, acoustic data - or, more accurately, aerodynamic data - about speech production; and on the other, they may help us to understand the control mechanisms underlying speech production.

The general results showed that, for the four talkers involved, talking with deficient oral sensation was not much different from their undisturbed talking. They tended to shift tongue carriage posteriorly; to slow speech rate; and to display minor imprecisions in articulation, consisting primarily of alterations in lip and tongue activity. Stop and fricative consonants were produced with slightly greater intraoral air pressures and were characterized by longer durations; scaling of effort during stop production maintained its power-law relation to air pressure.

The general description of intraoral air pressure variations by consonant class during normal (orally sensate) speech was very much like that described by others (Malecot, 1955, 1968; Subtelny et al. 1966; Arkebauer et al. 1967; Lisker, 1970). (a) The average pressures for fricatives and stops were similar, but the voiceless categories produced higher intraoral pressures - the sub-categories ordered as voiceless stops, voiceless fricatives, voiced fricatives, voiced

169

stops. This pattern was also obtained when oral sensation was interfered with, and the loss of sensation
did not change the average levels. (b) In normal
speech, intraoral pressures associated with consonants before primary stressed vowels and before secondary stressed vowels differed, on the average, by less
than one cm H_2O; the same pattern was found when the
talkers were anesthetized. (c) The pressures generated for consonants embedded in isolated words were
greater than for those in sentence contexts; this
difference vanished with anesthesia. (d) Differences
associated with place of articulation were small,
with a tendency for back consonants to have higher
pressures, independent of sensation condition.

The average durations of these consonants showed
patterns very like those in the air pressure data.
(a) Durations of consonants produced while anesthetized, however, tended to be longer than in normal
speech; the class differences are small (on the order
of 1-20 msec) but stable. (b) Consonants initiating
primary stressed syllables were longer than those initiating secondary stressed syllables. In other
words, the durations of consonants produced in the
control condition, in agreement with the finding that
speech was slower in the sensory deprived state; syllabic stress and context affected the duration of
consonants, making them longer before a stressed vowel and in isolated words.

The stop variants - that is, allophones - examined in the study included samples exhibiting such
features as lip rounding, dentalization, palatalization, nasal closure, lateral closure, nasal release,
lateral release, unaspirated release, intervocalic
voicing, and devoicing. In general, the voiceless
stop variants were produced with lower pressures and
shorter durations than the simpler syllable-initial
stops. Voiced variants, however, had the same average
pressures as the simple stops, but their durations
were shorter. The most deviant classes of productions were stops with nasal and lateral releases.
Their pressures were significantly lower and they

were significantly shorter than other classes - the release characteristics, more than place of articulation or voicing. When the pressures and durations of the control and anesthetized productions of the stop variants are compared, the relationships are similar to those observed for the simple stops: no difference in pressure, but a durational difference. (An exception is the duration of the palatized alveolar stops which is 35 msec. greater with anesthesia).

In the scaling task, the talkers produced syllables to correspond to a numerical magnitude suggested by the experimenter and the median production was used in the analysis. For each numerical magnitude, the geometric mean of the medians was calculated and a least-squares statistic was used to estimate the slope of the function relating effort to intraoral air pressures. When the magnitude of the effort is plotted against air pressure on log-log coordinates, the slope of the resulting function corresponds to the exponent of the power function governing the growth of the psychological (effort) magnitude. In this experiment the data approximate power functions (that is, straight lines in log-log coordinates) with slopes close to 2; the scaling of the control utterances gave slopes of about 1.8, while the scaling with anesthetized oral cavities produced slopes of about 2.3; (the pressures developed for /pa/ were always lower when anethesia was used, but /ba/ showed no such change). In general then, the exponent of the power function for growth of effort changed with the administration of anesthesia, but the talkers had no great difficulty in scaling their effort in a prothetic mode. The change in slope of the plotted averaged functions seems to reflect the uniqueness of talking without oral sensation, rather than the loss of ability to produce articulate speech. These results can be interpreted as good indirect evidence that intraoral air pressure (if it must be monitored through the oral mucosa) is not a primary feedback cue.

171

These experimental results demonstrate that, when oral sensation is eliminated, the production of consonants is prolonged and is characterized by greater pressures in the mouth. Such changes in production are grossly similar to those observed, for example, during emphatic speech. The usual explanation of the complex changes in fundamental frequency, intensity and duration that accompany emphasis is to assume that greater driving pressures (controlled, for example, by the thoracic musculature) are responsible. This increase in driving pressure can produce any or all of the observed changes and also produce a concomitant increase in the level of intraoral air pressure. In other words, the experimental results can be interpreted as meaning that, when deprived of oral sensation, a talker uses more effort in producing speech - effort being manifest as the increase of intrathoracic (or subglottal) pressure through the contraction of appropriate abdominal and/or thoracic musculature.

The question of whether it is appropriate to assign a significant role to changes in effort sufficient to counteract the effects of orosensory deprivation is ansered affirmatively, in part at least, by the scaling behavior of the talkers. When a sensation is absent in the oral cavity, the talkers' scaling behavior was little changed, and most importantly, did not depart from (log-log) linearity. These considerations appear to make untenable the suggestion by Malecot (1970) that changes in intraoral air pressure constitute an important parameter in the feedback control loop for articulation. This interpretation in terms of effort is speculative, of course, and alternative explanations based on more-easily specified parameters should be investigated.

The question of whether air pressure monitored at other levels in the speech system constitutes a primary control parameter is not eliminated by these findings. Wyke (1967) has suggested, for example, that the mechanoreceptors of the larynx are sensitive to increases and decreases in subglottal air pressure and that laryngeal adjustments are made on the basis of such changes. In this case, the level of intra-oral air pressure would be under the control of laryngeal adjustments that modulate the breath stream.

The present measurements of consonantal and over-all durations indicate that the timing of peripheral events, that is, the articulation of consonants, is modified when sensation in the mouth is eliminated. Such changes are compatible with the hypothesis that tactile information is important for consonant production (Perkell, 1969; Henke, 1967). The results also could be interpreted as meaning that myotactic information concerning closures and constrictions was not monitored adequately when anesthetized, and, therefore, the talkers produced speech more cautiously. Their slowing down of the speech-producing activities, however, was not sufficient to produce gross changes in the articulation of consonants, and consequently their general level of intelligibility was not changed.

Models of speech production using closed-loop feedback mechanisms usually are described as operating on a segment-by-segment basis. This generally is taken to mean that their control parameters are associated with the production of elements of about phoneme size. The segments that function in a given language, however, are not well characterized by invariant physical parameters nor articulatory descriptions; in fact, perceptable differences among allophones are quite common. This lack of physical invariance imposes a heavy burden on closed-loop control models, since they must account for the progressive and regressive assimilations that occur in a variety of contexts - that is, they must look backward and forward in time before concluding that a segment has been produced appropriately.

If the major contextual constraints on connected speech segments were highly determined by physiological factors, then, in spite of the complexity of articulatory behavior, intraoral air pressure might qualify as a candidate for the control of articulation.

Many contextual constraints are not explicable in terms of physiology alone, however, but seem rather to be characteristic of the language under consideration. While the prevalence of such language-specific influences on articulation is not well quantified, the phonetic literature contains examples enough to suggest that instances of nonphysiological constraints may be more common than clearly identified instances of phyiological constraints. If it is true that a great deal of the variability of segments is accounted for by language-specific rules, then there is no reason to believe, <u>a priori</u>, that the loss of oral sensation will interfere seriously with speech production. In the present cases, where the disturbances to speech under anesthesia were restricted essentially to minor adjustments of the tongue and lips, the generation of speech must have been primarily under the control of a sensing system other than a closed-loop one. This point of view seems compatible with the hypothesis that some open-loop component provides phonological information to the speech-control mechanism (MacNeilage, 1970).

References

Arkebauer, H.J., Hison, T.J. and Hardy, J.C. Peak intraoral air pressures during speech. J. Speech Hear. Res., 1967, 10, 196-208.

Atal, B.S. and Hanauer, S.L. Speech analysis and synthesis by linear prediction of the speech wave. J. Acoust. Soc. Amer., 1971, 50, 637-655.

Henke, W.L. Preliminaries to speech synthesis based on an articulatory model. Conf. speech Communication and Processing, Cambridge, Mass., 1967, Paper C5.

Itakura, F. and Saito, S. Analysis, synthesis telephony based upon the maximum-likelihood method. Proc. 6th International Congress on Acoustics, Y. Kohasi (Ed.), Tokyo, Aug. 21-28, 1968; Paper c-5-5.

Lisker, L. Supraglottal air pressure in the production of English stops. Lang. Speech, 1970, 13, 215-230.

MacNeilage, P.F. Motor control of serial ordering of speech. Psychol. Rev., 1970, 77, 182-196.

Malecot, A. An experimental study of force of articulation. Studia Linguistica, 1955, 9, 35-44.

Malecot, A. The force of articulation of American stops and fricatives as a function of position. Phonetica, 1968, 18, 95-102.

Markel, J.D. Formant trajectory estimation from a linear least-squares inverse filter formulation. (October, 1971) Monograph No. 7, Speech Communications Research Laboratory, Inc., Santa Barbara, California.

Perkell, J.S. Physiology of speech production: Results and implications of a quantitative cineradiographic study. Cambridge, Mass: The MIT Press, 1969.

Prosek, R.A. An evaluation of the role of oral sensation in consonant production. PhD thesis, Purdue University, 1971.

Stevens, K.N. Airflow and turbulence noise for fricative and stop consonants: Static considerations. J. Acoust. Soc. Amer., 1971, 50, 1180-1192.

Subtelny, J.D., Worth, J.H. and Sakuda, M. Intraoral pressure and rate of flow during speech. J. Speech Hear. Res., 1966, 9, 498-518.

Wyke, B. Recent advances in the neurology of phonation: Reflex mechanisms in the larynx. Brit. J. Disord. Communicat., 1967, 2, 2-14.

Chapter 5

DISCUSSION PAPER ON ACOUSTICS OF SPEECH
LINGUISTIC THEORY AND SPEECH RESEARCH

Sven Öhman

Uppsala University
Sweden

Professor Fujimura has presented a paper which is full of interesting facts about human speech and which also summarizes some of the most important experimental methods of our science. One point of particular significance which Fujimura's paper brings out and which needs reemphasis, I think, is the crucial role played by small computers in our work. In speech research, data still outbalances theory in large measure and we manage to confront theory with data only through a mixture of qualitative and quantitative comparisons. Because of the magnitude of the data collections that have to be considered, these comparisons are in general not possible to make without the use of small interactive computers equipped with special input/output and software facilities. To take just one example: the highly sophisticated and useful radiographic and palatographic techniques that Fujimura has developed and described here today, not only require a computer to be used efficiently in the collecting of data, but they produce data at rates so high that processing and analysis would be unthinkable without a specially programmed computer. Since it is precisely this sort of data we need, my feeling is, that work at the computer console will continue to be a basic ingredient in the daily life of the student of human speech in the foreseeable

177

future.

Having said this I must now turn to my main task here today which I understand to be that of discussing some of the assumptions Fujimura makes in his paper.

In particular, I should like to dwell on one specific point which Fujimura touches upon explicitly or implicitly in various contexts, namely why it is that we should worry at all about the physical aspects of language use. In view of the most recent developments in theoretical linguistics it is not at all clear that this aspect should carry much significance for an understanding of the nature of human language.

I will therefore not concern myself at this moment with the experimental details that Prof. Fujimura discusses but will instead make a few remarks on linguistic theory in relation to the sort of research Prof. Fujimura and I believe most of us here are interested in.

At a relatively early point in his paper, Prof. Fujimura states that our ultimate concern as students of speech is that of "understanding...the relation between the linguistic codes and the acoustical (and related) properties of speech phenomena." In other words, Fujimura seems to mean that the ultimate goal of our field of study is to find out how language materializes physically in oral-auditory communication. It is also moderately clear that he considers the grammatical and the physical aspects of language to be establishable at least relatively independently of each other and in particular that it is some variant of the generative transformational type of grammar he has in mind when he talks about "linguistic codes".

Since transformational theory has made great strides during the last decade, and since it claims to constitute the core of a complete theory of human linguistic behavior, there is every reason for us to ask where our own work fits into this theory and conversely how the theory can aid us in our researches. My own answer to both of these questions is quite neg-

ative. Some of the reasons for my negative attitude
are as follows.

A transformational grammar of some language pur-
ports to be an abstract characterization of the intrinsic linguistic competence of an idealized native
speaker of that language. It is not a theory of how
a speaker produces speech or of how a listener per-
ceives spoken words, but rather a formal summary of
the intrinsic knowledge that the speaker/listener is
supposed to possess about his language.

When one uses the word "knowledge" in this connection one is urged by transformationalists to remember that it is not knowledge in the sense of "con-
sciously reproducible facts" that is implied by the
term. It is rather the knowledge that lies behind
the native speaker's capacity to select grammatical,
in contrast to ungrammatical, expressions in order to
perform adequate speech acts in infinitely varying
speech situations. Moreover, one is not supposed to
think of this intrinsic linguistic competence of a
speaker as being something physical, such as a set
of possible states of the nervous system or a set of
behavioral dispositions or the like. On the contrary
a speaker's linguistic competence is said to be a
purely mental phenomenon.

The object of a transformational grammar is consequently something which is neither physical nor
necessarily available to conscious awareness by the
speaker himself. And what is worse, one's linguistic
competence need not even be directly reflected in
one's linguistic performance, since the latter is
often unconsciously blurred by a number of extralin-
guistic disturbance factors such as absentmindedness,
intoxication and so forth. This last mentioned state
of affairs has in fact led many linguists to base
their investigations almost entirely on their own
intuition about their own language and the neologism
"to intuit" seems now to be current in wide circles
as a term meaning "to sense a grammatical fact about
one's language".

Personally, I think most of what I have just re-

lated must be labelled as metaphysics. One must
strongly doubt, it seems to me, that the concept of
linguistic competence as explicated by transformational linguistics philosophers corresponds to any reality at all. There is certainly need for a concept of
linguistic competence, but it will have to be con-
strued so as to be empirically meaningful. In particular, it would be natural to reserve the term for
that which is meant when we say that someone has a
good (or bad) command of his language. That is, the
theory should allow us to talk about <u>degrees</u> of observable linguistic competence, which is at present
not possible in any direct way within the transformational approach.

The conceptual distinction between competence
and performance in transformational theory has a number of theoretical consequents which in turn have direct bearings on speech research. What I have in mind
here are questions concerning the nature of phonological entities such as the distinctive features, segmental phonemes, stresses, pitch accents and the like
on the one hand, and the nature of linguistic explanation on the other hand. To approach these questions
it is interesting to consider the ideological roots
of the competence/performance distinction itself.

Transformational theory is both a continuation
of and a reaction against the positivistic school of
linguistics which emanates from Leonard Bloomfield
and which is nowadays commonly called taxonomic linguistics. As is well known, a great deal of thought
was given within this school to establishing semi-
algorithmic procedures for the determination of structural features such as phonemes, morphemes and immediate constituents in any given corpus of linguistic
data.

When Chomsky formalized the notion of immediate
constituent by means of phrase structure grammars
and found that these grammars were inadequate for the
description of a great variety of simple and straight
forward grammatical regularities, the question arose
as to how the grammar formalism was to be extended in

order to make up for the deficit. As everyone knows, Chomsky proposed that a very potent type of rule, the grammatical transformation, was to be added to the phrase structure rules.

This extension immediately gave rise to a serious theoretical problem, namely that of limiting the definition of transformational grammar so as to exclude unrealistic applications. In other words, the transformation is a type of rule with such great possibilities of application, that it will in general allow many ways of accounting for any given set of linguistic data. This state of affairs thus left much room for subjective taste and ideosyncratic judgement in linguistic description, a circumstance that displeases the linguist who seeks in language an objective phenomenon obeying deterministic rules.

To avoid this situation Chomsky made what I consider to be the fundamental mistake of transformational theory. He proposed that there was to be a general linguistic theory the purpose of which was to constrain the form of any natural language grammar in such a way that unrealistic applications would always be objectively detectable and thus avoidable. The allegedly empirical basis of this general theory was, as I see it, the assumption that the universal linguistic ability of man is a very specific psychological phenomenon with strong limitations on its structure. In particular it was not to be seen as a product of general intelligence. Moreover, man's general language ability was thought of as chrystallizing as it were in the individual's acquisition of his mother tongue and as showing up as his intrinsic linguistic competence in the language in question. The linguistic competence of a native speaker is thus, according to the theory, the result of the interaction between the speaker's innate language ability and his particular linguistic environment. Therefore, the grammar is to reflect the competence, and the general theory is to reflect man's universal language ability. And since the latter is supposed to be highly constrained in some sense, the theory should correspond-

ingly constrain the form of grammars. We thus see
how Chomsky's line of thought brings about an apparent connection between the formalism for stating
grammatical rules and the structure of human language as a universal phenomenon. The metaphysical
idea of an intrinsic linguistic competence is constructed in order to justify this connection. Or,
one might say, the Chomskyan concept of an intrinsic competence was invented in order to meet the
demand for uniqueness in linguistic description.

Very much has happened in linguistic theory
since these decisive steps were taken. In particular, the body of language data that has been subjected to transformational analysis has increased
a great deal in syntax as well as in semantics and
phonology, and a number of slightly diverging sub-
schools have emerged within the transformational
camp. It seems obvious to me, however, that these
more recent efforts would lose much if not all of
their motivation if the Chomskyan ideas of an intrinsic linguistic competence and a highly specialized
universal language ability were given up. It would
be hard to understand otherwise why there should
be so much animosity concerning the "best" format
for a grammar.

Let us now look at some of the most confusing
consequences of transformational philosophy. One
immediate consequence is that since a speaker's linguistic competence is a mental phenomenon, this must
also be the case with all of its components. Hence,
in particular, all of phonology is mental, even such
rules as the lengthening of vowels before voiced obstruents and the like. Moreover, the distinctive
features of the elementary sound segments are mental.
They are entities that could never be measured by
some physical instrument. They can only be known in
the above mentioned mysterious sense of knowing. If
physical studies of speech have any relevance whatsoever, this relevance could only be remote and of
a corroborating kind.

Another consequence of mentalistic linguistics

becomes apparent when one studies generative formulations of the phonological regularities of some language such as for instance American English. Anyone
who has taken the trouble of working through Comsky
and Halle's now famous treatise on the sound pattern
of English, for example, must have experienced the
enormous abstrusity of the rule systems proposed
there for the stress and segmental regularities of the
language. I do not want to mention the many little
errors that the analysis contains. They are after all
relatively few in comparison with the enormity of the
task that the authors set themselves and in consideration of the many ingenious ideas that they managed
to work out. Of far greater significance, to my mind,
is the circumstance that the nontransparancy and complexity of the rules and of the derivation they entail
are necessary consequences of the philosophy that
every phonological regularity is in principle "known"
to the ideal speaker and must therefore show up among
the transformational rules, i.e., in the model of his
competence. Generative phonology in this form seems
to me to be a veritable <u>reductio</u> <u>ad</u> <u>absurdum</u> of the
whole theory.

The most serious problem with transformational
theory is, however, in my opinion, the position it
takes with respect to the explanation of linguistic
hhenomena in general. To take one example from phonology, Chomsky and Halle on the basis of their research on English propose as a universal principle
that whenever two consecutive phonological rules differ formally in a certain way the application of one
rule precludes the application of the other, i.e.,
they are disjunctively ordered. Now, if a language
displays a set of phonological regularities that depends crucially on the disjunctive ordering of certain rules, the proponents of transformational theory
feel that the universal principle of disjunctive ordering explains the regularity in question.

This is, to me, a source of constant bewilder-
ment. It is not so important in this connection
whether or not the principle of disjunctive ordering

or any other similar principle actually works when all
facts are considered. What seems so strange to me is
rather the idea that facts concerning human speech
communication should be explainable in terms of highly
abstract principles regulating the format of grammatical formulas. This is of course entirely in line
with the general philosophy of transformational theory.
It can nevertheless be doubted whether humanity will
ever agree to accept explanations which are not in
themselves understandable in terms of elementary
everyday experience. The success of classical physics
rests precisely on its ability to achieve this end.
Transformational theory, on the other hand seems here
to talk to us much like the notorious school teacher
who said to his students "All this may sound simple,
but wait until I have explained it to you!"

I do not mean, of course, that there is anything
wrong in proposing abstract universal principles of
grammar. Only that when this is done, these principles in turn will immediately call for an explanation in terms of the physical and psychological conditions to which the human use of speech is subject.
It is the apparent lack of feeling for this last step
that makes transformational linguistics so disappoint-
ing to me.

As I said earlier much of the force of transformational theory rests on the assumption that man's universal linguistic ability is a very specific and
constrained psychological capacity, and that consequently the linguistic competence of any individual is
necessarily subject to strong structural limitations.
This assumption has not been borne out by the results
of linguistic research. As more and more types of
linguistic structure have been considered, the variety
of formal devices to be admitted in grammatical statements has had to be gradually enlarged. It was therefore not surprising when Peters and Ritchie a few
years ago managed to prove that the formal apparatus
granted by the general grammatical model proposed in
Chomsky's "Aspects of the Theory of Syntax" is equiv-
alent in expressive power to the most general formal

184

languages known to logicians. Nor would it be surprising if a similar proof could be given concerning the formal language used in Chomsky and Halle's "Sound Pattern of English".

Given this situation the question concerning the best formalization of grammar becomes a question of convenience and purpose. From this I draw two conclusions. First that we no longer have any really strong reason for believing in some innate specific language capacity over and beyond general intelligence. And second, that we should choose our form of presentation of the data of language so as to maximize our understanding of what actually happens when people talk and listen to talk.

Brain physiologists sometimes say that the brain can be regarded as a general purpose computer which has a very large storage capacity though its basic operations are relatively slow and few in number. Specialization comes only at the periphery in the receptor and effector organs.

If this is so, our understanding of the structure of human language should be best promoted if we begin with careful studies of the physical limitations on speech production and perception. I see no reason for us to constrain our attention to the symbolic uses of vocal sounds in this connection. On the contrary the whole biophysical problem of vocal expression should be open for us.

It seems to me that the results summarized in Fujimuras paper represents a good start in this direction.

Chapter 6

THE UNITS OF SPEECH PERCEPTION

Ilse Lehiste

Department of Linguistics
The Ohio State University
Columbia, Ohio

INTRODUCTION

Speech perception is a vast topic that might be
approached in several different ways. Much interesting work has been done recently with regard to models
of speech perception. There is continuing interest
in the question of categorical perception and the differences in perception depending on whether or not a
listener is responding in the speech mode; related
questions involve the role of lateralization in speech
processing, and the relationship between speech perception and short-term memory. I have decided to lim-
it the topic to a survey of recent work concerning
the units of speech perception. It will occasionally
be necessary to relate these units to units of production; likewise, it will be impossible to refrain completely from discussing certain speech perception models. However, I shall not attempt exhaustive coverage
of these latter topics; in fact, it will not be possible to achieve exhaustive coverage even of the more
limited subject. However, I hope to touch upon some
of the more interesting theories and experimental
findings at the several levels at which perception
units may be established. I shall proceed from the
smallest to the largest, starting with the perception
of sub-phonemic phonetic differences and concluding

with clause-and sentence-level units and their relationship to syntax.

THE MINIMAL UNITS OF SPEECH PERCEPTION

Listening in the speech mode

One of the problems in trying to establish what
constitutes the minimal unit of speech perception is
drawing a boundary between the perception of signals
in a psycho-acoustic experiment (auditory processing)
and the perception of signals in a speech mode (phonetic processing). It is well known that an identical
physical stimulus may be perceived in two different
ways, depending on the psychological setting. For
example, the F2 transitions of a synthetic CV syllable
may sound as chirps of a bird or as glides in pitch,
when presented out of context; provided with a following synthetic vowel, they signal the point of articulation of the consonant preceding the vowel (Liberman 1970). The question is now whether listeners are
capable of distinguishing subphonemic phonetic detail
while listening in a speech mode.

One of the characteristics of listening in a
speech mode is the so-called categorical perception
of phonemes. This means that a listener's ability
to discriminate variations in the acoustic cue is much
better at the boundary of phone classes than within
the phone class (Liberman, Harris, Hoffman, and
Griffith, 1957; Liberman, Harris, Kinney, and Lane
1961; Stevens, Liberman, Öhman, and Studdert-Kennedy
1969). Presented with a set of simulated CV syllables
in which F2 transitions are separated by the same
frequency intervals, the listener groups the transitions according to the number of distinctive points
of articulation employed in his language; withing the
range, adjacent sounds are classified as 'same', and
crossing from one range to another, adjacent sounds
are classified as 'different'.

There are some problems with categorical perception. In early experiments, it appeared to work well

for consonants, but poorly for vowels. Categorical perception appeared to be associated with a discontinuity in articulation; in the case of vowels, there is no such articulatory discontinuity, which might explain a lack of categorical perception in vowels.

The problem has been recently re-considered by Chistovich and Kozhevnikov (1969-1970). It had been shown earlier (Fry, Abramson, Eimas and Liberman 1962; Stevens, Liberman, Öhman, and Studdert-Kennedy 1969) that listeners are capable of distinguishing among a large number of stimuli (synthetic vowels) which are classified by them in the same phonemic category. This result could be interpreted in two ways. One interpretation is that phonetic images of vowels form a continuum; in hearing a vowel, the listener 'locates' the stimulus on the continuum by reference to certain articulatory target positions kept in memory. The other interpretation is that a listener is capable of remembering, for a certain time, not only the phoneme which has been selected on the basis of the heard stimulus, but also some spectral characteristics of the sound. If the two stimuli which are being compared prove to be different phonemes, subphonemic spectral information is discarded (Chistovich, Fant, de Serpa-Leitão, and P. Tjernlund 1966; Chistovich, Fant, and de Serpa-Leitão 1966; Fujisaki and Kawashima 1968).

The subphonemic level

The experiments discussed by Chistovich and Kozhevnikov showed that in certain cases, man is capable of perceiving subphonemic phonetic differences even while listening in a speech mode. This suggests that minimal units of perception may be found at a subphonemic level. A proposal to that extent has been recently made by Wickelgren (1969(a), 1969(b), who submits 'concept-sensitive allophones' as candidates for the role of minimal perceptual units.

Wickelgren claims that sounds are determined by context in such a way that, for example, a /p/ pre-

ceded by /a/ and followed by /i/ is uniquely determined as the kind of allophone that follows /a/ and
precedes /i/, and such an allophone of /p/ is different from one that is both preceded and followed by
/a/.

There are several problems connected with this
model, some of which came up in connection with a
recent study by Lehiste and Shockey (1971). In this
paper, we explored the perceptual significance of
transitional cues in one or the other of the vowels
of a VCV sequence that are due to the influence of
the transconsonantal vowel. Öhman (1966) had shown
that the transitions from the first vowel in a VCV
sequence to the intervocalic consonant depend on the
quality of the second vowel. Likewise, there are
differences in the transitions from the same consonant to the same second vowel that depend on the quality of the first vowel. In our study, we used taped
VCV sequences (where V = /i æ a u/ and C = /p t k/)
in which either the first or the second vowel was
removed by cutting the tape during the voiceless
plosive gap. Although the transitional cues were
present, and were of the same kind and order of magnitude as those observed by Öhman, the listeners were
unable to recover the missing vowels from these modified transitional cues.

According to Wickelgren's model, the context to
which allophones are sensitive consists of one preceding and one following sound; thus a following /i/
in an /api/ sequence will not exert any influence on
/a/, although it will influence the realization of
/p/. The results of the experiment just reported
might be considered supportive of Wickelgren's claim;
although influence from the second vowel was physically insignificant. It would seem then that perceptually, the context to which allophones are sensitive
is indeed limited to one preceding and one following
sound.

There is another possible interpretation: the
transitions both to and from the intervocalic consonant are part of the consonant; thus it cannot be

190

claimed at all that V2 has affected VI, even though the transitions from VI to C have been modified.

The first interpretation is supported by the vowel data, but contradicted by certain consonant data obtained in the same experiment (Lehiste and Shockey 1971). Perceptually, the influence of the trans-consonantal vowel was insufficient to recover the missing vowel; thus allophones seem not to be sensitive to non-contiguous context. However, the first vowel in a $V_1 CV_2$ sequence is coded, according to Wickelgren's model, as $\#V_c$, the c being the same for different V_1's regardless of the quality, or even the presence, of V_2. In other words, to take a concrete example, the first /a/'s in /api/, /apa/, and /ap#/ should all be identically coded as $\#a_p$. It seems reasonable to assume that if the context-sensitive allophone is the minimal unit of perception, the context to which the allophone is sensitive should be perceptible. Thus the /p/ should be equally perceptible, i.e. equally recoverable, under all three conditions described above. Our experiments in consonant identification show extensive differences in identifiability between consonants that appear in final position as a result of elimination of the second vowel on the one hand, or as a result of having been produced by the speaker as unreleased final consonants, on the other. Although the modifications of transitions to an intervocalic consonant due to the quality of a following vowel were not sufficient to recover that vowel, they did have an effect on the identification of the consonant when the second vowel was removed.

The stimuli used in the final consonant identification experiment should have been identical: the left-hand context of the intervocalic consonants and the unreleased final consonants was the same, and the right-hand context was effectively removed by elimination of the releases. If identification was based only on left-hand context, we would have obtained identical scores. Since the scores were considerably different, perception must have been influenced by the anticipatory effect of the right-hand context, manifested within the segment preceding the consonant.

As a digression, I would like to remark that the claim that sounds are not sensitive to noncontiguous context cannot be upheld anyway in the light of historical sound changes. There are numerous processes which affect sounds, e.g. vowels, across intervening consonants and vice versa. For example, in the so-called palatal umlaut that has occurred in Germanic languages, there must have been a stage at which the /a/ of, say, /api/ was clearly distinct from the /a/ of /apa/. Whether the intervocalic consonants were involved or not is a moot question; it is difficult to prove or disprove whether in the Germanic languages the intervocalic consonant was first palatalized and then lost its palatalization after transmitting it to the preceding vowel. There exist instances however, in which a consonant that is otherwise susceptible to palatalization was not palatalized by a following high vowel under umlaut conditions.

Let us now return to the second possible interpretation: that the transitions are not part of the vowel at all, but part of the consonant. Then the vowel would consist only of the steady state. In principle, if a context-sensitive allophone is the basic unit of perception, the context to which it is sensitive should play a part in perception. In other words, if the transitions are part of the consonant, it should be possible to recover both the preceding and the following consonant in a C_1VC_2 sequence, given only the steady state of the vowel. We have not run such an experiment, but the recoverability of C_1 and C_2, in the correct order, from the steady state of the vowel seems implausible considering what is known of the effect of preceding and following consonants on vowel targets. For example, both a preceding and a following /r/ will lower the third formant of an interconsonantal vowel; but given only the steady state, it will not be possible to discover whether the lowering was due to left-hand or right-hand con-

192

text.

Wickelgren's hypothesis thus seems to be in need
of modification. It is clear that the effects of
coarticulation reach beyond contiguous sounds. On
the other hand, the context is not always perceptually recoverable. It may be that the 'context-sensitive' allophones fit a production model better than a
perception model. The physical modifications are undoubtedly there, but if the context of a context-
sensitive allophone is not perceptible, it seems un-
justified to assume that context-sensitive allophones
are the basic units of perception.

Considering allophones as minimal units of speech
perception is one way to approach a level of perception lower than the phoneme. Another is to consider
phonemes as "bundles" of distinctive features, and
to investigate perception at the feature level.
There is no question but that certain features can be
perceptually isolated from the "bundles" in which
they appear; e.g., voicing can be extracted from the
other characteristics of a voiced consonant. The
fact that features can be responded to apart from the
phonemes to which they belong supports the notion
that the brain is capable of parallel processing of
incoming information (Miller and Nicely 1955).

Parallel processing has been discussed in detail
in several recent publications (Chistovich and Kozhevnikov 1969-1970; Bondarko, Zagorujko, Kozhevnikov,
Molchanov, and Chistovich 1968 (translated by I.L.,
1970); Liberman 1970). In essence, it means that
the same physical signal (e.g. a frequency change in
the second formant) carries more than one kind of information (e.g. the phonetic value of a vowel and the
point of articulation of an adjacent consonant). A
corrollary assumption is that it is difficult, if not
impossible, to draw precise boundaries between acoustic segments in such a way that the first acoustic
segment would contain no information regarding the
perception of the second segment, and vice versa.

It will turn out that the first characteristic
of parallel processing encourages us to seek the min-

193

imal units of speech perception at a level lower (in a certain sense) than traditional allophones, while the second characteristic leads to the conclusion that the smallest units of perception must be located at a higher level - the level of something like a syllable. Let us consider both propositions in somewhat greater detail, and relate them to the role of phoneme-sized units in speech perception.

But first of all I should remark that an assumption of parallel processing would partly save Wickelgren's 'context-sensttive allophones' as minimal units in speech perception: in effect, the perception process could operate with information contained in several time segments, and the problem of non-contiguous influence could be ignored. On the other hand, the allophones would lose their unit-like character: their features, perceived separately and in parallel, would not necessarily be co-terminous, and instead of phone-like units (which one assumes 'context sensitive allophones' to be) we would be dealing with something like 'long components' (cf. Lihiste 1967, 1970, discussing Harris, 1944).

The question of the perception of sub-phonemic phonetic detail leads back to the question of categorical perception. To the extent that listeners are capable of distinguishing between stimuli falling within the same phonemic category, we are dealing with the perception of sub-phonemic phonetic detail. Reference was made above to the work of Chistovich et al. (1966(a), 1966(b)) which showed that listeners were able to make finer distinctions in vowels than those prescribed by their phonemic system. For evidence of sub-phonemic perception of a suprasegmental feature-duration I should like to quote Lisker and Abramson (1971). In their experiments with the duration of voice onset time, one of the authors serving as listener distinguished five clear labelling categories, while the phonemic system of English would provide only two.

The differential perception of duration leads to the question of the perception of temporal segments

194

in speech. Several phoneticians have expressed doubt
concerning the possibility of perceptual segmentation
of speech into units whose duration can be objectively established. It is, of course, known that acoustical signals are largely continuous; nevertheless, they also exhibit some drastic and abrupt
changes. The continuous nature of the clues signal-
ling the point of articulation has been used to argue that the minimal unit of perception is a unit of
the order of a syllable (for a recent summary, cf.
Liberman, Cooper, Shankweiler, and Studdert-Kennedy
1967). On the other hand, continuous speech signals
are perceived in ordinary listening as if they consisted of a sequence of discrete units (phonemes).
The question is whether the boundaries of these units
 - or a modified version thereof - can in some way be
associated with characteristics of the acoustic patterns. The basic question is thus whether it is possible to segment speech in a perceptually meaningful
way.
      The obvious place to begin is to consider sig-
nals that differ only in the duration of a segment,
in such a manner that the differences in duration are
not associated with any qualitative differences.
The voice-onset-time experiments provide one such
condition; they have shown both a possibility of categorical perception (which would serve as evidence
for the phonemic level) as well as subphonemic perception (providing evidence for the ability of the
ear to analyze duration in a phonetic rather than
categorical manner). Further evidence is provided by
languages with distinctive quantity.
      It is a linguistic fact that in some languages
the length of a vowel or consonant may have distinctive function. Experiments with synthetic speech
(Lehiste 1970(b)) show that listeners agree in a very
high degree in assigning linguistic labels to stimuli
(such as the duration of a voiceless plosive gap),
but also to match the stimuli with some kind of 'durational image', an abstract durational pattern characterizing a particular word type. If a difference

195

in duration of 10 milliseconds can switch 42% of the
listeners from one category of linguistic response to
another, the difference must be perceptually significant. Obviously it is impossible to tell, during
the voiceless plosive gap itself, whether the plosive is qualitatively shorter or longer; the listeners must be comparing durations, which means that
they must be using some fixed point of reference. I
submit that at least in languages with distinctive
quantity, abrupt changes in the manner of articulation serve as reference points with regard to timing judgments.

This is fully in accord with the notion that
speech is processed in parallel: whatever the process by which the duration of one segment is compared with that of another (or with a stored 'durational image'), it can very well take place at the
same time as the cues for point of articulation are
processed which are extracted from the same acoustic
signal (e.g. the same vocalic sound). In fact, all
suprasegmental information must be processed in a
similar way. For example, the presence of voicing
serves to establish the voicedness of a vocalic
sound at the same time as a possible fundamental frequency change taking place during the voiced segment
may signal a distinctive lexical tone. I have discussed the perception of suprasegmentals in detail
elsewhere (Lehiste 1967-1970; Lehiste, 1970(a)), and
shall not elaborate any further on this topic within
the present context.

There is additional, somewhat circumstantial,
evidence of the importance of the manner of articulation in speech perception. In a study of the perceptual parameters of consonant sounds, Sharf (1971)
established seven-point scales for duration, loudness,
frequency, sharpness, and contact. Substantial num-
bers of significant differences were obtained only
for duration comparisons based on manner of articulation; but since the contact parameter was specifically chosen to provide an indication of how well subjects related sounds to place of articulation, the

196

latter finding appears unsurprising). In an earlier study, Denes (1963) showed that manner of articulation carries by far the greatest functional load in the English sound system, and suggested that the acoustic correlates of manner might be used for segmentation in automatic speech recognition systems.

Perception of duration thus appears associated with the perception of manner of articulation. Both represent perception of phonetic detail which may or may not be distinctive. The perception of such phonetic detail serves to substantiate the claim that the minimal elements of speech perception must be located at the subphonemic level, which may thus be considered as established.

The phonemic level

The question is now whether the unit next in size is a phoneme-like unit or a syllable. The evidence for the psychological and perceptual reality of phoneme-like units has been summarized by Chistovich and Kozhevnikov (1970). Savin and Bever (1970) have argued for the "non-perceptual reality" of the phoneme. Let us review the arguments of Chistovich and Kozhevnikov first.

Much of the evidence for phoneme-like perceptual units comes from studies of categorical perception (cf. above). To the extent that the categorical perception idea is valid, the psychological reality of phonemes as perceptual units must be accepted. There is a connection between categorical perception and the motor theory of speech perception; both seem to apply better to consonants than to vowels (or to other signals of a continuous nature) (Liberman 1957; Stevens 1960; Liberman, Cooper, Harris, and MacNeilage 1962; Lane 1965; Liberman, Cooper, Shankweiler, and Studdert-Kennedy 1967; Studdert-Kennedy, Liberman, Harris, and Cooper (1970)). Chistovich and Kozevnikov (1969-1970) have shown, first, that vowels are also perceptible in a categorical fashion. Since the articulatory process involved is continuous rath-

197

er than discontinuous, this would argue against the motor theory. Second, they suggested that the number of categories in vowel perception may be larger than the number of traditional phonemes in the language; and further, that a listener is capable of remembering for a certain time not only a phoneme, but what they call 'timbre description' - subphonemic phonetic detail, which makes it possible to make distinctions within a category. The authors call their perceptual categories 'psychological phonemes'. It has been shown, for example, that Russian subjects classify [ɨ] and [i] as different psychological phonemes, although they are never encountered in the same environment and thus may be considered as constituting allophones of a single phoneme. Vowels between hard and soft consonants were classified by Russian subjects as belonging to different sound types, although they would again constitute positionally conditioned allophones according to classical phonemic theory.

Savin and Bever (1970) studied the order in which listeners make decisions at the phonemic and syllabic levels in the course of speech perception. Their method was to ask a listener to monitor a sequence of nonsense syllables for the presence of a certain linguistic unit, either a phoneme or a syllable (e.g. "bæb", "sæb") or a phoneme from that syllable: the syllable-initial consonant phoneme for some subjects (e.g. /b/ or /s/) and the medial vowel phoneme for other subjects (e.g. /æ/). Subjects responded more slowly to phoneme targets than to syllable targets (by 40 msec for /s-/, 70 msec for /b-/ and 250 msec for medial /æ/). Savin and Bever interpret these results as supportive of the view that phonemes are identified only after some larger linguistic sequence (e.g. syllables or words) of which they are parts. The reality of the phoneme, the authors say, is demonstrated independently of speech perception and production by the natural presence of alphabets, rhymes, spoonerisms, and interphonemic contextual constraints.

These results do not disprove the existence of a phonemic level of perception, and therefore the title of the paper by Savin and Bever ("The nonperceptual reality of the phoneme") appears somewhat misleading. Before the general conclusion is accepted, one would like to see what the reaction times to final consonants are, i.e. whether subjects would respond more slowly to a final /-b/ than to the syllable /sæb/. While not directly comparable to the reaction time experiments carried through by Fry (1970, to be discussed below), the results of Savin and Bever are sufficiently different from those of Fry to suggest additional studies.

It seems that a level of perception at which phoneme-like units are responded to should be recognized; it remains to relate it to the other levels of perception for which evidence has likewise been provided by studies of speech perception.

HIGHER-LEVEL UNITS OF PERCEPTION

Unitary perception of sequences of segments

The parallel processing of speech signals is compatible with the suggestion that the minimal unit of perception must be of the order of a syllable (Savin and Bever 1970; Liberman, Cooper, Shankweiler, and Studdert-Kennedy 1967). There is good evidence that the ear is particularly well suited to the perception of changes in acoustic parameters rather than their steady states (Abbs and Sussman 1971). Without going into details, let me just recall the experience of most researchers who have synthesized isolated vowels: produced on a monotone, the vowels frequently seem to occupy a borderline between speech-like and nonspeech-like stimuli, while the imposition of a fundamental frequency glide shifts the listener clearly into the speech mode. It is also well known that the majority of point of articulation cues of consonants are manifested in adjacent vowels. It seems thus reasonable to look for higher-level units

199

of perception beginning with sequences of two speech
sounds. The first major problem involves the perception of sequential order.

Wickelgren's idea of context-sensitive coding
could certainly explain the correct perception of
sequential order; but the notion of parallel processing, which seemed essential for upholding that
theory, appears to be incompatible with the decoding
of order from simultaneously received feature cues.
The perception of temporal order is a vast topic,
deserving a review on its own; I shall restrict myself in this survey to a few recent experiments
which shed some new light on the problem.

The mechanisms employed in the perception of
consonant clusters have been investigated in a series
of experiments by Bond (1971) and Day (1970(a), 1970
(b)).

The study by Bond (1971) deals explicitly with
the perceptually unitary nature of consonant clusters.
Bond studied 15 pairs of English words which differed
from each other only in the order of obstruents in
the cluster. The pairs /ps-sp/, /ts-st/ and /ks-sk/
were all represented five times (some examples:
task-tax, lisp-lips, coast-coats). The words were
produced by a male native speaker of English; randomized listening tests were constructed, in which
the signal was degraded by addition of white noise.
19 subjects took the listening test, writing down
what they heard. Five of the subjects took the test
a second time, producing a spoken response (a repetition) to each stimulus. These subjects' responses
were analyzed for reaction time in addition to being
scored for correctness. It was found that reaction
time was consistently faster for correct than for
incorrect responses; but the pattern of confusions
for written responses and spoken responses was essentially the same. It was further found that reversal errors were the most common errors. Bond argues
from this that minimal perceptual units must be larger than the phoneme. If consonant clusters were
perceived phoneme by phoneme, there is no reason for

200

the listener to reverse the order. To be sure, the
listener may occasionally be forgetful; but there is
no reason to suppose that he would be more likely to
forget the order of the consonants than to forget
one of the consonants. Since reversal errors were
much more common than substitution errors, some special perceptual mechanisms must be postulated for the
perception of consonant clusters. Bond's findings
thus confirm a suggestion made by Neisser (1967),
according to which a listener gradually learns to
distinguish a cluster like /ts/ from a cluster like
/st/, rather than perceiving a sequence of /t/ followed by /s/, or /s/ followed by /t/. Clusters of
this type thus seem to constitute a perceptual unit.

Day (1970(a)) studied phonemic fusion in dichotic
listening, in which listeners received two speech
stimuli at the same time with various relative onset
times. The stimuli differed in their initial consonants (e.g. /bæŋkət/ and /læŋkət/). On some trials,
either /bæŋkət/ or /læŋkət/ led by 25, 50, 75, or
100 msec; on other trials, both stimuli began at the
same time. Subjects reported hearing /blæŋkət/
regardless of which consonant led. When specifically asked to judge the temporal order of the initial
phonemes, most subjects reported hearing /b/ first,
no matter whether /b/ or /l/ actually led. Day concludes that instead of processing temporal order in
an accurate fashion, subjects responded to the stimuli
according to the constraints imposed by the phonological system of English. In English, stop + liquid
clusters are permissible in initial position, but
liquid + stop clusters do not occur. The responses
thus clearly imply the presence of a linguistic level
of processing.

A similar study was carried out with reversible
clusters (Day, 1970(b)). Since there are no reversible clusters in English in initial position, a final cluster was selected. The stimuli were /tæs/ and
/tæk/, whose fusion would yield acceptable English
words in either order, viz. /tæsk/ and /tæks/. All
trials were dichotic pairs, consisting of /tæs/ to

201

one ear and /tæk/ to the other ear. The onsets of
the syllables were aligned over a wide range of values: stimuli either started at the same time, or one
or the other stimulus led in steps of 5 msec to a
100 msec lead.

In contrast with the nonreversible case, temporal order judgement was very good when the cluster
could occur in either order in the language. One of
the temporal orders (/ks/) was somewhat more preferred. Day suggests that this may be due to the
fact that the acoustic shapes of stop consonants
undergo greater changes as a function of context than
do fricatives; thus the acoustic shape of /k/ in
/tæk/ may be more important that that of the /s/,
to the extent of biasing the perceived order of the
two phonemes. (I would suggest that segmental duration may have played a perhaps decisive part. The
stimuli were synthesized with equal duration given
to /æ/ in both /tæk/ and /tæs/. In actual speech,
/æ/ would be longer before a fricative; thus listeners may have been biased toward a /tæks/ response by
the relative shortness of the /æ/).

In a further experiment, subjects were asked to
decide which ear led, rather than which phoneme.
Performance on the ear task was much better: subjects were highly accurate, even though they were
language-bound on the phoneme task.

The difference between the results obtained with
nonreversible and reversible clusters is explained
by Day as follows. Two general levels of processing
are postulated: a linguistic level and a nonlinguis-
tic level. Correct temporal order may be represented
in the system at some point in time, but later stages
of processing mold this information to conform to the
linguistic structure of the language. Hence nonlin-
guistic information, concerning acoustic shape and
temporal order information is lost only after it en-
ters higher stages of linguistic processing.

Primary processing and linguistic processing

Day called the two levels of speech processing
which her experiments had isolated, "linguistic"
and "non-linguistic". It appears, however, that
both levels have to be further subdivided. Even at
the non-linguistic level, there is a difference in
perception depending on whether one is listening in
the "speech mode". Evidence for this is available
from many sources, among which are laterality studies (Studdert-Kennedy and Shankweiler 1970; Day and
Cutting 1970). I would like to call the processing
of an auditory signal in the speech mode "phonetic
processing". Attempts to separate auditory and phonetic modes of processing have been recently discussed by Fujisaki and Kawashima (1969) and by Pisoni (1971). The linguistic level suggested by Day
could perhaps be called the phonological level of
speech processing. At this level, information available to the listener about the phonological structure of the language (e.g. information concerning
permissible sequences) is interposed between primary
recognition and perceptual decision. The experiments
of Chistovich et al. (1966(a), 1966(b)) regarding
the mimicking and perception of vowels show the possibility of separating the phonetic and phonological
levels of perception, as do the experiments in the
perception of reversible and nonreversible clusters
by Day.
　　　There are higher levels within the linguistic
level of processing, and some attempts have been made
recently to explore them experimentally. A very intriguing set of experiments by Fry (1970) deals with
reaction time to monomorphemic and bimorphemic words
that are identical as to their phonemic composition.
Fry used the minimal pair lacks/lax, serving both as
speaker and listener. Responding 100 times to the
randomized stimuli, he made only 2 wrong responses to
50 occurrences of lax, and likewise only two errors
in responding to lacks - a result surprising to Fry,
who had not expected a subject to be able to respond

consistently to the difference between the two items.
The mean reaction times were 557 msec for lax and 518
msec for lacks, a difference that just misses significance at the .05 level of probability. Fry considers it worth noting that the direction of the difference points to a longer reaction time to the monomorphemic word.

Fry also tested the reaction time to longer sequences differing in the presence and absence of a
word boundary. The items were the two sentences It's
a sign of temporizing and It's a sign of temper rising, which are segmentally identical in Fry's pronun-
ciation. There were six errors in the perception of
50 presentations of temporizing and 3 in the case of
50 presentations of temper rising. Mean reaction
times (measured from the beginning of the syllable
/tem/ in each case) were 711 msec for temporizing and
858 msec for temper rising, a difference which was
significant below the .01 level of probability. The
item containing the word boundary thus took significantly longer to produce a response, although the
differnce in duration between the two items was negligible (30 msec in a total of 1430 msec).

Fry's starting assumption had been that processing time increases with the complexity of the task.
The results of the experiment with sentences support
this view; the two sentences differ in their syntactic structure, and it is quite probable that the syntactic level of processing was involved in addition
to primary processing. However, the results of the
lax - lacks experiment seem to imply that a monomorphemic word presents a more complex task that a bimorphemic one. This appears counter-intuitive; and
there might be alternate explanations to Fry's findings. If the results should be substantiated by
further experiments, it might be assumed that a bimorphemic word contains more information than a monomorphemic word and therefore can be processed faster.
If additional data should show that the effect observed by Fry may have been due to chance, it might
be concluded that there exists no separate morphemic

204

level of linguistic processing. Such experiments
were in fact carried through by Bond (1971). Bond
used ten minimal pairs, each pair consisting of one
monomorphemic and one bimorphemic word of the same
phonemic shape. Each pair of words composed a sub-
list, within which the two words were recorded in
random order, each word being produced ten times.
Care was taken to ensure that the speaker intended
the 'right' word every time. 29 listeners took the
test, which consisted of 200 stimuli. Reaction times
and correct scores were obtained by techniques similar to those used by Fry.

The over-all scores indicated that subjects were
not able to identify the words correctly at levels
significantly above chance. The mean scores ranged
from 45.1% for lax - lacks to 55.4% for lapse - laps.
When the responses of the subjects to each production
were analyzed, however, it was found that subjects
were very consistent in their responses to some of
the test items. Significant scores (at the .02 level)
were obtained for three items in the 20 productions
of members of the pair bard - barred (15.4%, 84.6%
and 15.4% correct), and one item each in the pairs
wade - weighed (100% correct), lax - lacks (18.2% correct), baste - based (85.7% correct) and mist - missed
(100% correct). As the scores show, while the subjects could be highly consistent in agreeing on a
particular response, they did not necessarily identify the word correctly; the identification scores for
utterances on which the subjects agreed on one response were still at chance level (57% correct).

There was no significant systematic difference
in reaction time between correct and incorrect responses. There was, however, some tendency for reaction time to be shorter to the bimorphemic word, as
Fry had discovered; the differences were not statistically significant.

This cannot be considered supportive of Fry's
findings, because reaction time differences become
meaningful only if the subjects can identify the
words correctly, which was not the case with Bond's

subjects. Bond explains the high degree of agreement
shown by the subjects in response to some of the
stimuli as follows. Faced with the task of the experiment, listeners develop a strategy for making use
of fine phonetic detail (duration, spectral characteristics of /s/ etc.). In this manner they arrive
at some consistent labelings. But since the ident-
ifications based on this strategy are equally likely
to be correct or incorrect, the strategy cannot be
considered to be part of ordinary speech perception.

Within the framework developed in this paper, I
would propose that we are dealing with phonetic processing rather than linguistic processing. The
perception of fine phonetic detail is certainly documented by Bond's results, but this information plays
no part in establishing a possible morphological
level within linguistic processing.

While the morpheme level evidently has to be
rejected as a level of processing within the level of
linguistic processing, it might be inquired whether
a word constitutes a perceptual unit at some level.
Fry's reaction time experiments provide some evidence
that the word is certainly not the minimum unit of
perception. In testing reaction times to 18 contrast like bid-big, or begin-began, Fry found that
in only three cases did the mean reaction time exceed
the total duration of the stimulus. In most cases,
subjects had no difficulty whatever in responding
before a word or syllable was complete. The processing mechnaism was evidently capable of dealing with
segments smaller than the whole syllable or word.

Whether the word constitutes a perceptual unit
does not emerge from Fry's experiment with sentences
containing the items temporizing - temper rising,
since in examples of this kind it is impossible to
separate lexical differences from syntactic ones.
However, certain techniques have been developed within the past ten years for studying the perception of
syntactic units, and the rest of the paper will deal
with perception at this level.

206

Perception of syntactic units

To a large extent, recent studies of sentence-level perceptual units go back to a seminal paper by Ladefoged and Broadbent (1960). In the research on which the paper is based, Ladefoged and Broadbent presented a series of tape-recorded sentences to various groups of listeners. During each sentence, a short extraneous sound (a "click") was present on the recording, and listeners had to indicate the exact point in the sentence at which the click occurred. Errors were large compared to the duration of a single speech sound; Ladefoged and Broadbent concluded that the basic unit of perception is larger than a phoneme, and that the listener does not deal with each sound separately but rather with a group of sounds. Subjective location of clicks, as reported by the subjects, differed from their objective location according to a regular pattern; Ladefoged and Broadbent argue that the points toward which the clicks were displaced constituted boundaries of perceptual units.

Fodor and Bever (1965) used the same technique to investigate the hypothesis that the primary units of speech perception correspond to the constituents of which a sentence is composed, i.e. the more abstract segments revealed by a constituent analysis of the sentence provided by the grammar of the language. Fodor and Bever found that clicks were attracted toward the nearest major syntactic boundaries in sentential material. The number of correct responses was significantly higher in the case of clicks located within constituents. Fodor and Bever consider these results supportive of the view that the segments marked by formal constituent structure analysis do in fact function as perceptual units, and that the click displacement is an effect which insures the integrity of these units: the units resist click intrusion.

In a subsequent study, Garrett, Bever and Fodor (1965) attempted to determine whether the earlier

results should be interpreted as reflections of the
assignment of constituent structure during the processing of sentences, or were rather effects of correlated acoustic variables (such as pause and intonation) which tend to mark constituent boundaries in
spoken language. They constructed and recorded pairs
of sentences for which some string of lexical items
was common to each member of a pair. The common
portions of each pair were made acoustically identical by cross-splicing, i.e. by splicing a recorded
version of a portion of one member of the pair to the
opposite member of the pair. When a spliced version
is paired with a copy of the original recording,
           (Example: A. (In her hope of marrying)
                           (Anna was surely impractical)
                       B. (Your hope of marrying Anna)
                           (was surely impractical).)
there are two sentences in which part of the acoustic
material is identical, but for which the constituent
boundaries are different. The results showed that
exactly the same acoustic signal was responded to
differently in every case, and the differences were
uniformly as predicted by the intended variation in
the constituent structure.
     Bever, Lackner and Stolz (1969) further tested
the hypothesis that the perceptual segmentation of
speech depends on transitional probabilities. The
fact that clicks are subjectively located at boundaries between clauses might be a reflection of the
low transitional probability between clauses rather
than a demonstration that syntactic structure is
actively used to organize speech processing. In this
experiment, subjects were asked to indicate the subjective location of clicks placed in sentences which
differed in terms of transitional probabilities between clauses. It was found that high-probability
sequences within clauses attract clicks, while low-
probability sequences do not. The authors interpret
these results as indicative that transitional probability has different effects within and between
clauses and thus is not a general mechanism for the

active segmentation of speech.

In another set of experiments, Bever, Lackner and Kirk (1969) found that within-clause phrase structure boundaries do not significantly affect the segmentation of spoken sentences, and that divisions between underlying structure sentences determine segmentation even in the absence of corresponding clause division in the surface phrase structure.

In most of these studies, subjects were ostensibly involved in only one task, namely click localization; but in fact they were performing a far more complex assignment. They had to listen to a sentence, pay attention to the click, remember the click location, and mark that on the written version of the sentence. The sentences were usually quite long; it seems obvious that we are dealing here with a complex interaction of perception and memory. Techniques used up to this point did not attempt to separate the effects of memory and perception.

Abrams and Bever (1969) attempted to minimize the effects of memory by giving the subjects a different task: pressing a key in response to a click. In a second presentation of the test sentences, subjects had to write the sentences and locate the click as before. Reaction times were thus obtained in addition to click localization data.

The results were somewhat ambiguous. Abrams and Bever had expected that clicks objectively occurring in clause breaks should receive faster reaction times than clicks in any other location. This turned out not to be so. There was also no systematic interaction between reaction time and subjective click location. Reaction time to clicks before clause breaks was affected by clause length and by familiarity with the sentence more than the reaction time to clicks after clause breaks. According to Abrams and Bever, this indicates that syntactic structure does systematically modify attention during speech perception. In sentences, the clause in a natural unit for internal perceptual analysis. During clauses one

listens to the speech and nonspeech stimuli; at the
end of clauses one encodes perceptually what was just
heard. Accordingly, a click at the end of a clause
is responded to relatively slowly, since it coincides
with the point of internal perceptual analysis of the
preceding sentence. At the beginning of a clause, a
click is reacted to quickly because it conflicts with
relatively little internal perceptual processing.

Abrams and Bever suggest further that the attentional system tapped by the reaction-time measure is
distinct from the behavioral process which produces
the systematic errors in click location. Immediate
reaction time interacts with the process of developing the internal perceptual organization of speech.
Listeners first organize the speech into major segments, then they relate the speech and click temp-
oraily. It is this latter process that maintains the
integrity of the speech units as revealed in the location of clicks.

In another study, Bever, Kirk and Lackner (1969)
tried to avoid conscious participation of the listeners altogether by measuring their galvanic skin response to shocks. In this experiment, subjects heard
sentences in one ear, during which a brief shock was
administered before, in or after the division between
two clauses. The galvanic skin response to shocks
objectively at the end of a clause was larger than
the response to shocks at the beginning of a clause.
Bever, Kirk and Lackner view this as confirmation of
the hypothesis that the syntactic structure of a
sentence can influence systematically the change in
skin resistance in response to a mild shock presented
during the sentence.

An independent effect was that galvanic skin
response to shocks at the end of a clause decreased
as a function of clause length; responses to shock at
the beginning of a clause were relatively unaffected
by the length of the preceding clause. According to
the authors, this supports the claim that listeners
respond to the syntactic structure of speech as they
hear it.

Fodor and Garrett (1971) revised the earlier view that click location is affected only by major constituent boundaries. Under appropriate conditions (when a listener is given more than the usual amount of time to consider a sentence), minor boundaries were found to affect click location. Fodor and Garrett suggest that assignment of minor constituent boundaries is a relatively late operation in the processing of sentences. If the listener has a chance for developing a more fine-grained analysis of the sentence containing a click, effects of minor constituent boundaries on click location are increased.

The series of studies just reviewed thus presents the following claims: listeners use grammar actively to impose syntactic structure on the speech stimulus as they hear it. Listeners respond in terms of the underlying structure of the sentence rather than its surface structure. Acoustic cues alone do not determine the boundaries of perceptual units.

Certain of these findings have been challenged in several recent studies. Abrams and Bever (1969) had found that subjects did not react faster to clicks placed in major constituent breaks than to clicks within the constituents. Holmes and Forster (1970) found exactly the opposite: reaction times to clicks at the major syntactic break of the sentence were faster than reaction times to clicks not at a break. This confirmed their hypothesis that processing load is a function of the surface structure of sentences, and that it decreases at major constituent boundaries.

The second result of the study by Holmes and Forster is likewise in direct contrast to the findings reported by Abrams and Bever: reaction times were slower when the click was in the first rather than in the second half of the utterance. Holmes and Forster interpret this result likewise in terms of differential processing loads. It is obvious that these results place in question the conclusions drawn by Abrams and Bever from their data.

Chapin, Smith and Abrahamson (1972, in press)

produced a detailed critique of Bever, Lackner and
Kirk (1969) who had claimed that underlying structure
sentences are the primary units of immediate speech
processing. Chapin, Smith and Abrahamson found that
clicks were attracted to major surface constituent
boundaries, even when these did not coincide with
the boundaries of underlying structure clauses. Another finding was that clicks are attracted to preceding constituent boundaries. This suggests an
overriding perceptual strategy in speech processing:
the listeners attempt to close constituents of the
highest possible level at the earliest possible point.

Bond (1971) studied both click localization and
reaction time, testing the hypothesis that subjects
segment an incoming sentence on the basis of stress
and intonation patterns. Reaction time is then pre-
diceted to be shorter to clicks between phonological phrases; it is also expected to be different to
clicks located in stressed syllables, as compared to
clicks placed in unstressed syllables.

When reaction time to clicks in stressed and unstressed syllables was compared, it was found that
reaction time was significantly faster to the click
located in an unstressed element, either in the consonant preceding the unstressed vowel or in the unstressed vowel itself. Subjects were much more accurate in locating a click when it occurred in a
stressed vowel than when it occurred in a consonant
or in an unstressed vowel (correct scores 46% vs.
12%). Clicks were thus much less likely to be 'attracted away' from stressed vowels than from unstressed vowels; the error responses, however, were
in the direction toward major boundaries.

Reaction time was also examined on the basis of
an 'intonation phrase', i.e. any phrase that was de-
marcated by a clear intonation curve. Reaction time
was found to be progressively slower as the click occurred further into the intonation phrase; thus there
is a correlation between reaction time and the position of the click within an intonation phrase.

Bond suggests that in sentence perception, the

listeners segment the sentence into phrases defined
on the basis of stress and intonation; they then
process the sentence further, to arrive at a syntactic analysis. Reaction time is apparently sensitive
to initial segmentation, while click localization is
sensitive to the final analysis.

The role of stress in the perception of sentence-level units

Bond's study did not attempt to separate the
parts played by stress and intonation. I conducted
an experiment, described below, to further investigate the role of stress in click localization.

The purpose of this experiment was to explore
the role played by suprasegmental features, especially stress, in the analysis of an incoming sentence.
If the assumption is true that linguistic processing
presupposes phonetic processing, it stands to reason
that stress and intonation are not ignored by a listener in the perception of a sentence. This, as may
be recalled, has been more or less generally assumed
since the 1965 paper by Garrett, Bever and Fodor
(cf. above).

It was decided to place clicks in identical positions within a sentence, varying the stress in such
a manner that the words within which clicks occurred
would appear both with and without stress, all other
factors being equal. If listeners react differently
to clicks placed in the same position under different
stress conditions, the role of suprasegmental factors
in perceptual processing will be confirmed.

In order to control stress and click placement
precisely, the experiment was carried through with
synthetic speech. The stimuli were produced at the
Bell Telephone Laboratories using the following
technique. A normal utterance was analyzed by a
formant-tracking program (Olive, 1971). The automatically tracked formants and fundamental frequency
were later modified by hand; changes in time, formant
structure, and fundamental frequency were produced by

213

a suitable computer program. The program allows the researcher to specify the frequencies of the three formants, the fundamental frequency, and the overall amplitude at each 10 msec sampling period. Specific changes that were made will be described below. The re-synthesis was produced by a digital hardware synthesizer (Rabiner et al., 1971). The entire process was controlled by a Honeywell DDP 224 computer (Denes, 1970).

The experimental technique used in the experiment differs from earlier methods in several ways. In most previous experiments, clicks had been recorded on the second channel of a two-track tape recorder, and the stimuli had been presented to listeners dichotically through headphones. Dichotic presentation introduced into the experimental situation a whole array of complicating factors, including competition between speech and nonspeech in relation to hemispheric specialization (Day and Cutting, 1970), and the problem of right- or left-handedness of the subjects. To avoid these probably unnecessary complications, the stimuli were recorded on full-track tape, with clicks introduced synthetically within the recording, and were presented to listeners over a good-quality loudspeaker in a sound-treated environment. It should be recalled that Ladefoged and Broadbent had likewise used a loudspeaker in their original experiment reported in 1960.

In most earlier experiments, listeners were required to write down the sentence that had been presented, and to indicate the position of the click on their own transcription. As was mentioned above, this technique introduces a memory component into the picture whose magnitude is difficult to estimate. It has been known for some time that the human short-term memory has a capacity of something like seven syllables (Miller, 1956). Memory units have been studied intensively by Johnson (1970), who found the 'chunks' of recall to be approximately the same size. In a recent paper, Gamlin (1971) has shown that subjects matched for intelligence may differ in their

214

short-term memory capacity, and that low short-term memory subjects structure sentences differently than high short-term memory subjects. Gamlin suggests that low short-term memory subjects may be forced by their memory limitations to process sentences into smaller syntactic units. Clearly most of the test sentences used in earlier click experiments have been long enough to overtax the short-term memory; thus it is entirely possible that the results confuse the sentence processing strategies with memory strategies.

The way chosen to eliminate the memorization problem was to use only one sentence with which the listeners became familiar during the introduction to the test, and to provide the subjects with written versions of the sentence. This represents again a return to the Ladefoged-Broadbent (1960) technique. In that study, subjects were presented both with unknown sentences over headphones, and with sentences that were written out and read out before the stimuli that contained the clicks were played over a loudspeaker. Ladefoged and Broadbent found that prior knowledge of the content of the sentence did not affect accuracy.

The sentence chosen for the experiment was one used by Bever, Lackner and Kirk (1969) in the experiment which provided the basis for their claim that the underlying structures of sentences are the primary units of immediate speech processing. The sentence, together with the phrase structure assumed by Bever et al., is as follows:

If (you (did ((call up) Bill))) (I (thank you (for (your trouble))))

Bever et al. placed clicks in the major clause break, in the middle of each of the two words immediately preceding the major break, and in the middle of each of the two words immediately following the major break. Separate results are not reported for this sentence, but one may assume the general conclusions to be applicable, i.e. that the boundary

215

after Bill attracted clicks, while boundaries within
the two clauses had no consistent effect on the subjective location of clicks.

The sentence was synthesized by the procedure
described above. The sentence was produced by a male
speaker with no special emphasis on any word and
without any pauses. After re-synthesis, the pitch
of the sentence was changed to monotone at 100 Hz.
Stress was then simulated on each of the four words
did, Bill, I, and thank. This was done by time expansion and by introducing a pitch inflection on the
appropriate word. The values of the parameters are
specified by the program at 10 msec intervals. In
time expansion, the number of sampling intervals is
specified to which a given word is to be expanded,
and the program interpolates the values of the parameters proportionately. The expansion factors had
been obtained previously by comparing the durations
of stressed and unstressed versions of the test
words in different productions of the sentence; they
were 25/33 for did, 32/58 for Bill, 16/34 for I
and 31/42 for thank.

The fundamental frequency contour applied to the
test word started at 100 Hz, rose to a peak of 111
Hz, and dropped back to 100 Hz. The peak of the contour was placed at the point of occurrence of the
fundamental frequency peak in a normal stressed production.

Clicks were produced by setting formant frequencies to I for one sampling period and introducing
random noise through the formants at an intensity
equal to that of the strongest vowel. The duration
of the clicks was 10 msec. Clicks were placed before, within and after each of the four words; the
clicks within words were located at the pitch peak.
With the method of time expansion used in the study,
the clicks remained in precisely the same position
relative to the word under both stress conditions.
A table of click placements and stress conditions is
given below.

TABLE I

SURVEY OF CLICK PLACEMENT

Stressed word	Test word	Click placement relative to test word		
		Before	Within	After
Did	did	X	X	X
	Bill	X	X	X
	I		X	X
	thank		X	X
Bill	did	X	X	X
	Bill	X	X	X
	I		X	X
	thank		X	X
I	did	X	X	X
	Bill	X	X	X
	I	X	X	X
	thank		X	X
thank	did	X	X	X
	Bill	X	X	X
	I		X	X
	thank		X	X

Two comments should be added. In order to simulate
stress on I, a glottal stop (with a duration of 17
sampling periods, i.e. 170 msec) was inserted before
I. In the sentence in which I carried simulated
stress, two click placements were used for the sequence Bill, I: a click was placed in the last frame
of Bill, immediately preceding the glottal stop. In

other instances, only one click placement was used
between words. This is true also of sequences of
Bill, I (i.e. the major clause break) in all other
cases in which I was not stressed, including those in
which Bill carried simulated stress.

The first part of the listening test was designed to check the effectiveness of the stress simulation. A set of ten randomized sentences was prepared, containing two productions each of the test
sentence produced on a monotone (and without time expansion, i.e., without stress simulation), and two
sentences each with stress placed respectively on did,
Bill, I, and thank. (The sentences contained no
clicks.) The listeners were asked to underline the
stressed word. The results are presented in the following table.

TABLE 2

SUBJECTIVE PLACEMENT OF STRESS,
DEPENDING ON STRESS SIMULATION
Scores in per cent

	Mono-tone	Stress on did	Stress on Bill	Stress on I	Stress on thank
If	4				2
you	4	4			
did	12	90	6	2	2
call	16	2	2	2	
up	16		2		
Bill	28		84	4	2
I				92	
thank	10	4	6		94
you					
for					
your					
trouble	10				

As may be seen from the table, the syllables on which simulated stress was placed were overwhelmingly accepted as being stressed. The neutral sentence provided two surprises. I had expected the word <u>did</u> to be judged as stressed, since it is lexically marked as emphatic; however, there was a wide scatter of responses, and the word judged relatively most frequently as stressed was the word <u>Bill</u>. It will be reported later that this word behaved in an unexpected way in other respects too. Whether its position before the clause break is in any way connected with this behavior has to remain a matter of conjecture; further experimentation is clearly needed to solve the problem.

After the first part of the test, some examples of sentences containing clicks were played to the listeners, and instructions were given to draw a slash line through that part of the sentence that contained the click. Subjects were informed that clicks could occur between words or within a word. Sample sentences with slashes were provided on the handout. The subjects then proceeded to the main part of the test, which contained the 41 stimuli in two different randomizations (for a total of 82 stimuli), balanced in such a way that each stimulus occurred once during the first half and once during the second half of the test. The whole test took approximately twenty minutes to complete. The test was administered singly or in small groups to 25 listeners, mainly graduate students and staff members of the Department of Linguistics of the Ohio State University. The results consist of 50 judgements per stimulus, for a total of 4,100 judgements. The results of the listening tests will be presented with reference to Tables 3, 4, and 5. The question of correct identification will be discussed first.

The evidence for the listener's analysis of the sentence in terms of underlying structure units had been largely derived from subjective localization of clicks at major syntactic boundaries. Specifically, it had been claimed that clicks objectively at such

boundaries were correctly located more frequently
than clicks placed elsewhere, and that clicks placed
elsewhere had a strong tendency to migrate toward the
major syntactic boundaries. This experiment contained sentences in which clicks were placed at various boundaries, including the major clause boundary.
The per cent correct identification of click location at various boundaries was as follows:

If (you (did ((call up) Bill)))   (I
      24.0   40.0   51.5   27.6
(thank you (for (your trouble))))
41.5   16.5

     The total number of clicks correctly identified
between Bill and I was 69 out of a possible 250 (5
sentences), or 27.6%. The total number of clicks
objectively placed in the boundary, but subjectively
shifted elsewhere, was 181, or 72.4%. Most of these
clicks were attracted into the following word, i.e.
into I. When I was unstressed, it attracted 37
clicks away from the boundary (from 150 possibilities,
3 sentences), and when it was stressed, 71(from 100
possibilities, 2 sentences). As far as attracting
clicks objectively located elsewhere, there were 150
such cases out of a possible 1800 (36 sentences),
which amounts to 8.3%

     Table 3 presents the average correct scores for
the subjective location of clicks objectively placed
in stressed and unstressed production of the words
did, Bill, I, and thank. The unstressed scores combine stresses on the three other words; e.g. unstressed did combines scores for instances in which
stress was simulated on Bill, I, and thank. A study
of the scores reveals a number of regularities.
There is a common pattern for the words did, I, and
thank, while Bill shows a highly divergent pattern.
Table 4 gives the average scores of the three words
with similar behavior.

TABLE 3

CORRECT SCORES (PER CENT)

Word	Objective click placement		
	Before	Within	After
did, stressed	16.0	68.0	62.0
did, unstressed	26.7	56.0	32.7
Significance of difference*	>.10	>.10	<.01
Bill, stressed	56.0	38.0	24.0
Bill, unstressed	50.0	64.7	32.7
Significance of difference	>.10	<.01	>.10
I, stressed	16.0	40.0	66.0
I, unstressed	34.7	24.0	33.3
Significance of difference	<.05	<.10	<.001
thank, stressed	28.0	78.0	22.0
thank, unstressed	46.0	43.3	14.7
Significance of difference	<.05	<.001	>.10
*See Spiegel (1961, p. 171)			

TABLE 4

CORRECT SCORES FOR DID, I, AND THANK (IN PER CENT)

Word	Objective click placement		
	Before	Within	After
Stressed	20	62	50
Unstressed	35.8	41.0	26.9
Significance of difference	<.10	<.05	<.001

In unstressed versions of did, I, and thank,
clicks placed before the word tended to be identified
more correctly than clicks placed in analogous position in stressed words. The difference is significant at the .10 level. Clicks within and after
stressed words were identified more accurately than
within and after unstressed words. This, too, is a
significant difference, with the significance increasing from the .05 level for position within the test
word to the .01 level for position after the test
word. The word Bill, however, shows the opposite result. In the case of Bill, the relationships between
the scores are reversed, although only the difference
between the scores for position within stressed and
unstressed versions of Bill reaches significance (at
the .01 level).

The various kinds of subjective shifts are shown
in Table 5.

Study of this table explains why clicks preceding stressed words received low correct scores:
there is an overwhelming tendency for such clicks to
be subjectively located within the stressed word. To
put it differently, stress attracts the click from
the preceding boundary into the stressed word. For
did, correct identification of a click before the
test word was 16%, compared to subjective shifts in
46% of the cases; for I, the 16% correct location of
the click occurring at the boundary contrasts with a
64% shift into the stressed word, and for thank, 28%
correct contrasts with a 64% shift. The subjective
shift in the case of I is particularly noteworthy,
since it involves a shift away from the major syntactic boundary, which supposedly attracts clicks and
certainly should resist their being attracted away.
Table 6 shows the level of significance of differences
in scores due to some of the shifts.

Table 6 requires some interpretation. It is obvious that the shifts from before a stressed word into the stressed word are highly significant. In some
instances, shifts from after the test word to the following word are also significant; but failure to

222

TABLE 5

CLICK PLACEMENT AND CLICK LOCATION
IN STRESSED AND UNSTRESSED WORDS (PER CENT)

Objective click placement	Subjective click location				
	Within preced- ing word	Before test word	Within test word	After test word	Within follow- ing word
Before did, stressed	8.0	16.0	46.0	8.0	2.0
Within did, stressed		10.0	68.0	16.0	6.0
After did, stressed		2.0	20.0	62.0	14.0
Before did, unstressed	11.3	26.7	50.7	2.0	0.7
Within did, unstressed	2.0	14.0	56.0	16.7	6.0
After did, unstressed	0.7	6.7	20.0	32.7	16.7
Before Bill, stressed	10.0	56.0	26.0	4.0	
Within Bill, stressed			38.0	48.0	6.0
After Bill, stressed		2.0	8.0	24.0	16.0
Before Bill, unstressed	9.3	50.0	26.0	8.7	0.7
Within Bill, unstressed	0.7	2.7	64.7	25.3	4.0
After Bill, unstressed			7.3	35.3	45.3

TABLE 5 - Continued

Objective click placement	Subjective click location				
	Within preceding word	Before test word	Within test word	After test word	Within following word
Before I, stressed	2.0	16.0	64.0	8.0	8.0
Within I, stressed		2.0	40.0	44.0	12.0
After I, stressed		2.0	20.0	66.0	12.0
Before I, unstressed	10.0	34.7	24.7	6.7	6.7
Within I, unstressed	2.0	17.3	24.0	22.0	28.0
After I, unstressed	1.3	9.3	3.3	33.3	50.7
Before thank, stressed	2.0	28.0	64.0	2.0	
Within thank, stressed	2.0	4.0	78.0		
After thank, stressed		2.0	36.0	22.0	20.0
Before thank, unstressed	9.3	46.0	33.3		
Within thank, unstressed	6.6	29.3	43.3	4.0	
After thank, unstressed	3.3	18.0	53.3	14.7	4.7

TABLE 6

DEGREE OF SIGNIFICANCE OF SUBJECTIVE SHIFTS

| Objective click Placement | Subjective shift (by one-half step) to | |
	Within test word	Within following word
Before did, stressed	<.01	
After did, stressed		<.001
Before did, unstressed	<.01	
After did, unstressed		>.20
Before Bill, stressed	<.001	
After Bill, stressed		>.20
Before Bill, unstressed	<.01	
After Bill, unstressed		>.20
Before I, stressed	<.001	
After I, stressed		<.001
Before I, unstressed	>.20	
After I, unstressed		<.05

TABLE 6 - Continued

| Objective click Placement | Subjective shift (by one-half step) to | |
	Within test word	Within following word
Before thank, stressed	<.001	
After thank, stressed		>.20
Before thank, unstressed	<.20	
After thank, unstressed		>.20

shift is equally important. This is not shown directly on this table, but can be realized by comparing Table 6 with Table 5. For example, the probability that a click objectively placed after stressed did would be attracted into the following word is exceedingly small; the reason for this is the high accuracy of click location in the position in general, and the fact that no stressed word ever followed did. It is the stressed words that attract preceding clicks; there was no comparable systematic tendency for clicks to be subjectively shifted from a preceding boundary to the middle of an unstressed word.

As regards the word Bill, the degree of significance shows the failure to shift in both cases in which the click was placed before the word.

Clicks objectively placed within a stressed word receive high correct scores and show little tendency to shift away. This tendency is greater in unstressed words. The direction of these shifts is not systematic in any way.

Clicks placed after stressed words are highly

226

identifiable. If they migrate, it is toward the following word. The tendency to shift into the following word is much more pronounced in the case of clicks
placed after unstressed words. After Bill and I, in
particular, the click was subjectively shifted to the
following word more frequently that it was correctly
located. Interestingly, this is the only instance in
which unstressed Bill shares the behavior of other
unstressed words; in all other respects, it seems as
if stress and lack of stress were reversed in the case
of Bill. The reason why clicks are not shifted to
the following word after unstressed did and thank is
most probably the lack of stress on the words immediately following the click.

Except for the matter just described, no particular regualrities seemed to be associated with the
position of the word relative to the beginning or end
of the sentence. The behavior of clicks associated
with Bill remains a problem calling for further
study.

The results of the experiment demonstrate that
stress does indeed have an effect on the subjective
location of clicks. Without trying to read too much
into the outcome of the limited experiment, I feel
justified in saying that click localization is more
sensitive to surface phenomena than has been previously assumed. The underlying structure of the
sentence remained the same during the experiment; if
the listeners somehow proceed directly to the analysis of underlying structures, clicks should have been
treated similarly in the same words, regardless of
their stressed or unstressed realization. Since
there were significant differences, one may conclude
that click localization is not exclusively dependent
on the underlying syntactic structure of the sentence.

SUMMARY AND CONCLUSION

In this paper, I have attempted to establish the
units of perception and the levels at which perception
operates. Evidence has been adduced for two basic

steps in perception: primary processing and linguistic processing. Primary processing consists of uditory processing and phonetic processing, which constitutes listening in a speech mode. There are several levels within the linguistic level, of which the phonological and syntactic level are considered better documented than a possible morphological level. Linguistic processing presupposes primary processing. Auditory processing must logically precede other levels of processing; phonetic processing is considered as presupposed by the other levels, but the possibility is admitted that phonetic and linguistic processing may proceed concurrently. The units at the various levels may differ in size, and there is extensive interaction between them, as there is, for example, between the phonetic and phonological levels on the one hand and the syntactic level on the other hand. Processing at the syntactic level presupposes analysis at the phonetic level, which seems to be largely suprasegmental. Parallel processing is accepted as part of the model, and a strict separation of levels is considered unwarranted.

ACKNOWLEDGEMENTS

I am grateful to the College of Humanities of The Ohio State University for releasing me from teaching duties during the autumn quarter of 1971, while this paper was being written. I wish also to express my appreciation to Dr. P.B. Denes and Dr. J.P. Olive of the Bell Telephone Laboratories for their help with the experimental part of this paper, to Dr. A.W.F. Huggins (of M.I.T.) and Dr. T. Smith (of the University of California, San Diego) for their challenges and suggestions, and to my research assistants Linda R. Shockey and Richard P. Gregorski for their help in administering the listening test.

References

Abbs, J.H., and H.M. Sussman. Neurophysiological
    feature detectors and speech perception: a dis-
    cussion of theoretical implications. J. Speech
    Hearing Res., 1971, 14, 23-36.

Abrams, Kenneth, and Bever, Thomas G. Syntactic
    structure modifies attention during speech per-
    ception and recognition. Quarterly Journal of
    Experimental Psychology, 1969, 21, 280-290.

Bever, T , Kirk, R., and Lackner, J. An autonomic
    reflection of syntactic structure. Neuropsych-
    ologia, 1969, 7, 23-28.

Bever, T.G., Lackner, J.R., and Stolz, W. Transition-
    al probability is not a general mechanism for
    the segmentation of speech. Journal of Exper-
    imental Psychology, 1969, 79, 387-394.

Bever, T.G., Lackner, J.R., and Kirk, R. The under-
    lying structures of sentences are the primary
    units of immediate speech processing. Percep-
    tion and Psychophysics, 1969, 5, 225-234.

Bond, Z.S. Units in speech perception. Working Pap-
    ers in Linguistics, 1971, No. 9, viii-112.
    Computer and Information Science Research Center
    Technical Report Series, OSU-CISRC-TR-71-8.
    The Ohio State University, Columbus, Ohio.

Bondarko, L.V., Zagorujko, N.G., Kozhevnikov, V.A.,
    Molchanov, A.P., and Chistovich, L.A. A model
    of speech perception by humans. Academy of the
    Sciences of the U.S.S.R., Siberian Section:
    Nauka, Novosibirsk. Translated by I. Lehiste,

Working Papers in Linguistics, 1968, No. 6, Ohio State University, Columbus , 88-132.

Chapin, Paul G., Smith, Timothy S., and Abrahamson, Adele A. Two factors in perceptual segment-ation of speech. Journal of verbal Learning and Verbal Behavior, 1972 (in press).

Chistovich, L., Fant, A., de Serpa-Leitão, A., and Tjernlund, P. Mimicking of synthetic vowels. Speech Transmission Laboratory Quarterly Pro-gress and Status Report, 1966(a), 2, 1-18.

Chistovich, L., Fant, G., and De Serpa-Leitão, A. Mimicking and perception of synthetic vowels, Part II. Speech Transmission Laboratory Quart-erly Progress and Status Report 3, 1-3.

Chistovich, L.A., and Koxhevnikov, V.Z. Perception of speech. In Voprosy teorii i metodov issled-ovanija vosprijatija recevyx signalov, Lenin-grad; Translated as L.A. Chistovich et al. Theory and methods of research on perception of speech signals. JPRS 50423, 1970.

Day, Ruth S. Temporal order judgements in speech: are individuals language-bound or stimulus-bound? Paper presented at the 9th Annual Meet-ing of the Psychonomic Society, St. Louis, November, 1969. (Haskins Laboratories), 1970(a) SR-21/22, 71-87.

Day, Ruth S. Temporal order perception of a revers-ible phoneme cluster. Paper presented at the 79th meeting of the Acoustical Society of Amer-ica, Atlantic City, 21-24 April, 1970(b).

Day, Ruth S., and Cutting, James E. Perceptual com-petition between speech and nonspeech. Paper presented at the 80th meeting of the Acoustical Society of America, Houston, 3-6 November, 1970.

Denes, Peter B., On the statistics of spoken English. J. Acoust. Soc. Amer., 1963, 35, 892-904.

Denes, Peter B. On-line computers for speech research. Transactions of the IEEE on Audio- and Electro-acoustics, December, 1970, Vol. AU-18, 4, 418-425.

Fodor, J.A., and Bever, T.G. The psychological reality of linguistic segments. Journal of Verbal Learning and Verbal Behavior, 1965, 4, 414-420. Also in: L.A. Jakobovits and M.S. Miron (eds.), Readings in the Psychology of Language. Englewood Cliffs, N.F.: Prentice-Hall, Inc. 1964, 325-332.

Fodor, J.A., and Garrett, M.F. "A consolidation effect in sentence perception. Research Laboratory of Electronics, M.I.T. Quarterly Progress Report, 1971, 100, 182-185.

Fry, D.B. Reaction time experiments in the study of speech processing. Nouvelles Perspectives en phonétique, Institut de Phonétique, Université Libre de Bruxelles: Conferences et Travaux, 1970, Vol. I, 15-35.

Fry, D.B., Abramson, A.S. Eimas, P.D. and Liberman, A.M. The identification and discrimination of synthetic vowels. Language and Speech, 1962, 5, 171-189.

Fujisaki, H., and Kawashima, T. The influence of various factors on the identification and discrimination of synthetic speech sounds. Reports of the 6th International Congress on Acoustics, Tokyo, 1968, 2, B-95-98.

Fujisaki, H., and Kawashima, T. On the modes and mechanisms of perception of speech sounds. Paper presented at the 78th meeting of the Acoustical Society of America, San Diego, 1969, November 4.

Gamlin, Peter J. Sentence processing as a function of syntax, short term memory capacity, the meaningfulness of the stimulus and age. Language and Speech, 1971, 14, 115-134.

Garrett, M., Bever, T., and Fodor, J. The active use of grammar in speech perception. Perception and Psychophysics, 1965, 1, 30-32.

Harris, Z. Simultaneous components in phonology. Language, 1944, 20, 181-205.

Holmes, V. and Forster, K. Detection of extraneous signals during sentence recognition. Perception and Psychophysics 7, 1970, 5, 297-301.

Johnson, Neal F. The role of chunking and organization in the process of recall. Psychology of Learning and Motivation, 1970, 4, New York: Academic Press, 171-247.

Ladefoged, P., and Broadbent, D.E. Perception of sequence in auditory events. Quarterly Journal of Experimental Psychology, 1960, 12, 162-170.

Lane, H. The motor theory of speech perception: a critical review. Psychological Review, 1965, 2, 275-309.

Lehiste, Ilse. Suprasegmental features, segmental features, and long components. Actes du Xe congrès international des linguistes, Bucarest, 1967: Editons de l'academic de la Republique socialiste de Roumanie, Bucarest, Vol. IV, 1-7. (1970)

Lehiste, Ilse. Suprasegmentals. Cambridge: M.I.T. Press, 1970(a).

Lehiste, Ilse. Experiments with synthetic speech concerning quantity in Estonian. Proceedings of the 3rd International Congress of Fenno-Ugricists, Tallinn, 1970(b) (in press).

Lehiste, Ilse and Shockey, L. The perception of coarticulation. Two papers presented at the 82nd meeting of the Acoustical Society of America, Denver, 1971, October 20.

Liberman, Alvin M. Some results of research on speech perception. J. Acoust. Soc. Amer., 1957, 29, 117-123.

Liberman, Alvin M. The grammars of speech and language. Cognitive Psychology, 1970, 1, 301-323.

Liberman, A.M., Cooper, F.S. Harris, K.S. and MacNeilage, P.F. A motor theory of speech perception. Proceedings of Speech Communication Seminar, Stockholm, Session D-3, 1-10, 1962.

Liberman, A.M., Cooper, F.S.,,Shankweiler, D.P., and Studdert-Kennedy, M. Perception of the speech code. Psychological Review, 1967, 74, 431-461.

Liberman, A.M., Harris, K.S., Hoffman, H., and Griffith, B. The discrimination of speech sounds within and across phoneme boundaries. Journal of Experimental Psychology, 1957, 54, 358-368.

Liberman, A.M., Harris, K.S., Kinney, J. and Lane, H. The discrimination of relative onset time of the components of certain speech and nonspeech patterns. Journal of Experimental Psychology, 1961, 61, 379-388.

Lisker, L., and Abramson, A.S. Distinctive features and laryngeal control. Language, 1971, 47,

767-785.

Miller, G.A. The magical number seven, plus or minus
two: Some limits on our capacity for processing
information. Psychological Review, 1956, 63,
81-97.

Miller, G.A., and Nicely, P.E. An analysis of perceptual confusions among some English consonants. J. Acoust. Soc. Amer., 1955, 27, 338-352.

Neisser, Ulric. Cognitive Psychology. New York:
Appleton-Century-Crofts, 1967.

Öhman, S.E.G. Coarticulation in VCV utterances. J.
Acoust. Soc. Amer., 1966, 39, 151-168.

Olive, J.P. Automatic formant tracking by a Newton-
Raphson technique. J. Acoust. Soc. Amer., 1971,
50, 661-670.

Pisoni, David B. Very brief short-term memory in
speech perception. Paper presented at the 82nd
meeting of the Acoustical Society of America,
Denver, 1971, October 19.

Rabiner, L.R., et al. Digital formant synthesis.
Paper 23C8, Proceedings of the 7th International
Congress on Acoustics, Budapest, 1971, Vol. 3,
157-158.

Savin, H.B., and Bever, T.G. The nonperceptual reality of the phoneme. Journal of Verbal Learning
and Verbal Behavior, 1970, 9, 295-302.

Sharf, Donald J. Perceptual parameters of consonant
sounds. Language and Speech, 1971, 14, 169-177.

Spiegel, Murray R. Theory and Problems of Statistics.
New York: McGraw-Hill, 1961, 171.

Stevens, KN.N   Toward a model for speech recognition. J. Acoust. Soc. Amer., 1960, 32, 47-55.

Stevens, K.N., Liberman, A.M., Öhman, S.E.G., and Studdert-Kennedy, M.   Cross-language study of vowel perception. Language and Speech, 1969, 12, 1-23.

Studdert-Kennedy, M., and Shankweiler, D.   Hemispheric specialization for speech perception. J. Acoust. Soc. Amer., 1970, 48, 579-594.

Studdert-Kennedy, M., Liberman, A.M., Harris, K.S., and Cooper, F.S.   Motor theory of speech perception: A reply to Lane's critical review. Psychological Review, 1970, 77, 234-249.

Wickelgren, Wayne A.   Context-sensitive coding, associative memory, and serial order in (speech) behavior. Psychological Review, 1969(a), 1, 1-15.

Wickelgren, Wayne A.   Context-sensitive coding in speech recognition, articulation and development. In K.N. Leibovic, ed., Information Processing in the Nervous System. Springer: New York-Heidelberg-Berlin: Springer, 1969(b) 85-95.

Chapter 7

DISCUSSION PAPER ON SPEECH PERCEPTION

Wayne A. Wickelgren

Department of Psychology
University of Oregon

My comments on Dr. Lehist's paper are organized primarily into two sections: (a) serial vs. parallel processing in speech recognition. First, I will argue that speech production involves a special kind of mixture of both serial and parallel processing, though the observable output of the speech production process makes the serial aspect of speech production much more obvious than the parallel aspect. Second, I will argue that speech recognition also involves a special kind of mixture of serial and parallel processing, but with parallel processing overwhelmingly more important at linguistic levels below the word.

Throughout this paper I will be defending the position that the context-sensitive allophone representative is the important unit at the segmental level in both speech recognition and articulation. In my opinion, context-sensitive allophones subserve the proposed functions of both syllables and phonemes better than do syllables and phonemes, at the segmental level in speech perception and production. However, I strongly suspect that representatives of context-free phonemes play an important role in the child's acquisition of context-sensitive allophones in articulation. Furthermore, the concept of the phoneme plays an important role in the definition of the context-sensitive allophone.

I assume that the units of representation in the lexicon (dictionary) of a language are concepts, not words or morphemes. By this I mean that every different meaning of a word will have a different unit representing it in the lexicon. In addition, a word made up of two morphemes such as "blackbird" will often not be represented by two morpheme units, "black" and "bird", but rather by one concept unit, "blckbird". However, in some cases, such as the representation of singular vs. plural forms of a concept, I would assume that a plural concept such as "birds" is represented by the conjunction of two concept representatives, "bird" and "plural". A regular past tense verb, such as "walked" is probably represented by "walk" and "past", etc. In addition, I assume that two "synonymous" meanings of different words have at least somewhat different representation at the concept level, though all semantically similar concepts presumably have strong associations between them or overlapping "semantic feature" representation in the concept system, etc.

To communicate concepts by speech, we must translate concepts into a sequence of articulatory gestures which result in a temporally distributed speech wave form. For the moment, let us ignore the difficulty involved in segmenting speech at any articulatory, acoustic, or auditory-sensory level, and make the assumption that a concept (word) is represented by a set of structural (articulatory and auditory) units at some lower phonetic level(s) of the nervous system.

In the past, linguistics has always considered the structural (phonetic) analysis of a concept (word) to be an ordered set of nonoverlapping segments. Occasionally, it has been argued that the immediate segmental constituents of words are syllables, but more frequently the assumption has been that the immediate constituents of words are phonemes. In either case, the representation of a word is by an ordered set of "context-free" segments. By "context-free", I mean that the same segments can appear in a large variety of different segmental contexts. That is to say, the /s/ phoneme in the word "struck"

238

is the same /s/ phoneme as in the words "pass" or
"pensive". The word must be represented by an ordered set of such segments (phonemes), because, frequently, the same segments (phonemes) in a different
order represent a different word. Of course, there
are a number of phonological restrictions and differential statistical probabilities of one segment (phoneme) following another segment (phoneme) in the language, but this fact is not represented in the phonetic "spelling" of any word in the lexicon.

Recently, Wickelgren (1969(a) and (b)) proposed
a rather different type of immediate constituent analysis of concepts (words) at a "segmental" level.
Wickelgren proposed that a word like "struck" be represented by an unordered set of context-sensitive
allophone representatives such that each allophone
representative was essentially an ordered triple of
immediately adjacent phonemes in the phonemic spelling of the word. Thus, the spelling of the immediate
constituents of the word "struck" would be

$$\#s_t, \ s_{t_r}, \ t_{r_\Lambda}, \ r_{\Lambda}k, \ \Lambda k\#.$$

For convenience, the context-sensitive allophonic spelling of the word "struck" has been written in
the obvious order. However, the representation of
"struck" can be by the unordered set of context-sensitive allophones at some level of the nervous system,
since the order of the context-sensitive allophones
can be uniquely reconstructed from associations in
long-term memory. Clearly, the association from $\#s_t$
will be strongest to s_{t_r} of all the context-sensitive
allophones in the word, and the association from
s_{t_r} will be strongest to t_{r_Λ} of all the allophones in
the word etc. Thus, a simple left-to-right assoc-
iative generation process will reconstruct the order
of these context-sensitive allophones from the unordered set. Note that the immediate phonetic constituents of words by this theory are context-sensitive.
The selection of one constituent for a word places
restrictions on what other constituents can be selected in the spelling of the word. Another way to say
this is that the immediate phonetic constituents are

239

overlapping, rather than non-overlapping as in the
case of phonemic or syllabic spelling. Although a
context-sensitive allophonic spelling of a word does
dictate some particular order in the articulation
of the phonetic constituents, these allophonic constituents overlap to a certain limited degree (in terms
of phonemes, each constituent overlaps its two immediate left and right neighbors). Thus, the order of
the constituents is not like the segments of a tape
so much as it is like the links of a chain, each of
which interlocks with two adjacent links. Another
useful analogy is that the context-sensitive allophone
is like a piece in a linear jigsaw puzzle with notches and tabs that exactly fit the tabs and notches on
the correct left and right hand pieces. It may be
somewhat missleading to refer to context-sensitive
allophones as segmental representatives at all. Perhaps context-sensitive allophones should be called
links or "linkments" (the latter by analogy to "segment"). I will not pursue further this attempt to
add another word to the English lexicon.

Presumably, at still more peripheral levels of
the nervous system, a particular context-sensitive
allophone activates a particular set of motor feature
representatives that control the muscles of the vocal
tract. Also, at a peripheral auditory level, sets of
auditory feature representatives are associated with
each context-sensitive allophone for the purposes of
speech recognition. I will have very little to say
regarding either the auditory or articulatory feature
levels of the speech articulation and perception processes in this paper.

In addition, I will have nothing to say in this
paper concerning historical linguistics and phonology.
Although it is not necessarily true, it seems very
plausible to me to assume (as I do) that the processes
governing changes in the sound system of a language
are very different from the processes controlling
performance in speech recognition and articulation
by a competent adult speaker. In agreement with Ladefoged (1970), I believe that a large number of phono-

240

logical laws are essentially laws of historical linguistics, not rules that function in the recognition
or production of speech. However, also in agreement
with Ladefoged, I suspect that some phonological
rules (e.g., regular plural formation, regular past
tense formation) are rules which do function in adult
speech production and recognition processes. Unfortunately, I have not given sufficient time to these
matters to make discussion in the present paper
worthwhile. In any event, the casual observation by
Lehiste of nonadjacent contextual influences in historical linguistics seems to me to be not clearly
relevant to the possible role of context-sensitive
allophonic coding in adult speech performance.

SERIAL AND PARALLEL PROCESSES IN SPEECH PRODUCTION

Lehiste cites Öhman (1966) who showed in VCV
sequences that the transition from the first vowel to
the following consonant depended on the nature of the
second vowel. In agreement with the terminology of
Daniloff and Moll (1968), let us call this an example
of "forward" co-articulation. Öhman (1966) also demonstrated that the transition from the intervocalic
consonant to the second vowel depended upon the nature of the first vowel. Following the terminology of
Daniloff and Moll, this is an example of "backward"
co-articulation. It is almost universally assumed
that backward co-articulation effects can be explained
entirely by mechanical inertial factors in which
changes in the state of contraction of articulatory
muscles lag behind the arrival and termination of
neural commands to an articulatory muscle persist
through subsequent segments unless directly contradicted by a command to an articulatory muscle.
Forward co-articulatory effects cannot be explained by assuming that the neural commands for each
segment are not delivered strictly in succession,
but rather are delivered in an overlapping (shingled)
manner to the articulatory muscles. A somewhat
vaguer "explanation" of forward co-articulation is

that there is forward "planning" of a larger portion
of the utterance than a single segment.

In my opinion, the most attractive explanation
of at least some forward co-articulatory effects is
the "priming" mechanism suggested by Lashley (1951),
in which all of the segments in a phrase are partially activated (primed) before beginning to fully activate any single segmental representative. Lashley
considered this priming process to be necessary in
order to account for anticipatory errors in pronun-
ciation. Wickelgren (1969(a) and (b)) points out
how the priming process, in conjunction with the assumption that the segments are context-sensitive allophones, provides a mechanism for articulation of
an entire phrase as an automatic process at a "lower"
phonetic level without continued direction by the
higher cognitive (syntactic and semantic) level.
This would permit the cognitive level to be planning
the next phrase while the phonetic level of the nervous system was directing the articulation of the
previously planned phrase. MacKay (1969, 1970, 1971)
has more fully developed the necessary characteristics for this priming process and carefully documented the power of this priming process in explaining a
variety of speech errors. MacKay's error analyses
indicate the need to assume a temporal gradient of
priming with the greatest degree of priming being for
the next segment to be uttered, the next greatest
degree for the following segment, etc.

MacKay assumes that this gradient of priming is
achieved by a scanner passing over representatives of
successive segments arranged in a non-associative
buffer memory. However the associative-chain theory
proposed by Wickelgren (1969(a) and (b)) for speech
articulation provides a completely natural mechanism
for achieving exactly this type of priming gradient.
Consider the associative chain of five consecutive
context-sensitive allophones for the word "struck" as
shown in Fig. 1. During articulation of $_str$, the
representative of $_str$ will be maximally activated,
but it will be sending impulses "downstream" in the

chain to further increase the degree of activation of $+r_\Lambda$ above the level produced by the prior phrase priming process (selection of the unordered set of context-sensitive allophones). This heightened activation (priming) of $+r_\Lambda$ should result in some degree of heightened priming of $_r\Lambda_k$, and so on to the end of the associative-chain. This would provide precisely the gradient of activation that MacKay's analysis indicates is necessary in order to account for the distribution of a variety of speech errors as a function of segmental (phonemic or allophonic) distance.

An illustration of the qualitative characteristics of this priming process for each of the five context-sensitive allophone representatives in the word "struck" as a function of time is shown in Fig. 2. Note that in Fig. 2 all of the context-sensitive allophones in the unordered set for the word "struck" start off at a positive level of priming due to the phrase priming process that occurred when word representatives at the concept level selected the appropriate unordered sets of context-sensitive allophone representatives at the segmental level. In turn, each of the successive context-sensitive allophone representatives in the word is raised to a level of maximum activation. At any given point in time, the degree of activation is maximal for the current context-sensitive allophone representative, next highest for the immediately following context-sensitive allophone representative, next highest for the following allophone representative, etc. Allophone representatives that are not a part of the unordered set for any word to be articulated in the phrase are at the lowest level of activation of all, arbitrarily called zero level of activation. After a previously-primed allophone representative has been articulated it is inhibited and returned to zero degree of activation, unless that allophone representative has been "doubly primed" (primed twice in conjunction with two occurrences in the phrase). In this latter case, it is necessary to assume the al-

243

lophone representative returns to the level appropriate for a singly-primed allophone representative. For phrases of any reasonable length in English, this repetition of an allophone representative in a phrase will occur only very rarely.

An extremely interesting experiment by Ladefoged and Silverstein (1970) on the speed with which a subject can interrupt a currently-articulated utterance to begin a new utterance provides evidence for precisely the type of phrase priming postulated by Wickelgren (1969(a) and (b)). Ladefoged and Silverstein found that there were no differences in the speed with which subjects were able to stop saying what they intended to say and start saying something else as a function of where the cue to do this was given, provided it was given <u>during</u> the utterance. That is to say, there were apparently no stress-linked or syntax-linked differences in ease of interrupting speech during the articulation of a phrase. However, during a period just <u>prior</u> to the subject's beginning articulation of the utterance, the subject responded much more slowly to the cue (as long as 750 msec before the utterance vs. an average of 350 msec during the utterance). Ladefoged and Silverstein interpreted their results to indicate that, prior to beginning an utterance, the speaker was planning the articulation and could not readily plan another utterance. By this same token, it must be assumed that during articulation of the utterance, this higher syntactic and semantic (concept) planning level is free to plan the articulation of another utterance and not involved at all in the ongoing control of articulation of the current utterance. This latter assumption accounts for the absence of any syntax-linked differences in ease of interruption during the utterance.

Priming (or some process like priming) seems necessary in order to account for the more remote forward co-articulatory effects such as described by Daniloff and Moll (1968). However, with the assumption of context-sensitive allophonic coding in speech articulation, priming is not necessary in order to

244

account for the more remote forward co-articulatory effects such as described by Daniloff and Moll (1968). However, with the assumption of context-sensitive allophonic coding in speech articulation, priming is not necessary in order to account for the more immediate forward co-articulatory effects such as those observed by Öhman (1966). In VCV utterances, Öhman apparently found no effects of the first vowel on the steady state formant levels for the terminal vowel and no effects of the terminal vowel on the steady state formant levels for the initial vowel. Thus, all of the co-articulatory effects observed by Öhman can be characterized as being effects of the initial and terminal vowels on the intervocalic consonant. The capacity for such immediate context-conditioned variation is an obvious consequence of the assumption that the segmental units are context-sensitive allophone representatives, rather than phoneme representatives. Clearly, the context-sensitive allophone representative for $_\alpha b_u$ will be different from that for the context-sensitive allophone $_o b_u$. Since the segmental representatives of the consonant are different in these two cases, the consonant can be different in both its initial and terminal transitions. There is no necessary reason within context-sensitive coding theory to assume that the only effect of a prior segment would be upon the initial portion of the subsequent segment, though it is reasonable to assume that co-articulatory effects will have some gradient of this type.

According to the theory developed in this section, speech articulation involves a combination of serial and parallel processes. Phrase priming may be an entirely parallel process, that is to say, all of the allophones for all of the words in the phrase may be primed simultaneously. Alternatively, as suggested by Wickelgren (1969(a)), each word in the phrase may be primed in its appropriate temporal order. However, the priming of the segments of each word consists of the simultaneous priming of all of the allophones in the word (parallel process). In

245

any event, the maintenance of this priming for all of
the allophone representatives in the entire phrase
during articulation of the phrase is assumed to be a
parallel process. The succession of maximally activated allophone representatives clearly has the
primary character of a serial process, but the existence of a priming gradient induced by the associative-chain is once again a parallel process. The
advance priming of immediately succeeding allophone
representatives provides an extremely natural mechanism, within an associative-chain theory, by which a
certain degree of temporal overlap in the neural commands for successive segments might be achieved.

SERIAL AND PARALLEL PROCESSES IN SPEECH RECOGNITION

Correlation of recognition of different segments.

Lehiste raises an interesting criticism of the
context-sensitive coding theory in speech recognition
based on the data of Lehiste and Shockey (1971).
Lehiste argues as follows:
"It seems reasonable to assume that if the context-sensitive allophone is the minimal unit
of perception, the context to which the allophone is sensitive should be perceptible. Thus,
the /p/ should be equally perceptible, i.e.
equally recoverable, under all three conditions
described above." (These three conditions are
/api/, /apa/, and /ap#/.)
Lehiste and Shockey (1971) investigated the identifiability of each vowel and consonant segment in a
V_1CV_2 sequence both when the sequences were intact
and when either the first or second half of the utterance was removed by cutting the tape during the voiceless plosive gap (the consonants were either /p/, /t/,
or /k/).

To examine the validity of Lehiste's assertions
regarding context-sensitive coding in perception, it
is necessary to discuss the presumed operation of context-sensitive allophones in speech recognition, in

246

some detail.

From a perceptual point of view, the context-sensitive coding theory asserts that the acoustic features which contribute to the recognition of adjacent context-sensitive allophones must be to some extent overlapping in time of occurrence. To illustrate this, consider the hypothetical representation shown in Fig. 3.

Fig. 3 illustrates one possible set of distributions for the density of features for each allophone in the word "struck". The feature densities shown in Fig. 3 are surely incorrect in a number of respects. First, since by various approximate measures of phoneme duration at a peripheral articulatory and acoustic level, the different types of phonemes differ in their relative durations, it is likely that the spread of the distributions of features for different context-sensitive allophones would have to be assumed to be somewhat different as well. Fig. 3 shows all of these spreads to be approximately equal, and this is probably false. In addition the unimodal "normal-type" distributions shown in Fig. 3 are just a wild guess as to the approximate form of the distributions. Nevertheless, for present purposes, the overlapping feature-density distribution shown in Fig. 3 are completely satisfactory.

Note that in Fig. 3 the cues for recognizing the allophone $/_s t_r/$ occur at the same time as many of the cues appropriate for recognizing the allophone $/\#s t$ and the allophone $/_t r_\Lambda/$. In Fig. 3, there is even some temporal overlap between the features for $/_s t_r/$ and the features for $/_r \Lambda_k/$, though the decision to represent the spreads in this manner was made purely arbitrarily to illustrate the possiblity of some more remote interaction that is nevertheless consistent with the formulation of context-sensitive allophones as the basic units in perception. It would be simpler to assume that non-adjacent allophones had no temporal overlap in their features, but I have no way of knowing that this is true at the present time. The point is that the representation shown in Fig. 3 is

247

perfectly consistent with the basic idea of context-
sensitive coding in terms of phoneme triples, and
yet it does yield some temporal overlap in the features for allophones separated by one intervening allophone. However, I think that it is contradictory
to my context-sesitive coding theory to have temporal
overlap in the features for allophones separated by
two or more intervening allophones.

One should be careful to note that the existence
of some temporal overlap between two adjacent or non-
adjacent context-sensitive allophone representatives
does not imply that the features that contribute to
the recognition of each allophone during this region
of temporal overlap are the same. Indeed, these
features may have nothing in common whatsoever.
Chances are, considering what we know about "transitions" between successive phonemes (allophones) that
the cues for immediately adjacent context-sensitive
phonemes (allophones) do have much in common in addition to their time of occurrence. Undoubtedly, it
is often the case that many of the same features
contribute to the recognition of immediately adjacent
context-sensitive allophones.

Presumably, the features that contribute to the
recognition of any given context-sensitive allophone
are somewhat redundant. That is to say, one can fail
to perceive some of these features (as a result of
either external or internal noise) and still be able
to activate the correct context-sensitive allophone
representative. This somewhat complicates the interpretation of any experiment in which the recognizability of an allophone (phoneme) was investigated as
a function of cutting a tape recording at various
points or adding different types of noise, etc. Certainly, one cannot assume that eliminating any particular time segment during the region of positive feature density for any particular allophone would necessarily reduce recognition of that allophone, especially under conditions that otherwise produce very
high intelligibility for the allophone.

Excluding the possibility of attentional fluc-
tuations or other confounding factors in speech recognition, context-sensitive coding makes the prediction that the recognizability of adjacent phonemes
should be positively correlated. The cues for adjacent phonemes undoubtedly have much in common, at a
minimum they have time of occurrence in common. Thus,
many factors that influence the recognizability of
one allophone must also affect the recognizability of
an immediately adjacent allophone. If zero or negative correlation is found for the recognizabilities
of immediately adjacent phonemes, it would be a serious disconfirmation of context-sensitive coding in
speech perception.

Looking at it from a somewhat different point of
view, if one has activated the internal representatives (recognized) $/_s t_r/$ then one ought, logically,
to know that the immediately prior phoneme was /s/ and
the immediate subsequent phoneme was /r/. One would
not know from this what the exact context-sensitive
allophones were for the immediately prior and succeeding segments, but one ought to be able to write down a
all three phonemes, given only the recognition of the
medial context-sensitive allophone. Of course, it is
possible that although this information is logically
present in the nervous system, people do not make use
of it in speech recognition, but this seems extremely
unlikely.

However, this raises the point that, because one
has recognized a single phoneme from an utterance of
several phonemes, one cannot assume (in fact it would
be unreasonable to assume) that this has occurred
because the individual has activated the particular
context-sensitive allophone representative appropriate
for that phoneme. Presumably, if a subject can only
identify a single phoneme from some utterance, he has
not maximally activated any single context-sensitive
allophone representative consistent with that phoneme.
Rather he has activated a set of context-sensitive
allophones appropriate for that phoneme, but no single
member of this set (no single context-sensitive allo-

249

phone representative) has been activated more than
the others. This would permit him to say that a particular phoneme had occurred, but not to say what the
immediately prior or succeeding phonemes were.

In light of the above discussion, we are now in
a position to evaluate the validity of Lehiste's comments concerning the significance of the Lehiste and
Shockey experiment for context-sensitive coding
theory. For the purposes of discussing the Lehiste
and Shockey experiment I will use an illustration
similar to that of Fig. 3 for one of the V_1CV_2 triples used by Lehiste and Shockey. Fig. 4 illustrates
the approximate feature density for each consecutive
context-sensitive allophone in the V_1CV_2 utterance
/api/. The dotted vertical line illustrates the
approximate position of the plosive break at which
Lehiste and Shockey made cuts in the tape under conditions for presenting either /ap/ or /pi/.

As Fig. 4 illustrates, presenting only /ap/
from the triple /api/ by means of a cut at the plosive break might have very little effect on the recognizability of the /a/ phoneme. This is because
very little of the features necessary for the recognition of /a/ occur to the right of the plosive
break. However, these features may be critical for
the identifiability of /#ap/ as a particular context-
sensitive allophone. Furthermore, the degree of
overlap between successive allophones shown in Fig.
4 is a wild guess. The percentage of features for
/#ap/ to the right of the plosive break may be considerably greater than that shown in Fig. 4.

Presumably in those cases when subjects were
only able to identify the initial vowel of such an
utterance, the cut did interfere with some features
that were critical for maximally activating the particular allophone /#ap/. However, under these conditions, it is still quite possible that the subjects would have sufficient information necessary to
identify the initial vowel as /a/. This occurs in
context-sensitive coding theory because a variety of
allophones appropriate to the phoneme /a/ have been

activated more than the allophone appropriate for any other phoneme. When this happens, one is able to identify the phoneme, but not its immediate phonemic context. Clearly, with the break occurring in the middle of the feature density distribution for /api/, one has surely reduced the intelligibility of the /api/ allophone and also the /p/ phoneme (class of [p] allophones).

Again it should be emphasized that context-sensitive coding theory does not predict that it is impossible to recognize one phoneme without recognizing its immediately adjacent phonemes. This would be an absurd prediction in any event. Context-sensitive coding theory ought to predict a positive correlation between the recognizabilities of immediately adjacent phonemes, under many conditions. This positive correlation should occur primarily under conditions of rapidly articulated speech (normal speaking and hearing conditions). In the Lehiste and Shockey experiments, which was modelled after that of Öhman (1966), the initial and terminal vowels were quite prolonged. This provided extremely good steady-state formant cues for the recognizability for the initial and terminal vowel phonemes, no matter what was done to the transition to and from the intervocalic stop consonant. Under such conditions, because of the foregoing remarks regarding redundancy of features for the recognizability of any allophone or any class of allophones (phoneme), one would expect very low or even zero correlations between the recognizabilities of adjacent phonemes. Thus, more careful examination of correlations between the recognizabilities of adjacent phonemes in experiments such as that of Lehiste and Shockey would be rather inappropriate for the evaluation of context-sensitive coding theory. However, it should be emphasized that a repetition of the Lehiste and Shockey experiment (or, even better, of experiments involving somewhat longer phoneme sequences in nonsense utterances) at normal speaking rates ought to provide a strong test of the context-sensitive coding theory in speech perception.

Lehiste and Shockey found that subjects could not operate above chance in identifying a terminal vowel, given the initial vowel and the transition to the intervocalic consonant. Similarly, they found that subjects could not operate above chance in identifying the initial vowel, given the terminal vowel and the transition from the intervocalic consonant. These findings suggest that whether or not there is any overlap in the time of occurrence of the features for these non-adjacent vowel phonemes, the features appropriate for recognition of each vowel are not overlapping in their character. Thus, the context-conditioned variation that occurs in a transition to the intervocalic consonant from the initial vowel as a result of the nature of the terminal vowel does not provide a cue for the recognition of the terminal vowel. Analogous statements can be made for the case of the recognizability of the initial vowel as a function of the transition from the intervocalic consonant to the terminal vowel. If this is found to be generally true of non-adjacent phonemes, then one can strengthen the prediction of context-sensitive coding theory to the effect that, with nonsense utterances, only the recognizability of the immediately adjacent phonemes will be positively correlated. Recognizability of phonemes separated by one or more intervening phonemes should have zero correlation according to this formulation. Of course, such zero correlations between the recognizabilities of non-adjacent phonemes should only be found in nonsense utterances. To the extent that subjects can identify words from a subset of all the phonemes or allophones in the word, this will induce a positive correlation between the recognizabilities of any pair of phonemes in the word. This occurs because the subject knows the phonemic and allophonic constituents of the particular words in his lexicon.

To clearly understand the operation of context-sensitive coding in speech perception, one must note the many ways in which a context-sensitive coding theory of speech perception departs from the more fam-

iliar model of serial recognition of successive, non-
overlapping, phoneme-sized segments. Since the features appropriate for the identification of each allophone overlap in time (and probably also in character), it is natural, and indeed necessary, to as-
sure that all of the allophone detectors are operating in parallel. That is to say, the acoustic cues
provide input simultaneously to all appropriate context-sensitive allophone representatives. It must
be assumed that the temporally distributed input for
any particular context-sensitive allophone representative can be summed up to some maximum period of
time.

When all of the acoustic cues for a particular
word such as "struck" have been received at the con-
text-sensitve allophone level, there will be some
distribution of degrees of activation imposed on all
of the context-sensitive allophone representatives.
For the word "struck" under conditions of high intelligibility, this would mean that the particular five
allophone representatives shown in Fig. 3 would be
maximally activated. These allophone representatives
would be strongly associated with the representative
of the word "struck" at the concept level, producing
maximal activation of this word representative, rather
than any other word representative. As noted before,
during delivery of the features for the word "struck",
heightened activation of the $/_s t_r/$ allophone representative ought to increase the activation of the sets
of all $/_s +/$ and $/_+ r_/$ allophone representatives,
since each allophone representative in these sets
should be strongly associated to the $/_s t_r/$ allophone
representative. Thus, the input to each allophone
representative need not be assumed to be entirely
from the lower auditory feature level, but could also
be partly from association between allophone representatives at the segmental level. In addition, an
activated allophone representative may be partially
activating different concept representatives which,
in turn, could produce associative feedback to the
allophone representatives appropriate for those words.

253

It is difficult to make quantitative predictions from such a complex theory of the speech recognition process. However, it is clear that this type of system provides maximal use for speech recognition of the information in the acoustic signal.

Clearly, the theory is asserting that the speech recognition process is largely parallel, except for the fact that the acoustic cues for a word are to some extent spread out in time. It is the activation of a sufficient proportion of the unordered set of allophone representatives in a word that produces recognition of that word, not the activation of an ordered set of allophone, phoneme, or syllable representatives. Freeing the speech recognition process from the necessity of recognizing segments in temporal order greatly increases the power and flexibility of the speech recognition system. For one thing, it makes right-to-left effects possible in addition to left-to-right effects.

Recognizing the order of segments

It is obviously critical that we perceive the order of the phonemes within a word, in some manner, since the same phonemes in different orders often constitute different words. The context-sensitive coding theory asserts that the order of phonemes is represented by an unordered set of context-sensitive allophones (overlapping phoneme triples). In this theory, the context sensitivity of the successive allophone segments is the key to the representation of their order.

The context-sensitive coding theory of the representation of segmental order is directly supported by experiments such as that of Warren, Obusek, Farmer, and Warren (1969) which showed that human beings are extremely poor at recognizing the order of even an extremely short series of context-free elements such as hisses, buzzes and tones. Human beings apparently do not have much ability to represent the order of rapidly occurring events (durations of several 100

254

msec) unless such event sequences have occurred fre-
quenlty in the past. Presumably frequent exposure to
sequences of different events permits the establish-
ment in the organism of units that represent something like overlapping triples of events (context-
sensitive coding).

It is interesting to contrast the Warren, et al.
findings with the findings of Yntema, Wozencraft, and
Klem (1964) on short-term memory for lists of rapidly
spoken digits. The lists in the Yntema, et al. study
were random orderings of a set of eight digit names
stored in a computer. The phonemes within the computer-spoken digits, of course, exhibit co-articulatory effects within the name for the digit. However,
the transitions from one digit name to the next digit
name in no way exhibit co-articulatory effects, since
the same context-free digit name was used in all sequences and at all positions in the computer-spoken
list of digits. Nevertheless, at rates where Warren,
et al. found subjects completely unable to perceive
the order of context-free hisses, buzzes, and tones,
Yntema, et al. found subjects perfectly able to perceive the order of digits up to three or four digit
lists (rates of two or four digits per second). Variations in rate in the Yntema, et al. study were achieved by introducing blank spaces between digit names.
The digit names were always limited to a hundred milliseconds in length (which is a speeded-speech representation of each digit). Thus, intelligibility
could certainly be improved if the auditory cues for
each digit occupied the entire 250 msec at the four
per second rate. This would undoubtedly have improved
ordered memory span performance even more. Thus,
there is a sharp contrast between the results for digit sequences and the results for sequences of hisses,
buzzes, and tones. In the latter case, the order of
even three or four such sounds could not be perceived
above chance level at the rate of 250 msec per sound
even when the sequence was repeated over and over again for as long as the subject desired before making
his order judgement! Surely, if subjects listened to

a list of "context-free" digits over and over again
they could achieve memory spans of at least seven or
even more such digits.

From the standpoint of context-sensitive coding
theory, one either has to assume: (a) that one can
have context-sensitive coding of (multiphonemic) dif-
it names, so that one has a representative for $/_25_4/$
which is different from the representation of a $/5/$
in any other context of (b) that the terminal and
initial phonemes of each digit name are entering into
context-sensitive allophone representation, without
the context-conditioned variation of the transitions
between them being present. In either case, there is
no context-conditioned variation (co-articulatory
cue) to signal the context-sensitively coded segments. Co-articulatory cues are very useful cues
for context-sensitive segments, but they are by no
means logically necessary for context-sensitive coding to work. Context-sensitive coding is most basically a theory of the representation of the ordering
of segments in terms of temporally overlapping units.
Context-sensitive coding of an ordered list of segments is possible even if the segments exhibit complete acoustic and articulatory invariance across all
different contexts. Of course, such context-conditioned acoustic transitions constitute particularly
good cues for the recognition of each context-sensitive unit (allophone or whatever). However, this
does not prevent the recognition of a context-sensitive unit in the absence of such transitional cues.

Feedback from concept level to segment level in speech
speech recognition

Experiments by Warren (1970) and Warren and Obusek (1971) provide important evidence for the existence of the previously postulated feedback from
the concept (word) level to the segment level in
speech recognition. In these experiments, a single
phoneme, such as /s/, or an entire syllable, /gis/,
was removed completely (including transitions to and

and from the segment) from the word "legislatures"
and replaced by a cough, tone, or buzz. Subjects
were not only able to correctly recognize the word,
but also appeared to automatically fill-in the missing segment at a phonetic (allophonic) level. Subjects reported that no segment was missing, that they
"heard" the missing phoneme(s). Furthermore, they
were unable to judge accurately which segment was deleted, even when they were guaranteed that some segment had been deleted! Since subjects can recognize
nonsense materials, we know that we are not denied
conscious access to the phonetic (subconcept) level
for perceptual judgements. Furthermore, under other
conditions (when the gap was left as a silent interval not filled-in with any extraneous noise), subjects
were able in the Warren experiments to accurately
judge which segment was missing. Thus, the inability
to judge the position of the missing segment under
the initial set of conditions provides evidence that,
under some conditions, the feedback from the concept
level to the context-sensitive allophone level can,
in conjuntion with random noise input, be sufficient
to activate the missing context-sensitive allophone
representatives. As mentioned previously, representation of a word in terms of an unordered set of
context-sensitive segment representatives makes possible the efficient realization of this feedback
from the concept to the segmental level, since the
time at which a segment is activated is not important
for the representation of the word at the segmental
level.

Reaction time to segments of different size

The Savin and Bever (1970) experiment cited by
Lehiste, and to a lesser extent the similar experiment of Warren (1971), provide additional evidence
for the theory that the context-sensitive allophone
is the basic unit of perception, rather than the
phoneme. In the Savin and Bever experiment, subjects
were to monitor a sequence of nonsense syllables for

257

either a single initial consonant phoneme /b/ or for
an entire nonsense syllable that began with the phoneme /b/. Subjects responded more quickly to the
syllable than to the initial /b/ phoneme in every
case. The results were replicated with initial /s/
and for a medial vowel, /ae/. Of course, these results do not provide support for the context-sensitive allophone over the syllable as the minimal
segmental unit for speech perception. What these
results do suggest is that the minimal unit of speech
perception is larger in temporal scope than the phoneme. Strong support for the context-sensitive allophone as the unit responsible for this effect, rather
than the syllable, would come if the reaction time
could be shown to decrease as one increased the phonemic size of the target from one to three phonemes
(for syllables longer than 3 phonemes), but not
to decrease for further increases in the phonemic
length of the target (up to the length of the entire
syllable).

References

Daniloff, R., and Moll, K. Coarticulation of lip
    rounding. Journal of Speech and Hearing Res-
    earch, 1968, 11, 707-721.

Ladefoged, P. The phonetic framework of generative
    phonology. UCLA Working Papers in Phonetics
    No. 14, March, 1970, 25-32.

Ladefoged, P., and Silverstein, R.O. The interrupt-
    ibility of speech. UCLA Working Papers in
    Phonetics No. 14, March, 1970, p. 10.

Lashley, K.S. The problem of serial order in behav-
    ior. In L.A. Jeffress (Ed.), Cerebral Mechan-
    isms in Behavior. New York: Wiley, 1951.

Lehiste, I., and Shockey, L. The perception of co-
    articulation. Two papers presented at the 82nd
    meeting of the Acoustical Society of America,
    Denver, October 20, 1971.

MacKay, D.G. Forward and backward masking in motor
    systems. Kybernetik, 1969, 2, 57-64.

MacKay, D.G. Spoonerisms: The structure of errors
    in the serial order of speech. Neuropsychol-
    ogia, 1970, 8, 323-350.

MacKay, D.G. Stress pre-entry in motor systems.
    American Journal of Psychology, 1971, 84, 35-51.

Öhman, S.E.G. Coarticulation in VCV utterances:
    Spectrographic measurements. Journal of the
    Acoustical Society of America, 1966, 39, 151-168.

Savin, H.B., and Bever, T.G. The nonperceptual real-
    ity of the phoneme. Journal of Verbal Learning
    and Verbal Behavior, 1970, 9, 295-302.

Warren, R.M. Perceptual restoration of missing
    speech sounds. Science, 1970, 167, 392-393.

Warren, R.M. Identification times for phonemic
    components of graded complexity and for spelling
    of speech. Perception and Psychophysics, 1971,
    9, 345-349.

Warren, R.M., and Obusek, C.J. Speech perception
    and phonemic restorations. Perception and
    Psychophysics, 1971, 9, 358-363.

Warren, R.M., Obusek, C.H., Farmer, R.H., and Warren,
    R.P. Auditory sequence: Confusion of patterns
    other than speech or music. Science, 1969, 164,
    586-587.

Wickelgren, W.A. Context-sensitive coding, assoc-
    iative memory, and serial order in (speech)
    behavior. Psychological Review, 1969(a), 76,
    1-15.

Wickelgren, W.A. Context-sensitive coding in speech
    recognition, articulation, and development.
    In K.N. Leibovic (Ed.), Information Processing
    in the Nervous System. New York: Springer-
    Verlag, 1969, 85-95.

Yntema, D.B., Wozencraft, F.T., and Klem. L. Immed-
    iate serial recall of digits presented at very
    high rates. Presented at the meeting of the
    Psychonomic Society, Niagara Falls, Ontario,
    October, 1964.

260

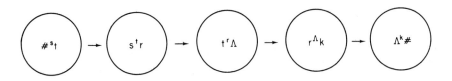

Fig. 1. Associative chain of context-sensitive allophone representatives for the word "struck."

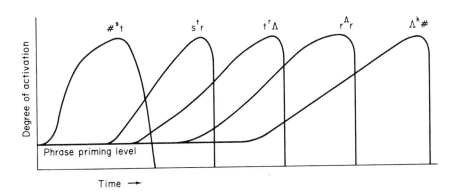

Fig. 2. Hypothetical approximate degree of activation of context-sensitive allophone representatives in articulation of the word "struck." Note that, in general, one cannot assume that all allophone representatives have approximately equal duration of maximal activation at any given rate of talking.

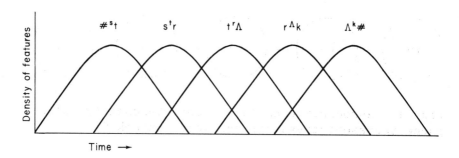

Fig. 3. Approximate density of features for recognition of each context-sensitive allophone in the word "struck."

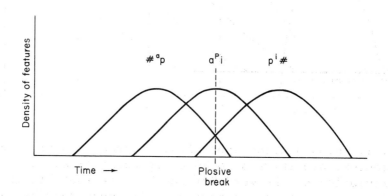

Fig. 4. Approximate density of features for recognition of each context-sensitive allophone in the nonsense word "api."

Chapter 8

DISCUSSION PAPER ON CORTICAL FUNCTIONING

H. Goodglass

School of Medicine
Boston University
Boston Massachusetts

Many avenues of approach have been taken in the
effort to infer the organization of language in the
brain. Each has its own advantages and limitations.
The work that has come out of the Montreal Neurological Institute is unique in that careful controlled
experimentation is combined with the study of precisely delineated operative removals. These studies
have shown that verbal memory deficits are produced
by temporal lobe removals on the left side and that
certain non-verbal deficits, particularly in visual
memory and music are produced by similar removals on
the right. Further, Dr. Milner's research has shown
convincingly that the contribution of the hippocampus
to short term memory is similarly lateralized.

Dr. Kimura, while working in Dr. Milner's laboratory introduced what has become the most popular
technique for the lateral representation of language
- the method of dichotic listening. This appealing-
simple procedure, in the hands of another of Dr.
Milner's students, Donald Shankweiler, has been used
to show that the phonological components of speech
are differentially lateralized and that it is primarily the consonants which put the left hemisphere's
speech analyzer to work.

Certain limitations on the generality of Dr. Milner's evidence arise from the population being studied. These are largely patients with early atrophic

lesions of the right or left temporal lobe. Such les-
tions, as we have seen, may produce shifts from the
genetically predisposed laterality of either hand
preference, or of language dominance, or both. Even
when language dominance has not been shifted, the
presence of non-functional brain tissue in the language zone results in a deviant allocation of developing language functions in the brain.

Recognizing the anomolies in brain dominance
caused by these lesions, Dr. Milner has scrupulously
checked out language dominance as distinct from handedness by means of the intracarotid amytal test.
This is undoubtedly the most revealing indicator
available of the probable effect of an operative re-
moval, but it is not quite the same as the effect produced by an ablative lesion. Further, we do not know
how the effects of the Wada Test compare, in the case
of pathologically shifted or rearranged language dominance, with those in the normal right or left hander

The second qualification is in no way a reflection on the validity of Dr. Milner's results. Namely, that by avoiding operative intrusion on the language areas proper, these studies succeed in telling
about the overall laterality, but not much about the
internal organization of language function. For the
source of this latter information, we must turn to
the accumulation over 100 years of haphazard experiments of nature and accident through which lesions
of vascular, traumatic or neoplastic origin have
occurred in the language zone and in which there has
been an opportunity for more or less careful behavioral study of the results. Thus, in order to gain
the advantage of knowledge about the interrelation-
ships among the components of language, we must accept the disadvantage of dealing post hoc with hap-
hazardly produced lesions.

I would like to supplement Dr. Milner's presentation by talking about these effects of natural and
traumatic lesions of the language areas themselves:
in other words, about aphasia. Particularly, I would
like to outline the knowledge about the organization

of components of expressive and receptive language -
spoken and written, based on injuries which have selectively damaged various zones and structures within
the overall anatomical language area.

Our original concept of brain laterality for
language, in fact, arises from the observation of the
effects of these lesions. These effects are dramatic, sometimes complete, and almost entirely one-sided.
A patient who suffers major injury to the left cortical language area experiences a massive impairment
of language function affecting all modalities. A
similar injury in the right hemisphere has no dis-
cernible effect on speech, reading or writing. I
will shortly discuss the deviations from this rule
and their relation to handedness, and in doing so
point out some of the problems in drawing parallels
between the data from natural lesions and those from
such experimental procedures as dichotic listening,
cortical stimulation, and the Wada Test.

It is curious to realize that while the association of aphasia with brain injury is recognized in
the earliest recorded medical literature, its almost
unique association with left sided injury escaped
notice until little over 100 years ago, Paul Broca
being credited with the first public report of this
finding. However, Broca also discovered the first
exceptions - patients who became aphasic after a
right hemisphere lesion. These people turned out to
be left handers. The simple classical doctrine of
cerebral dominance thus came into being - namely that
the left hemisphere controls speech for left-handers.
As exceptions to this rule began to accumulate it
became clear that only about one percent of normal
right handers developed aphasia from lesions ipsil-
ateral to the preferred hand. However, several series showed that for left handers, a lesion in either
hemisphere stood an equal change of producing aphasia.
The best such series was published in 1969 by Gloning
et al., based on 57 right handers and 57 non right
handers matched, on the basis of post mortem examination, with respect to lesion size, location, and

265

type. This series is important because every case, whether positive or negative for aphasia is included. While not all lesions were in the language area, there is a matched lesion in the right hemisphere group for each left hander. The resulting distribution showed <u>no aphasia</u> in any of the right handers with a right sided lesion but clear aphasia in 15 of the 32 with left sided lesions. For the left handers, the results are very dramatic. Eighteen of the 25 are aphasic with lesions on the right and 19 of 32 are aphasic with lesions on the left. For the left handers, then, as far as susceptibility to aphasia goes, <u>each</u> hemisphere shows a rate comparable to, if not greater than, the <u>left</u> hemisphere of the right handers. Namely, with lesions equally distributed to left and right, there would be twice the proportion of left handed as of right handed aphasics.

Comparing these results with findings from the Wada Test and dichotic listening experiments, we find some puzzling discrepancies. Thus, Milner, Branch, and Rasmussen reported in 1966 that 70 percent of left handers had exclusively left sided aphasic reactions and only 15 percent (17 of 117) had an aphasic reaction bilaterally. In contrast 92 percent of 95 of right handers showed exclusively left sided aphasic reactions. Obviously then the Wada Test is sensitive in some way to the differential language representation in the brain. While it is the best experimental indicator now available it still seems to behave differently from a natural lesion. The dichotic listening technique is obviously also sensitive in some way to lateral asymmetry for language, but with this technique there is little or no reliable difference between right and left handers. Both groups show about 80% of individuals with right ear superiority for words. Clearly, dichotic listening is not yet suitable as an individual diagnostic test of brain laterality in normals, although it is useful as a research tool and as a diagnostic tool in cases of brain injury, where unequivocally one-sided results may be obtained.

266

Now I would like to shift my discussion to the selective disturbances of language seen with injuries to specific structures within the left language area. All of our knowledge in this area comes from destructive lesions which effectively ablate a part of the brain. Stimulation of the exposed cortex, while effective for mapping the speech area, does not selectively impair the components of language as does an ablative lesion.

At the risk of oversimplifying, let us consider those systems which correspond on the one hand to linguistically definable levels of organization and, on the other hand to the anatomical zones related to them. We will start with two of these anatomico-functional relationships. The first is the storage and recognition of the acoustic sequences composing the phonemes, syllables, and words of a language and the arousal of semantic associations to them. Reasonably enough, these functions are selectively disturbed by injuries to the posterior portion of the temporal lobe, an auditory association area immediately adjacent to Heschl's gyrus, i.e., adjacent to the primary auditory sensory area of the left cerebral cortex. This region is called Wernicke's area, for the neurologist who identified it as critical for the integrity of auditory comprehension.

On the output side, the most clearly identifiable system is the one responsible for the implementation of the phonological rules of the language via the activity of the articulatory apparatus. The zone which usually develops this function is the anterior speech zone called Broca's area - again, logically enough, located near the base of the primary motor strip in the cortex, adjacent to the area controlling movements of the mouth and tongue.

These two subsystems are often independently damaged. However, the clinical manifestations of such selective injuries only begin to be described by the narrow concepts of motor encoding on one hand and auditory decoding on the other. In fact the anterior and posterior aphasic syndromes are most dis-

267

tinctive because of their differential <u>speech output</u> patterns. In listening to these patterns one is struck by additional autonomous features. These features correspond to two more linguistic dimensions: those of syntax and lexicon.

It is noteworthy that the dissolution of syntax is associated with the anterior, or Broca's area lesion, which, as we have seen, impairs articulation. Beyond articulation, however, we find that the ability to initiate and maintain a flow of speech is impaired, so that output is effortful, and produced word-by-word, as well as being phonologically distorted. The breakdown of grammar is very real, and not merely an economy of effort. Speech content reverts to isolated nouns, so that the statistical frequency of this part of speech is greatly increased over normal; sentences revert to holophrastic form, much like those of a young child. Auxiliary verbs drop out of speech, verbal inflections are lost and sentence structure, at best, sticks to the overlearned S-V-O sequence. The patient seems to have forgotten how to form other English sequences even when he attempts to repeat a model. Thus, in a functional sense we may say loosely that the phonological and syntactic levels of speech output are represented in the anterior portion of the speech area. More precisely — that lesions in this zone are more likely to be manifested by phonological and syntactic deficits, with a relatively well preserved level of comprehension.

In contrast, as we listen to the speech output of the patient with the posterior lesion a totally different set of abnormalities stand out. To begin with, articulation is facile, initiation of speech is uninhibited, and long strings of grammatically organized words may be produced, sometimes at greater than normal rates. The content, however, is extremely low in information because the patient cannot supply substantives, but fills out his speech with repetitious, circumlocutory expressions, often replete with neologisms and semantic anomalies. In fact, when we

present objects for him to name to visual confront-
ation, we confirm that he has greatly reduced access
to his lexicon. A short quote from the speech of
such a patient will illustrate what I mean. The
patient is telling about a picture-situation in which
two small boys are stealing cookies behind their
mother's back.

"Well this is mother is away here working her
work out o' here to get her better, but when she's
looking, the two boys looking in the other part.
One their small sile into her time here. She's
working another time because she's getting, too. So
the two boys work together an one is sneakin' around
here, making his work and his further funnas his
time he had."

This patient, in spite of his apparent verbal
fluency could name absolutely nothing to visual con-
frontation. But in addition to these deficits, this
typical speech sample tells us about another apparent language function of the temporal lobe: namely,
monitoring, selection, and control.. It is as though
the intact phonatory and grammatical capacities of
the Broca's area subsystem are turned loose and al-
lowed to run free without benefit of purposeful word
selection or orientation to a semantic goal.

While access to the lexicon is particularly damaged by destruction of Wernicke's area, this particular deficit, i.e., word-finding, is the most difficult to assign to a particular lesion site. It is a
part of virtually all aphasic syndromes. However, it
often appears as a nearly pure disorder with injuries
at the far posterior portion of the temporal lobe,
that is at the temporo-parietal juncture.

The complex composed of Wernicke's and Broca's
areas with their inter-connections can be considered
as the central core for the speech mechanism. They
do not, of course, originate the intellectual content of speech, nor provide the initiative or motivation to speak nor deal with the multi-modal concepts
to which a perceived message refers, nor the relationship between the concepts. What can we expect if this

central mechanism is left undamaged, while the brain peripheral to it is destroyed? The ability to repeat without understanding and to recite memorized sequences would remain untouched when all purposeful communication is destroyed. While this syndrome has been recognized and in fact attributed by many writers to the isolation of the speech system from the non-linguistic cognitive apparatus, a most dramatic confirmation of the relationship was published a few years ago with autopsy findings by Drs. Geschwind, Quadfasel and Segarra.

The organization of the cerebral substrate for written language is quite complex. It seems to reflect the fact that the normal speaker acquires reading and writing on the basis of his previously established oral comprehension and speech. The neural systems which underlie oral language, therefore, comprise a necessary part of the system for written language. Typically, injury of the auditory language association cortex - i.e., injury to Wernicke's area, damages both reading and writing. Injury to the anterior speech zone, or Broca's area, damages writing very severely; reading less severely.

There is, however, a crossroad area in the brain which is sensitive for written language only, with little, if any effect on speech. This is the angular gyrus, located at the juncture of the posterior temporal lobe and lower parietal lobes. If reading can be considered to require an association between visual and auditory signals, this region has evolved in a most logical location, half way between the auditory and visual association areas.

It would be oversimplifying the picture to suggest that all available anatomical evidence supports the model I have outlined. While the primary motor and sensory systems are wired into the brain with little leeway for individual variation, this degree of invariance does not apply to the distribution of functions in the language association areas. The plasticity of the brain in response to early lesions or to very slow growing lesions of later life is ev-

idence of this. As a result, there is considerable
variation in individual symptoms produced by similar
lesions, within the general framework I have described. In some individuals the functions of the
language zone seem quite diffusely organized, so
that an injury which usually produces a discrete,
standard deficit will instead produce an ill defined,
general diminution of language. This diffuseness is
particularly characteristic of the right hemisphere
of left handers.

The many lines of evidence which converge to form
our present concept of language and the brain cannot
be summed up in a short discussion. A more complete
treatment would bring in the dramatic evidence supporting the anatomic associationist model which comes
from the disconnection syndromes - the "pure aphas-
ias" and the unilateral aphasic phenomena produced by
callosal section. By way of unsolved problems, we
should mention the dissociation between languages
in polyglot aphasics and between phonetic, syllabic,
and idiographic modes of communication, as seen in
the writing of Japanese aphasics and the manual communication of the deaf.

References

Geschwind, N., Quadfasel, F.A., and Segarra, J.M.
    Isolation of the speech ara. Neuropsychologia,
    1968, 6, 327-340.

Gloning, I., Gloning, K., Haab, G., and Quatember, R.
    Comparison of verbal behavior in right-handed
    and non-right-handed patients with anatomically
    verified lesions of one hemisphere. Cortex,
    1969, 5, 43-52.

Milner, B., Branch, C., and Rasmussen, T. Evidence
    for bilateral speech representation in some non-
    right handers. Transactions of the American
    Neurological Association, New York: Springer,
    1966.